Emotion, Affect, Sentiment:
The Language and Aesthetics of Feeling

Edited by
Andreas Langlotz and Agnieszka Soltysik Monnet

D1676825

SPELL

Swiss Papers in
English Language and Literature

Edited by
The Swiss Association of University Teachers of English
(SAUTE)

General Editor: Lukas Erne

Volume 30

Emotion, Affect, Sentiment:

The Language and Aesthetics of Feeling

Edited by

Andreas Langlotz and Agnieszka Soltysik Monnet

narr
VERLAG

Bibliografische Information der Deutschen Nationalbibliothek

Die Deutsche Nationalbibliothek verzeichnet diese Publikation in der Deutschen Natio-
nalbibliografie; detaillierte bibliografische Daten sind im Internet über http://dnb.dnb.de
abrufbar.

Publiziert mit Unterstützung der Schweizerischen Akademie der Geistes- und Sozial-
wissenschaften.

© 2014 · Narr Francke Attempto Verlag GmbH + Co. KG
Dischingerweg 5 · D-72070 Tübingen

Internet: http://www.narr.de
E-Mail: info@narr.de

Umschlagabbildung und Einbandgestaltung: Martin Heusser, Zürich
Foto: Edvard Munch, The Scream (1893)
© The Munch Museum/The Munch-Ellingsen Group / 2014, ProLitteris, Zürich
Druck und Bindung: Laupp & Göbel, Nehren
Printed in Germany

ISSN 0940-0478
ISBN 978-3-8233-6889-2

Table of Contents

General Editor's Preface

SPELL (Swiss Papers in English Language and Literature) is a publication of SAUTE, the Swiss Association of University Teachers of English. Established in 1984, it first appeared every second year, was published annually from 1994 to 2008, and now appears three times every two years. Every second year, SPELL publishes a selection of papers given at the biennial symposia organized by SAUTE. Non-symposium volumes are usually collections of papers given at other conferences organized by members of SAUTE, in particular conferences of SANAS, the Swiss Association for North American Studies and, more recently, of SAMEMES, the Swiss Association of Medieval and Early Modern English Studies. However, other proposals are also welcome. Decisions concerning topics and editors are made by the Annual General Meeting of SAUTE two years before the year of publication.

Volumes of SPELL contain carefully selected and edited papers devoted to a topic of literary, linguistic and – broadly – cultural interest. All contributions are original and are subjected to external evaluation by means of a full peer review process. Contributions are usually by participants at the conferences mentioned, but volume editors are free to solicit further contributions. Papers published in SPELL are documented in the *MLA International Bibliography*. SPELL is published with the financial support of the Swiss Academy of Humanities and Social Sciences.

Information on all aspects of SPELL, including volumes planned for the future, is available from the General Editor, Prof. Lukas Erne, Département de langue et littérature anglaises, Faculté des Lettres, Université de Genève, CH-1211 Genève 4, Switzerland, e-mail: lukas.erne@unige.ch. Information about past volumes of SPELL and about SAUTE, in particular about how to become a member of the association, can be obtained from the SAUTE website at http://www.saute.ch.

Lukas Erne

Acknowledgements

The essays in this volume were selected from among the best presentations delivered at the biennial conference of the Swiss Association of University Teachers of English (SAUTE), which took place in Lausanne in April 2013. The theme for the event was *Emotion, Affect, Sentiment: The Language and Aesthetics of Feeling* and featured a broad range of papers by literature scholars, linguists and medievalists. We are grateful to the funding bodies, SAUTE (SAGW), UNIL and CUSO, who made the conference possible. And we would like to thank the conference participants, who made it a highly memorable and rewarding experience, especially the four plenary speakers: Nancy Armstrong (Duke), Jonathan Culpeper (Lancaster), Stephanie Trigg (Melbourne) and Paul Stenner (Open University, UK). The editors of this volume would also like to express a very warm "Thank you so much!" to Juliette Vuille, who not only helped plan and organize the conference as a third member of our team, but designed the original poster and provided invaluable good cheer and calm competence at every step of the way. The conference would certainly not have been the success it was without Juliette's great many personal and professional contributions. We would also like to thank the student assistants and exchange students who contributed to preparing the programme booklet, staffed the registration desks and helped in innumerable ways during the conference: Harley Edwards, Georgia Guenzi, Philipp Lindholm, Célia Méhou-Loko, Raphaël Meyer, Catherine Oakley, Eleftheria Tsirakoglou, Marie-Emilie Walz and Rebecca Woods. We are very grateful to Valeriya Vershinina, who prepared the index for this volume, and to Martin Heusser, who designed the cover. We would like to thank Keith Hewlett for his meticulous proof-reading and rapid preparation of the camera-ready copy. It is always a pleasure to work with you, Keith! Thanks also to Lukas Erne, the General Editor, for prompt and helpful instructions. And finally, we thank the National Museum in Oslo for the cover image of Edvard Munch's *The Scream* and ProLitteris for permission to reproduce it.

Introduction

It is a truism that we seek to express ideas, thoughts and attitudes through language and aesthetic forms of communication including fine art, film, theater, poetry and others. But then the behaviors and experiences that define our very existence cannot be captured in conceptual and rational terms alone. Rather it is another truism that we are thoroughly shaped and influenced by the powerful domain of emotion, affect, and sentiment. However, although nobody would deny the fundamental impact that emotionality has on our existence, until recently it has received much less scholarly and scientific attention than the cognitive and social dimensions of human life. This fact can probably be explained by a central phenomenological paradox surrounding emotions, affects, and sentiments. Despite their undeniable presence, they are fuzzy, evasive, and poorly graspable aspects of our experience. This pervasive and all-encompassing yet conceptually slippery force of emotionality is nicely reflected in Edvard Munch's painting *The Scream* (1893).

The image illustrates the potentially profound impact of emotion on an individual. The depicted persona screams with its mouth wide open and its hands covering the sides of its face, performing a gesture of emotional intensity. This emotional state, however, is not bound to the internal psychological world of the screamer nor is it reduced to its expression in the form of screaming. Rather the emotional experience is all encompassing, it blends with his/her environment as aesthetically represented through the swirls and curved lines – an ocean of affect – surrounding the protagonist; the whole context seems to be shaken with fear and/or pain. But despite being thoroughly emotional and affect-laden, the painting also demonstrates the highly evasive and conceptually inaccessible nature of affective experience. Due to the absence of sound in imagery, the audible force of the scream is merely alluded to vi-

Emotion, Affect, Sentiment: The Language and Aesthetics of Feeling. SPELL: Swiss Papers in English Language and Literature 30. Ed. Andreas Langlotz and Agnieszka Soltysik Monnet. Tübingen: Narr, 2014. 11-25.

sually. The same is true for the actual feeling of fear or pain. Phenom-
enologically, the feeling remains hidden to our immediate perceptual
and conceptual grasp. It is metonymically represented and pointed to
through aesthetic means of visual expression, yet we cannot perceive its
essence, i.e. the very feeling of fear or anguish that the screamer is suffering from. Like the two figures in the background of the image, we
cannot directly connect to the figure's emotional world. In fact, we cannot even know what kind of emotion the screamer is feeling; the painting has been interpreted variously as representing a scream of fear, anxiety, despair, or psychic anguish. If we examined any if these terms more
closely, we would discover even more ambiguity and disagreement
about what they mean to different people at different times and in different cultural spaces and scholarly disciplines. While being puzzling and
inherently paradoxical, Munch's painting thus reveals emotionality to be
a communicatively, culturally, and aesthetically represented, mediated as
well as constructed phenomenon by its very nature. Rather than limiting
the study of emotion, affect, and sentiment to the domain of psychology, this invites literary, historical, and linguistic approaches.

It is instructive to look at the different words we used in the title of
this volume. Arguably, all are synonyms, yet each term comes not only
with its own set of meanings (sometimes overlapping, sometimes opposed) and genealogies, but also with very different cultural baggage and
implications. For example, the first, *emotion*, is perhaps the most neutral
and wide-ranging of the four. Descended from Latin by means of the
French *émouvoir*, the term evokes motion or agitation, a stirring up from
a placid state. In this light, emotion is activity, energy, almost a synec-
doche for life itself in its positive aspects, or a force of disruption and
violence in its negative connotations. With the word *feeling*, important
distinctions come creeping in. A Germanic word, *felen* in Middle English, *feeling* was and still is associated with the sense of touch, and by association, with perception. Thus, immediately, a contrast between a
more active and passive understanding of the experience of being
moved or feeling something emerges. In addition, some scholars would
introduce a further distinction, locating feeling in subjective and individual experience, while allowing emotion a more conceptual and social
definition, as "social and cultural practices" (Ahmed 9). Hence, scholarly
attempts to schematize and theorize feelings have generally preferred to
use the word *emotion*, as in Robert Plutchik's influential model of the
"emotion wheel." The eminent American psychologist posited eight
primary, universal and hard-wired human emotions: anger, fear, sadness,

disgust, surprise, anticipation, trust, and joy, organized neatly into opposed pairs (Plutchik 109).

One notable exception to this trend of associating feeling with individual experience would be Raymond Williams' notion of "structures of feeling," which has been highly influential as an attempt to articulate the relationship between personal and collective affective formations. Not simply an individual feeling or emotion, a structure of feeling is a "particular quality of social experience and relationship, historically distinct from other particular qualities, which gives the sense of a generation or of a period" (Williams, *Marxism and Literature* 131). As Sue Kim, author of *On Anger*, argues, Williams is not referring to what we think of as emotions, which are already named, defined and overdetermined, but to the "unnamed-while-lived set of experiences, feelings, thoughts, values, etc. – emergent or pre-emergent formations – that characterize a particular generation in a given historical moment" (61). As a Marxist critic, Williams was interested in how lived experience is shaped by yet exceeds existing social structures and formations, and he chose the word *feeling* in order to "emphasize a distinction from more formal concepts of 'worldview' or 'ideology'" (132). Yet Williams' use of the term also exceeds what we think of as feelings, encompassing "characteristic elements of impulse, restraint and tone [and] specifically affective elements of consciousness and relationships" (132). The conceptually tricky terrain between the individual and the social that Williams attempts to capture with the term structure of feeling brings us to a more recent attempt to navigate the liminal spaces between the personal and the public, and the subjective and the autonomous: affect.

The term that has most powerfully captured the scholarly energies of the new interest in emotionality has been *affect* itself. We hear of the "affective turn" in disciplines across the social, human and even so-called hard sciences. Part of a larger turning away from the linguistic turn in the humanities, though perhaps simply another turn of the screw, the affective turn has seen a revived interest in the biological sciences, evolutionary theory and even Darwinism, or more specifically, Darwin's *The Expressions of the Emotions in Man and Animals*. Along these lines, the affective turn has been particularly fueled by evidence revealing the fundamental connections between "lower-level" emotionality, "higher-level" rational thinking, and good judgment (e.g. Damasio, Goleman). In fact, in tandem with other questions raised by postmodernism and the notion of the posthuman, affect theory has been intensely interested in the boundaries between the human and nonhuman, including human and animal, and human and cybernetic. Yet, even the term "affect theory" has not emerged from a single coherent set of foundational ideas or texts. On the contrary, there are at least two distinct vectors of theoretical force in affect theory, one based on interest in affect as innate and biological, derived from Silvan Tomkins' work and exemplified in Eve Kosofsky Sedgwick and Adam Frank's 1995 essay, "Shame in the Cybernetic Fold," and another tendency based rather on Gilles Deleuze and Felix Guattari, such as Brian Massumi's "The Autonomy of Affect" (also 1995).[1] Yet both share an insistence on distinguishing affect from emotion, identifying the latter as socially and linguistically (over)-determined, and defining affect instead as pre-linguistic and pre-conscious "forces or intensities . . . that circulate about, between, and sometimes stick to bodies and worlds" (Seigworth and Gregg 1). Theorists of affect like Brian Massumi or Lauren Berlant use the term to explore the complex resonances and encounters between bodies, subjects, and the social and physical world they live in, but this line of inquiry tends to pass over individual subjects and favor a depersonalized approach that often takes the political for its object instead. Thus, one of Massumi's best known essays, "The Future Birth of the Affective Fact," is about the manipulation of a sense of threat by the Bush administration, while Berlant's work consistently revisits a nexus of concepts including citizenship, sexuality, the public sphere, and national belonging. In short, although the affective turn is a wide constellation of developments, and the word *affect*, a Latinate word that derives from *afficere* ("to act upon, influence, affect, attack with disease"), means different things to different scholars, there is a tendency – which resonates well with the etymological root of the word, which assumes an external source – to use affect to discuss the experience of embodied cognition in the world.

This brings us to the final word of the title, *sentiment*, a word that may seem very old-fashioned compared to the currently sexy *affect*, but which may serve to remind us that even intellectual turns have a history. Long before affect emerged to help us think about embodied cognition, sentiment had been doing exactly that for nearly two centuries (as had the Aristotelian notion of *catharsis* well before that). A cognate of the Latin *sentire* (to feel), and derived from the French *sentement* (personal experience or feeling), *sentiment* became entangled in the eighteenth century with the words *sympathy* and *sensibility*. Francis Hutcheson and Adam Smith found in sentiment not only a theory of individual benevolence

---

[1] Social psychologist Paul Stenner identifies *three*, adding also the resurgence of psychoanalytical ideas in the social sciences, such as Ian Craib's "Social Construction as a Social Psychosis" (Stenner 8).

and compassion, but a basis for thinking about the social order. Questions of ethics and epistemology were closely tied to sentiment, and issues of cultural relativism versus human universalism were often channeled through discussions of sentiments and emotions (e.g. the David Hume/Immanuel Kant split in moral philosophy). Issues of aesthetics became vitally and essentially imbricated with the question of emotion, judgment and the grounds for collective life. In literature and the arts, sentimentalism reigned as a dominant mode for much of the eighteenth and nineteenth centuries, and endures in the continuing importance of melodrama as a narrative form (as Linda Williams has argued).

Modernism imposed an important break on the sentimental culture of the nineteenth century, both in the USA and UK and across Europe, looking back to Romantic notions (specifically from Kant) such as the "sublime" and the "transcendental," investing art with a kind of secular sacred force, and developing quasi-religious aesthetic concepts such as the epiphany (a term with a long Christian genealogy). In reaction to the highly emotionalized reception of art in the nineteenth century, modernist criticism tended to strive for a disinterested and more scientific or universalist attitude, hence the banishment of emotion from reading by the New Critics with the Affective Fallacy. It was not until feminism and postcolonial theory began to dismantle the modernist canon and its aesthetic value system that it was possible to look at the cultural work of emotion and sensation seriously again. This was done in the 1970s by critics such as Peter Brooks, Thomas Elsaesser, and Jane Tompkins, among many others. Thus, work on melodrama and sentimental culture in the fields of American Studies, film theory, theater history, and literature all paved the way for the current surge of interest in affect and emotion across the disciplines.

In April 2013, the English Department at the University of Lausanne hosted the biennial SAUTE conference to engage with this complex domain of emotionality and to scrutinize the general question of how affect, emotion, sentiment are related to language and aesthetics. It invited researchers in English and American literature, medieval studies, and linguistics to exchange new ideas, test innovative approaches, and analyze a multitude of texts and linguistic data. Since investigations into human emotionality ask for interdisciplinary contact between disciplines from the humanities and cognitive sciences and in light of the recent interest on the part of literature, medievalist, and linguistic scholars in cross-disciplinary inquiry, we also invited Paul Stenner, Professor of Social Psychology at the Open University in the UK, to give a keynote lecture on the "affective turn" as viewed from his field of research. The presentation focused on a particularly interesting aspect of affect theory, namely, *liminality*. In *The Affect Theory Reader*, Melissa Gregg and Gregory J. Seigworth propose that affect is "born in *in-between-ness* and resides as accumulative *beside-ness*" (2, italics in original). Stenner drew on anthropologist Victor Turner's work on rites of passage and the philosopher A. N. Whitehead's theory of experience to argue that affect is literally a liminal state, and therefore a phenomenon of transition. Observing that whereas traditional societies had carefully structured rites of passage and modern societies have few or none, Stenner proposed that the result is a tendency toward "permanent liminality." Following Victor Turner's claim that some of the features of traditional liminal situations have been taken over by "liminoid experiences associated with theater and art," Stenner explored the possible connections between contemporary art, the "affective turn," and the "conditions for an experiential confrontation with what it means to be a human being" that are created by liminality and a suspension of conventional structures. He ended his keynote lecture by pointing out that many of the positive qualities attributed to liminality by Turner resemble the way in which affect is currently celebrated by writers of the affective turn: as an event rather than a state or structure, as a potency or potential that can disrupt existing structures, as about community rather than society, etc. (see also Stenner and Moreno-Gabriel, "Liminality and affectivity" 13). The keynote was well received and several delegates incorporated Stenner's reflections into their contributions to this volume. Thus, interdisciplinary from the start, the conference covered a wide range of approaches and touched on issues such as the affective turn in literature, Romantic and Modernist aesthetics, the history of emotions, melodrama and the Gothic, reception aesthetics, attitudes, impoliteness, and medicine. The present volume comprises a selection of the best papers presented at the conference.

Literature

The first essay, Nancy Armstrong's "When Sympathy Fails: The Affective Turn in Contemporary Fiction," makes a boldly historical argument, taking as a point of departure the recent trend of fictional protagonists – such as Ishiguro's Kathy in *Never Let Me Go* – who resist or refuse the sympathetic identification traditionally produced and managed by the novel. Instead of ascribing this emergence to a recent historical event, however, Armstrong proposes that we consider the new forms of affect that emerged in the nineteenth century as life was re-defined by Darwin. Armstrong thus engages with the recent affect theorists' interest in the relationship between science and cultural formations, navigating deftly between Jane Austen, Franz Kafka and a range of contemporary writers to show that affect remains at the heart of the English novel, but in a radically new configuration. In this new formation, the novel transforms inhospitable places, such as those the protagonists inhabit, into liminal sites that allow these protagonists to survive their deaths as individuals or integrated identities and to experience new forms of self. With this provocative argument, Nancy Armstrong revisits the ideas that form her most influential work – such as the notion of the novel as a disciplinary institution – and reflects on the consequences for that argument of the most recent trends in contemporary fiction.

The next literature essay (the fifth essay in the volume) takes us into the heart of sentimental culture in the eighteenth century. In "The Affectionate Author: Family Love as Rhetorical Device in Eighteenth-Century Conduct Books for Young Women," Erzsi Kukorelly examines women's conduct guides to see how affection is deployed rhetorically as a disciplinary technique. Focusing on how young women are enjoined to comply with the conduct rules laid down in the texts in exchange for the love and affection of their elders, the author argues that eighteenth-century conduct books transform feelings of love into exchangeable commodities: parental love into advice, and filial love into good conduct. In contrast, Enit Steiner's "Exuberant Energies: Affect in *Vathek*, *Zofloya* and *The Giaour*" examines the darker side of eighteenth century sentimental culture, namely, Gothic fiction, and specifically the Orientalized Gothic. Like Kukorelly, Steiner focuses on the political and social dimensions of the representation of emotion, but looks at texts that stage a "vehement defiance" of eighteenth century family and institutions, plunging readers into stories of emotional excess, violence and perversion. If conduct books propagated compliance and discipline through affection, the Orientalized Gothic novel represented a site of resistance to the "domestic realism" and sentimental values that dominated British literature of this period.

The next two papers can also be viewed as companion pieces, even if dealing with rather different periods and texts. Sangam MacDuff's "Joyce's Transcendental Aesthetics of Epiphany" and Francesca de Lucia's "Awe, Terror and Mathematics in Don DeLillo's *Ratner's Star*" both examine the aesthetics of the transcendental and sublime that Modernism inherited from Romanticism. MacDuff argues that the literary epiphany, as conceived by Joyce in *Stephen Hero*, is not a wholly secular or subjective experience, but is informed by a Romantic aesthetics of transcendence. Joyce's modernist text is thus deeply indebted to Kant's theory of the sublime, while reimagining that sublimity not in moral law or nature but in language. De Lucia also argues that Don DeLillo's *Ratner's Star* draws on Romantic ideas about sublimity and specifically about the feeling of awe, but locates these in mathematics and scientific research rather than language. Drawing on Robert Plutchik's theory of emotions, Mary Jane Rubenstein's analyses of awe, as well as Kantian notions of the sublime, de Lucia explores the ambivalent emotions linked to modern experiences of the sublime, ranging from fear and paranoia to awe and sensations of redemption.

Medieval Studies

While giving the impression of a timeless motive, Munch's *The Scream* is a modernist painting emerging at a historical period when the relationship between the individual, nature, and society became radically redefined, with humans encountering themselves encaged in increasingly impersonal, bureaucratic and aggressive political machineries, denaturalized and increasingly technologized urban societies, and secularized psychological spaces of introverted self-reflexivity. Accordingly, the painting can be read as the emotional outcry of the modern individual who feels estranged, distorted, and diseased by the environment he/she finds him/herself in. Congruent with this interpretation, the Foucauldian notion that emotions and sentiments have a history has inspired a growing body of scholarly works that conceive "emotions as habits that can be produced through cultural scripts" (McNamer). The medieval period provides fertile ground for a study of social and cultural changes in emotional behavior. The present volume contains two contributions written by medievalists who engage with the question of how historical context influences and shapes the very idea of emotionality and how it patterns habits of affective engagement.

Stephanie Trigg's essay is centrally interested in the history of feeling. But rather than exploring a traditional medievalist topic, she focuses on the emotional reception of Chaucer by the romanticist Samuel Taylor Coleridge. Coleridge's affective experience when reading the most famous English medieval poet provides a scholarly test ground for Trigg to discuss how emotional stances towards literary works are subject to historical change and how such shifts can be read as reflections of the particular emotional habits of receptive textual communities. The essay thus establishes an interesting dialogue between the fields of literary reception – Chaucer reception in particular – histories of feeling, and the changing emotional orientations of literary criticism. In line with Reddy's concept of the "emotional utterance" (Reddy 104-105) that is employed by Trigg, literary criticism at different historical periods can be said to produce different types of emotive utterances about literary works, which are reflexive of the emotional habits adopted by the literary critics at a given point in time. Along these lines, our own reading of Munch's *The Scream* can be seen as an emotive utterance that probably unveils the analytical and emotionally-distanced orientation of present-day academic discourse in the humanities.

Daniel McCann's paper can also be associated with Munch's painting as it pulls us into the medieval conceptualization of fear. More specifically, the author discusses the two opposed appraisals of this emotion in medieval medicine and medieval theology. While the former rather seems to tie in with present-day classifications of fear as a negative emotion, the latter regards it as a suitable means to enhance the health of the soul and to prepare it for the union with God. These positive conceptions of fear are revealed through a close reading of Walter Hilton's *Scale of Perfection*. McCann's paper is also highly interesting from a contemporary perspective on emotion theory because it shows that competing theories of emotions – even of basic emotions such as fear – have a long tradition is Western thought. In addition, the essay reveals how such theories are closely connected to the ideological frameworks (medicine versus theology) in which they are embedded.

Linguistics

Human beings are not able to interact with one another, let alone communicate or learn a language, without showing a fundamental, if not innate, sense of empathy (Malloch and Trevarthen). But although human language and emotionality seem to be fundamentally intertwined, the complex connections between language and emotion have yet to be systematically explored in (English) linguistics (Foolen et al., Wilce). In this volume four innovative essays contribute highly interesting substance to fill this research lacuna. They address the role of emotions and affect in impolite language use, compare the use of expletives in Irish and British English, discuss the cultural relativity of emotional language and emotion concepts, scrutinize the meta-communicative reflections on emotional experiences by medical students, and test the emotional stances towards different Varieties of English as conveyed through the attitudes of Swiss students of English.

The essay presented by Culpeper, Schauer, Marti, Mei and Nevala takes us to the heart of emotional experience in language use. Focusing on how impoliteness affects interlocutors, the study pursues the more particular research question of which feelings members from different cultural backgrounds (England, Finland, Germany, Turkey and China) refer to when reporting on impolite speech events that they found themselves in. The article thus engages with the central question of how language use is sanctioned through an underlying emotional substrate that is of fundamental importance to distinguish between polite or impolite utterances. Empirically, the paper reveals parallels between the different cultures with regard to more general, higher-level emotion categories, but it also points to salient differences on the lower level of more specific emotional subcategories such as sadness. Thus, there seem to be both general and culture-specific trends in managing (im)politeness emotionally. Along these lines, the paper pulls us into the long-standing debate concerning the universality versus cultural-relativity of emotional experience. Theoretically, the study develops a convincing argument for including a cognitive dimension of appraisal that links the use of impolite language to (moral) judgments of inappropriateness which then trigger corresponding emotional reactions. This cognitive layer of evaluating speech events is bound to conceptions of norm through the notion of "sociality rights" as well as personal integrity through the concept of "face." The paper thus opens a window into the complex nexus between the emotional, cognitive, social, and linguistic components underlying linguistic interaction. To build an interpretative link between this essay and Munch's *The Scream*, we could see the screamer's emotional reaction as his/her judgment of the unacceptable social-interactional environment that he/she finds herself in. Following the logic of the paper, however, screamers from different cultures would react to this environment differently, not all of them would scream necessarily or scream as loudly as the others.

An alternative cross-cultural perspective on emotionality in language use is offered by Patricia Ronan. In her essay, she scrutinizes the use of religious expressions such as *Jesus!* or *My God!* and body-related swearwords as in *Fuck!* These expletives are used in English to signal the high emotional involvement of the speaker. With regard to *The Scream* they could thus be directly connected to what the screamer shouts out in reaction to his/her feeling state. Anchoring her study in the pragmatic classification of speech acts, most importantly expressives, the author is centrally interested in comparing the use of religious and *f*-word expletives in Irish and British English. This comparison is highly interesting because it provides scientific ground for investigating cultural differences in emotional expression between different varieties of a given language rather than between different languages alone. Along these lines, the study manages to bring variational pragmatics into contact with the ethnolinguistic study of emotion words. Ronan yields her results by employing a corpus-linguistic method, which allows her to compare quantitatively the occurrence of religious oaths and swearwords in the ICE Ireland and ICE Great Britain corpora. And indeed, the study reveals interesting differences in the (relatively rare) use of expletives in the two cultures, which point to culture-specific preferences of evoking religious and body-related connotations for communicating the emotional force of an utterance.

Varieties of English are also put on center stage by Sarah Chevalier. But rather than analyzing the linguistic communication of emotionality through these varieties, she focuses on the emotional stances that language users adopt towards them. The study thus approaches the nexus between language and emotion from the perspective of language attitudes. In particular, the author is interested in the attitudes held by Swiss students. But why Swiss students rather than native speakers of English? Chevalier takes the Swiss context as a test ground to find out whether the increasing importance and the increasingly positive evaluation of regional varieties of English by native speakers are also reflected in the emotional stances adopted by the students in Switzerland. This research question is pertinent since the increasing accessibility of different varieties of English to Swiss students through media channels and their high degree of mobility is likely to cause a greater exposure to "Englishes" rather than the traditional variety of standard British English formerly taught at schools. The study reveals that the students' affective relationship to different types of English is dynamically shifting indeed. This is highly interesting because macro-sociolinguistic developments in the English-speaking world also seem to leave their traces in the private emotional landscapes of non-native speakers of the language. The essay thus provides an important insight into the relationship between changing linguistic norms and their attitudinal substrates in an increasingly globalized world. In line with the aesthetics of *The Scream* it captures the dynamic and fluid interrelation between the external and the internal dimensions of affect.

Miriam Locher and Regula Koenig explore links between language and emotional experiences on the meta-communicative level of health discourse. By analyzing the content of written reports of British medical students, they investigate how the future doctors reflect on their communicative experiences when interacting with patients as part of their training. Locher and Koenig show emotion, affect, and sentiment to be one central theme highlighted by the students. Accordingly, the authors describe the range of emotion words used by the students and point to the variety of nonverbal cues that are described by them when giving their accounts of or when re-enacting the emotional experiences they felt when engaging with the patients. They are moved by the interlocutors' medical histories, by difficult cases, and by the patients' reactions within doctor-patient talk. In addition, they sometimes feel uneasy when it comes to communicating their own affective states within these encounters. Locher and Koenig's study can thus be nicely related to the *The Scream*. Like the screamer medical students often find themselves in emotionally charged or stirred up social environments. Probably, their spontaneous affective reactions would cause them to scream and express their empathy with the patients. However, the students have to learn to manage their emotional engagement with their interactors. Rather than screaming loudly, they have to adopt a controlled and somewhat detached position similar to the two figures in the background of Munch's painting. In this vein, this essay is fundamentally connected to the question of what forms of emotional expression and emotional "language" are supported and sanctioned by a given sociocultural context and which ones are regarded as dispreferred or unacceptable.

Media

The final essay brings us back to theories of melodrama but in the context of contemporary popular culture. Agnieszka Soltysik Monnet's "Political Emotions: Civil Religion and Melodrama in Spielberg's *Lincoln*" examines Steven Spielberg's recent biographical film about Abraham Lincoln in order to show how it weaves together melodrama and elements of civil religion to create a potent experience of national mythopoesis. Thus, like many of the other essays on literature in the volume, Soltysik Monnet's argument engages with the political and cultural uses of affect, examining how the cinematic choreography of affect can serve complex ideological interests. In keeping with the interdisciplinary spirit of the volume, the author offers a textual and dramaturgical reading of the film but also draws on sociology for tools to think about the interplay between emotions and national symbols such as Abraham Lincoln. More to the point, Soltysik Monnet demonstrates how melodrama, and its conventionalized staging of sympathetic identification for a virtuous victim-hero, remains one of the most important narrative modes in American popular culture. In a sense, this is not surprising, considering the importance that suffering has come to have in twentieth-century definitions of individual and collective identity. Collective victimhood has served as a key element in political formations, and individual trauma has assumed the role in discourses of subject-formation that sexuality once had. It is no coincidence then that *The Scream* is sometimes referred to as "the modern Mona Lisa." If La Giaconda's enigmatic smile, so full of possibilities as well as self-satisfaction, is the defining image of the European Renaissance, then what more fitting as an icon for modernity than Munch's anguished screamer?

*

As can be seen from this first glance at the essays in this volume, the evolving field of emotion, affect and sentiment provides an array of fascinating phenomena to be approached from a variety of perspectives offered by English and American literature, medieval studies and English linguistics. The field is ripe with new ideas, readings, and methods and we are proud to present some of this innovation in this volume. Therefore, we cordially invite the readers to join in the academic debates initiated at the SAUTE conference and to embark on the emotional, affective, and sentimental journeys that have led to this book.

Andreas Langlotz and Agnieszka Soltysik Monnet

References

Ahmed, Sarah. *The Cultural Politics of Emotion.* New York: Routledge, 2004.

Berlant, Lauren. "The Subject of True Feeling: Pain, Privacy and Politics." *Cultural and Political Theory.* Ed. Jean Dodi. Ithaca: Cornell University Press, 2000. 42-62.

———, ed. *Compassion: The Culture and Politics of an Emotion.* New York: Routledge, 2004.

Brooks, Peter. *The Melodramatic Imagination: Balzac, Henry James, Melodrama, and the Mode of Excess.* New York: Columbia University Press, 1985.

Clough, Patricia T. and Jean Halley, eds. *The Affective Turn: Theorizing the Social.* Durham: Duke University Press, 2007.

Craib, Ian. "Social Construction as a Social Psychosis." *Sociology* 31.1 (1997): 1-15.

Damasio, Antonio. *Descartes' Error. Emotion, Reason, and the Human Brain.* London: Penguin, 1994.

Darwin, Charles. "The Expression of the Emotions in Man and Animals" (1872). *From So Simple A Beginning: The Four Great Books of Charles Darwin.* Ed. Edward O. Wilson. New York: W. W. Norton and Company, 2006. 1255-1478.

Elsaesser, Thomas. "Tales of Sound and Fury." *Imitations of Life: Explorations of Melodrama.* Ed. M. Landis. Ohio: Wayne State University Press, 1991. 44-79.

Foolen, Ad, Ulrike M. Lüdtke, Timothy P. Racine, and Jordan Zlatev, eds. *Moving Ourselves, Moving Others: Motion and Emotion in Intersubjectivity, Consciousness and Language.* Amsterdam: John Benjamins, 2012.

Goleman, Daniel. *Emotional Intelligence: Why It Can Matter More than IQ.* New York: Bantam Books, 1995.

Gregg, Melissa, and Gregory J. Seigworth, eds. *The Affect Theory Reader.* Durham and London: Duke University Press, 2010.

Kim, Sue. *On Anger: Race, Cognition, Narrative.* Austin: University of Texas Press, 2013.

Malloch, Stephen, and Colwyn Trevarthen. *Communicative Musicality. Exploring the Basis of Human Companionship.* Oxford: Oxford University Press, 2009.

Massumi, Brian. "The Future Birth of the Affective Fact: The Political Ontology of Threat." *The Affect Theory Reader.* Eds. Melissa Gregg and Gregory J. Seigworth. Durham and London: Duke University Press, 2010. 52-70.

———. "The Autonomy of Affect." *Cultural Critique* 31 (September 1995): 83-110.

McNamer, Sarah. *Affective Meditation and the Invention of Medieval Compassion.* Philadelphia: University of Pennsylvania Press, 2010.

Plutchik, Robert. *The Emotions.* Boston: University of America Press, 1991.

Reddy, William. *The Navigation of Feeling: A Framework for the History of Emotions.* Cambridge and New York: Cambridge University Press, 2001.

Sedgwick, Eve Kosofsky, and Adam Frank. "Shame in the Cybernetic Fold: Reading Silvan Tomkins. *Shame and Its Sisters: A Silvan Tomkins Reader.* Eds. Eve Kosofsky Sedgwick and Adam Frank. Durham: Duke University Press, 1995. 1-28.

Seigworth, Gregory J., and Melissa Gregg. "An Inventory of Shimmers." *The Affect Theory Reader.* Eds. Melissa Gregg and Gregory J. Seigworth. Durham and London: Duke University Press, 2010. 1-25.

Stenner, Paul. "On Liminal Feelings and Feeling Liminal: A Psychosocial Rethinking of the 'Turn to Affect.'" Paper presented at the University of Lausanne, April 2013.

——— and Eduard Moreno-Gabriel. "Liminality and affectivity: The case of deceased organ donation." *Subjectivity* 6.3 (2013): 229–253.

Tompkins, Jane. *Sensational Designs: The Cultural Work of American Fiction, 1790-1860.* New York and Oxford: Oxford University Press, 1985.

Wilce, James M. *Language and Emotion.* Cambridge: Cambridge University Press, 2009.

Williams, Linda. *Playing the Race Card: Melodramas of Black and White from Uncle Tom's Cabin to O. J. Simpson.* Princeton: Princeton University Press, 2001.

Williams, Raymond. *Marxism and Literature.* Oxford: Oxford University Press, 1977.

When Sympathy Fails: The Affective Turn in Contemporary Fiction

Nancy Armstrong

This essay considers how and to what effect contemporary novels – as demonstrated by Ishiguro's *Never Let Me Go* – are altering the generic form that traditionally elicits a sympathetic response. I focus on protagonists with inhuman features that make it all but impossible for us to imagine ourselves positioned as they are on the frontier where autobiography converges with biology, i.e., the organism's endeavor to keep on living. Rather than attribute this change to another, ostensibly "real" event – say, the Holocaust or 9/11 – I turn to nineteenth-century fiction and social theory and identify a new form of affect that emerged alongside the biological redefinition of human life.

Given that for almost 300 years human protagonists capable of mirroring the reader's norms and values have earned the sympathy of a mass readership, why would a novelist ever abandon this component of the novel form? Yet, a number of contemporary novelists have done exactly that. Rather than representative men or women, these novelists offer protagonists that might be described as human "extremophiles," a term for biological life forms that survive under conditions thought to be incapable of sustaining life.[1] I use this term in order to call attention to

---

[1] Cooper uses this term to explain how the biosciences, in rethinking the limits against which biological life was previously defined, have also redefined its law of evolution as "autopoetic rather than adaptive." I see the anomalous protagonist rising to challenge, as Cooper does, the optimism attending biotechnical capitalism's appropriation of the evolutionary process.

Emotion, Affect, Sentiment: The Language and Aesthetics of Feeling. SPELL: Swiss Papers in English Language and Literature 30. Ed. Andreas Langlotz and Agnieszka Soltysik Monnet. Tübingen: Narr, 2014. 27-49.

protagonists – like J. M. Coetzee's Michael K., Kazuo Ishiguro's Kathy H., W. G. Sebald's Austerlitz, Indra Sinha's Animal, or Lauren Beukes's Zinzi December – who embody human norms and values that apply to no one but that one character. In view of the international popularity of these novelists, the radical singularity of their protagonists indicates nothing short of a disconcerting sea change. This transformation of the novel form coincides with the development of a major trend within several disciplines to rethink the source and operations of human emotion, or "affect." I plan to contribute to this interdisciplinary conversation by showing how a novel that replaces the norm-bearing protagonist with an anomalous human being transforms the sympathetic identification that novels have traditionally demanded of their readers.

I take as a given that the novel form that rose to dominance among literary genres was the one whose protagonists persuaded readers to imagine their own possibilities for achieving gratification within a set of social norms (see Armstrong). Over the span of three centuries, novels in ever-increasing numbers and in very different ways put representative flesh on these norms, charged them with emotion, subjected them to judgment, and periodically revised them. Such novels may offer objects of desire and standards of behavior that later seem ridiculously out of tune with the reader's own time in history. To continue to be read, they have nevertheless continued to convince readers that a line could and should be drawn indicating exactly where culture confronted nature and made instinct bow to the interests of community. No matter how and where a given novel sets such a line, three centuries of protagonists who assume human shape in relation to that line have made the idea of a world without some principle of normativity virtually unthinkable.

To mount a sustained challenge to the principle of normativity itself, a novelist must break the circuit of desire and self-confirmation in which we expect to participate when we pick up a novel. Kafka does this so memorably that he comes first to mind as a novelist known for writing not novels so much as fables, parables, or what Deleuze and Guattari have called a minor literature. Critics consider J. M. Coetzee the contemporary novelist who most resembles Kafka in this respect. But when we find an increasing number of Anglophone novelists doing much the same thing, it is not so easy to dismiss them *all* as courting marginality; they are reformulating the center. By altering the novel form in so basic a way, these novelists require their readers to question what novel readers have always taken for granted. Without some basis for identification, what does compel us to engage these protagonists? How do they recalibrate the circuit of feeling in which novels have routinely

hailed us as novel readers? In that the feeling they elicit necessarily precedes our response, how is this protagonist revising the reader's response to human behavior? To address these questions, I shall begin
with a theory of sympathy once considered sufficient to explain how
novels make us feel.

How Novels Feel

I read Adam Smith's 1759 *Theory of Moral Sentiments* as a rather transpar-
ent effort to defend Locke's liberal individual against the invasive surges
of feeling that could transform otherwise powerless people into a dangerous mob. As Foucault describes the problem in the first chapter of
Discipline and Punish, the increasing frequency with which spectacles of
punishment incited riots made it only too apparent that the masses were
more likely to identify with the victim on the scaffold than with the
government that choreographed these elaborate displays of its power.
The emotion generated by such an event was considered capable of in-
filtrating the mind through the body, swaying rational individuals to
abandon their own self-interest and become one with the crowd. Smith
proposed "sympathy" as a solution to the problem of how to promote
feelings that strengthened common bonds without eroding individual
judgment.
    This is how Smith did it: Even if we see our brother suffering on the
rack, he observed, we cannot feel what he feels, for the very reason that
each of us inhabits an autonomous bubble of consciousness. However
inclined to imagine ourselves in the other person's position, we can't be
in two places at once and will consequently feel only a faint approximation of that individual's suffering. Smith asks us to think of our capacity
to feel for other human beings as something like emotional capital that
accumulates as we vicariously experience pleasure or pain. This accumu-
lation both enriches and refines our character. As we inquire into the
cause of another's suffering or joy, we naturally develop a standard of
value and learn to invest our feeling in that person in proportion to the
cause of his or her emotion. This standard provides the basis of self-
mastery. In evaluating the emotional responses of others, we cannot
help but become aware of how an individual with mastery of his emotions would evaluate our own behavior. Once we can imagine being the
object of his gaze, we have taken this "impartial spectator" into our
breasts and as good as adopted its normative viewpoint as our own
(Smith 156). Let me offer an example from Jane Austen's *Northanger*

Abbey that shows how central this process is to the heroine's maturation
and thus to the novel itself.

Amused at his houseguest's fondness for gothic fiction, Henry Til-
ney encourages Catherine Moreland to anticipate the same sensational
phenomena at Northanger Abbey as those that terrify the heroine of
Radcliffe's *The Mysteries of Udolpho*. When a few key objects in her bedroom do uncannily match Henry's description, Catherine responds with
"breathless wonder" (Austen 123). The physical symptoms of her excitement multiply as she reaches into the "further part of the cavity" of
an old Japanese cabinet and grasps a manuscript sure to contain a lurid
account of captivity and abuse. Her "feelings were indescribable," the
narrator tells us, describing them quite well in terms that suggest erotic
arousal: "Her heart fluttered, her knees trembled, and her cheeks grew
pale" (124). At this point, she is so thoroughly captivated by the objects
Henry has embellished that her emotional response outstrips her cognitive control. By light of day, however, Catherine discovers that the cause
of all this fuss is nothing more than several laundry lists left behind by a
careless servant, and she hastens "to get rid of those hateful evidences
of her folly, those detestable papers then scattered over her bed" (126).
As she turns on herself in shame for having taken Henry's bait, Catherine adopts what she imagines to be his view of her behavior. He in
turn assumes the role of normative spectator, now a function of her
self-reflection.

This is the socializing effect of shame. To serve as the butt of a joke,
an individual must be reducible to a body, its parts, or its drives. The
resulting type or caricature produced must nevertheless be recognizably
human to fall so short of meeting the criteria for full humanity. In order
to create the conditions in which Catherine would be likely to mistake
fiction for fact, Henry must first have imagined himself in Catherine's
place and let himself be guided by her infatuation with gothic fiction. To
make this leap of imagination, he had to be at once sensitive to Catherine's excesses and sufficiently detached to view them critically. In contrast to the conventional jokester and resembling nothing so much as
Smith's "impartial spectator," Henry's exercise of his superiority does
not degrade but improves the object of sympathy. His joke enables
Catherine to see herself as he would see her were she not behaving so
inappropriately in the privacy of her bedroom. This leap of imagination
trumps her sympathetic bond with Radcliffe's heroine as it affords her a
critical perspective on her behavior worthy of Henry and his sister's
company. Austen uses a similar process to redirect the sympathy of her
readers onto a proper object. Guided by her free indirect style, we with-

draw our emotional investment from gothic heroines in order to experience the more refined pleasure that comes with ironic distance from
Catherine's scene of shame.

Let us now fast-forward from Austen's late eighteenth-century country house to the twenty-first century boarding school for future organ
donors in Kazuo Ishiguro's *Never Let Me Go,* and compare the impact of
Henry's joke on Austen's protagonist with that of Madame the headmis-
tress on Ishiguro's narrator, Kathy H.:

> As she came to a halt, I glanced quickly at her face. . . . And I can still see it
> now, the shudder that she seemed to be suppressing. . . . And though we
> just kept on walking, we all felt it; it was like we'd walked from the sun right
> into chilly shade. . . . Madame was afraid of us. But she was afraid of us in
> the same way someone might be afraid of spiders. (35)

This encounter interrupts the sympathy born of first-person narration.
By giving the power of narration to someone whom normative society
considers less than fully human, Ishiguro persuades us temporarily to
accept the alien view as normative. Madame's involuntary shudder trou-
bles that identification by recalling us to the commonsense awareness
that as novel readers we actually belong to Madame's world. Ishiguro
has calibrated Kathy's perspective so that we cannot fully share the de-
humanizing impact of Madame's shudder. But who among us could
acquiesce to the conditions of Kathy's existence? Her casual use of an
estranging idiolect – "carer," "donor," "completion," "normals," "deferral," and so forth – indicates that she not only accepts her subhuman
status as given, but also prides herself on an ability to function under
conditions we would find intolerable.

Austen's free indirect style enfolds us in a single community as we
ascend with Catherine from the position of the butt of the joke to the
ironic perspective of the gentleman jokester. By contrast, Ishiguro positions his reader between Madame's involuntary shudder and Kathy's
acquiescence to her biological destiny, both of which we partially share,
neither of which earns our unqualified sympathy. Smith himself called
attention to the exclusionary function of sympathy when he acknowledged that class differences limit the reach of sympathy: "The fortunate
and the proud wonder at the insolence of human wretchedness, that it
should dare to present itself before them, and with the *loathsome aspect* of
its misery presume to disturb the serenity of their happiness" (Smith 64,
my italics). In confronting a spectacle of human "wretchedness" that
exceeds his capacity for identification, the "fortunate and proud" individual responds with disgust. Where Smith clearly disapproves of class

contempt, he elsewhere suggests, when dealing with the failure of sympathy in the abstract, that it is only natural for one to see phenomena "which have their origin in the body" as "*loathsome* and disagreeable" (Smith 35, my italics). Like the "fortunate and proud" observer, then, Smith, too, shifts the source of involuntary "disgust" onto "the loathsome aspect" of the object that elicits it. Ishiguro challenges this tenacious commonplace, when he portrays the normative observer as committed in theory to educating clones and yet unable to suppress a shudder at the thought that one of her protégées might brush against her.

It makes a kind of sense that Smith's man of taste and judgment should respond with disgust when confronted with the "wretched" condition of the very poor, but what makes Madame shudder is not nearly so apparent. Her own efforts to reform the institutions for raising clones have ensured that Kathy H. is a superbly healthy though undereducated child who shows none of "the loathsome aspect" of her subhuman condition. Unable if not unwilling to imagine herself in Kathy's position, Madame relocates the cause of her involuntary disgust in the child. Given that both Madame and Kathy H. are subject to the baleful affect that pervades the novel, however, its source is neither in the eye of the beholder nor in the object beheld but in the novel that has engineered the failure of sympathy. Reversing the logic of Smith's emotional economy, the exchange between Madame and Kathy H. diminishes the humanity of each. As Madame shudders, Kathy H. feels a chill, which she recalls years later as beginning "a process that kept growing and growing over the years until it came to dominate our lives" (37). That "process" also strains our relationship as readers to both Kathy and Madame. The two unwittingly conspire to reproduce the assumption that only rights-bearing individuals are fully human. This assumption designates certain people as disposable and then doubles their mortification by rendering them eager to remain invisible. By eliciting something akin to disappointment, if not disgust for their inadvertent collaboration, the novel eliminates the ironic position that passes for impartiality in Austen. For lack of this self-confirming resting place, the affect rising from the collapse of sympathy has nowhere to go, no target but the novel itself. This is the mark of the contemporary novel: its use of the anomalous protagonist to turn the novel form against itself.

To understand this act of aesthetic sabotage, we must fill in the historical gap between Austen and Ishiguro. I propose to do so by identifying a change in the cultural function of the feeling that arises from the failure of sympathy. Virtually indistinguishable from disgust and contempt, Smith considered this feeling either a visceral reaction to spoiled or desecrated flesh or an expression of class arrogance. Over the course of the nineteenth century, however, we can observe his opposition between natural disgust and social contempt folding in on itself to emerge as loathing, both an instinct common to man and animal in Darwin's later work and a cultural response to people, food, and practices that obscured differences essential to group identity in Victorian anthropology. The emergence of such loathing as an affect that originated paradoxically in both nature and culture tells us that, between Darwin's time and ours something has altered the composition of the affective glue that held such a community together. The basis for fellow feeling consequently shifted from positive identification, or what that feeling embraces, to negative identification, or what a group must reject as capable of destroying its identity. As the means of updating as well as naturalizing normativity, the novel obviously played an important role in this transformation. Using Austen and Ishiguro as the beginning and end points of this larger historical process, I now want to look at key points in between, where certain novels began to think their way outside the box that Smith describes as sympathy.

The Touch of the Fuegian

Let us assume with Michel Foucault that during the nineteenth century, as new institutions of education and remediation made individuals perpetually anxious about controlling themselves, normativity itself became the primary means of government. The disciplinary mechanisms that produced this self-supervisory self needed something to supervise and found it in the terrifying drives and compulsions presumed to originate in the biological body. Thus, as Foucault explains in *The History of Sexuality*, volume I, the nuclear family and its protectorate, liberal society, gradually reorganized themselves around the abnormal potential harbored within each child in order to apply all the parental and social pressures necessary for normal development. Foucault wants to see abnormal individuals as the genealogical displacement of earlier monsters that violated natural categories – hermaphrodites, Siamese twins, and the like (*Abnormal* 38-39). Looking at the nineteenth century through the bifocal lens of psychiatry and the law, he describes the Victorians' preoccupation with monstrosity as their way of distinguishing normal people from those who were biologically but not psychologically human and thus ineligible for individual rights. In this sense, then, the abnormal individual was not really an individual at all because he or she was as manifestly incapable as a child of observing the norms codified and implemented by the great social institutions of the century. By calling attention to the fact that any number of human beings could not be held responsible for their actions, the Victorian obsession with human abnormality arguably created a problem. But the curious deviations that leapt off the pages of sensational journalism and psychiatric case studies also solved a problem; they made abnormality seem more fascinating and normalcy more necessary than ever before. This did not hold true for human life that fell outside the normal / abnormal binary. Such forms of human life asserted biological continuity exactly where the Victorians felt it was essential to establish difference. Where the identification of abnormal individuals had a stabilizing effect on normative society, manifestations of this other form of difference (as Foucault explains in the lectures published in English as *"Society Must Be Defended"*), called into question the very basis of liberal society.

Mary Shelley's *Frankenstein* appeared the same year as Austen's *Northanger Abbey* and gives us a protagonist obsessed, at the expense of all ties to home and family, by an ambition to create human life scientifically. Frankenstein's attempt to manufacture a biological man traumatizes every individual who encounters the result. It is not the creature itself so much as Frankenstein's loathing that reshapes both his life and the novel form that tells his story. When he saw his theory come to life, Frankenstein felt that he could not "endure the aspect of the being I had created" and had to rush "out of the room" (Shelley 39). Though biologically human, versed in the classics of Western literature, and a student of the manners of well-socialized human beings, this creature instantly repulses everyone who happens to set eyes on him, just as he does his creator. Shelley's narrative stages a sequence of such encounters that eliminates the possibility of a rapprochement between the new scientific definition of man and a traditional concept of humanity.

In formulating a biological definition of human life, Charles Darwin arguably followed in Frankenstein's footsteps, as did the most prominent psychologists and physicians of Darwin's time. George Henry Lewes was among those who argued that the rational mind itself was part of a complex network of nerves that could receive sensations from stimuli and respond without any intervention on the part of conscious decision-making (67-69). Throughout his major theoretical works, Darwin maintained that if even the simplest organisms could respond to sensations, then sympathy must be part of our biological makeup and as such did not require Adam Smith's leap of consciousness in order for us to feel what other people feel; that capacity was part of our biological heritage.[2] To make his point, Darwin called attention to Smith's failure to account for "the fact that sympathy is excited in an immeasurably stronger degree by a beloved than by an indifferent person." Better to assume that our sympathy for other human beings comes from "an instinct, which is especially directed towards beloved objects, in the same manner as fear with animals is especially directed against certain enemies" (*Descent* 823). When he made sympathy a natural impulse, Darwin limited fellow feeling to the kin group and confined the kin group to those to whom one instinctively feels attached. The importance of this change in the basis for human sociability cannot be overestimated. Where Smith had attributed sympathy almost exclusively to individual consciousness and human culture, Darwin put our positive social instincts on a continuum with the antisocial instinct of "fear," which in "*animals* is especially directed against certain enemies" (*Descent* 823, my italics). Thus where Smith had proposed sympathy as perhaps the most important curb and corrective to natural impulses, Darwin insisted that natural affection for kin might actually collaborate with a group's antisocial impulses toward rivals in the struggle for survival. The people of Tierra del Fuego caused him to violate the conviction that human and animal emotions sprang from a single source in nature.

As the narrator of the epic *Voyage of the Beagle* (1839), Darwin regarded his chiefly non-human subject matter with the same kind of fascination he later brought to the intricate labor of the honeybee, as well as with an awe he subsequently expressed when contemplating the grandeur of the system that had created so many subtle and spectacular differences (*Origin* 760). Thus it comes as something of a shock when Darwin suddenly abandons his sense of wonder at the creatures of South America and takes to denigrating the human inhabitants of Tierra del Fuego. His account of his first encounter with these people suggests that he participated reluctantly in what was obviously a greeting ritual:

> Their very attitudes were abject, and the expression of their countenances distrustful, surprised, and startled. After we had presented them with some scarlet cloth, which they immediately tied round their necks, they became good friends. This was shown by the old man patting our breasts and making a chuckling kind of noise, as people do when feeding chickens. I walked

---

[2] The recent insights of psychologist Antonio Damasio support Darwin's claim that human emotions have their roots in the sensitivity that is basic to biological life: "Unicellular organisms are 'sensitive' to threatening intrusions. Poke an amoeba, and it will shrink away from the poke" (Damasio 257).

with the old man, and this demonstration of friendship was repeated several
times; it was concluded by three hard slaps, which were given me on the
breast and back at the same time. He then bared his bosom for me to return
the compliment, which being done, he seemed highly pleased.

(*Voyage* 190)

Here, we see Darwin attributing emotion to his host while withholding
his own. Were it not for the affect that enters his account by way of the
Fuegian's touch, we might mistakenly consider Darwin an impartial
spectator to the encounter. But physical contact with the Fuegian would
seem to trigger the negative feelings that radiate outward and blight his
ensuing description of the surrounding landscape: "The entangled mass
of the thriving and the fallen [trees] reminded me of the forests within
the tropics – yet there was a difference: for in these still solitudes,
Death, instead of Life, seemed the predominant spirit" (*Voyage* 194).
This affect intensifies, as the "atmosphere" of Tierra del Fuego seemed
to Darwin as hyperbolically "blacker than anywhere on earth" and the
"channels [of the Strait of Magellan] appeared from their gloominess to
lead beyond the confines of this world" (*Voyage* 195).[3]

Consistent with the logic of his theory, Darwin maintains that what
differentiated the Fuegian from European man also enabled the former
to survive in this unwholesome environment (*Voyage* 199). But inconsis-
tent with that logic is the sudden introjection expressing his incredulity
"that they are fellow-creatures, and inhabitants of the same world" with
himself (*Voyage* 196). Contempt mounts as he recalls that their "hideous
faces [are] bedaubed with white paint, their skins filthy and greasy, their
hair entangled, their voices discordant, and their gestures violent" (*Voyage* 197). But their disheveled appearance is the least of it. What really
turns Darwin's emotional stomach is the Fuegian practice, "when
pressed in winter by hunger, [to] kill and devour their old women."
Adding insult to injury, the source of this information was a Fuegian
boy who "imitated [the old women's] screams as a joke, and described
the parts of their bodies which are considered best to eat" (*Voyage* 197).
Though otherwise unable to "put [himself] in the position of these sav-
ages, and understand their actions" (201), Darwin seizes on this anec-

---

[3] This sudden turn of a world full of life into a world of death anticipates Melanie
Klein's notion of the self as one formed and held together defensively. These defenses
are of two basic kinds: "The defences against [persecutory] fears are predominantly the
destruction of the persecutors by violent and secret and cunning methods." The second
defence takes the form of "sorrow and concern for the loved objects" to which she
gives "a simple word derived from everyday language – namely, . . . 'pining' for the lost
object" (151). A melancholic mix of anger and sorrow is indeed in evidence here.

dote as an occasion to identify with the object of the Fuegian's tasteless joke: "Horrid as such a death by the hands of their friends and relatives must be, the fears of the old women, when hunger begins to press, are more painful to think of" (*Voyage* 197). This momentary flash of sympathy with the victim intensifies disgust for the Fuegian jokester until, as he puts it, "I got to hate the very sound of their voices" (*Voyage* 207). This intense and pervasive aversion was certainly not Darwin's problem alone.

By the last three decades of the nineteenth century, novels were regularly tapping the power peculiar to this aversion and offering bizarre quasi-supernatural explanations for its cause. In this context it makes sense to see Robert Louis Stevenson's *The Strange Case of Dr Jekyll and Mr Hyde* as an attempt to account for an anti-social reaction so immediate and yet intense that it defies psychological explanation. Hyde is another botched scientific experiment aimed at purifying man's moral and intellectual thoughts and feelings of the human impulses that drag them down. All who lay eyes on Hyde take "a loathing to the gentleman at first sight" and some "turn sick and white with the desire to kill him" (Stevenson 7). Yet witnesses are at a loss to explain exactly why Hyde elicits this "loathing": "There is something wrong with his appearance," one explains, "something downright detestable. I never saw a man I so disliked, and yet I scarce know why. He must be deformed somewhere; he gives a strong feeling of deformity, although I couldn't specify the point'" (Stevenson 9). Compare this to the scene in Oscar Wilde's *The Picture of Dorian Gray,* where Basil Hallward, once society's favorite portrait painter, witnesses the changes that have mysteriously disfigured his painting of the irresistibly handsome young man: "An exclamation of horror broke from the painter's lips as he saw in the dim light the hideous face on the canvas grinning at him. Here was something in its expression that filled him with disgust and loathing" (131). Monsters who disfigure human nature beyond recognition do not last long; for they are doubly dismissed in these late Victorian romances. They not only vanish. The supernaturalism that marks their entry and departure from the novel also allows the reader to dismiss these monsters as unreal. What cannot be so easily dismissed, however, is the affect that they unleash. Aggravated by "real-life" accounts of Jack the Ripper, Sacher-Masoch, and the like, the loathing embodied in these monsters does not redefine human nature so much as extend its definition beyond the limits of the knowable.

Against this background, it seems oddly significant that in the concluding paragraphs of *The Descent of Man* (1871), Darwin resurrects the Fuegian male in a form resembling these literary monsters. He fashions various details from the *Voyage of the Beagle* into a figure of "savage" man so void of positive social instincts and so given over to anti-social behavior that it could not be mistaken for that of a merely underdeveloped or abnormal human being. The Fuegian difference was of another magnitude. Although Darwin had no trouble pushing conventional morality aside in order to map the social instincts inherited from animal forebears onto a continuum from affection to hostility, he regarded the Fuegian's anti-social behavior as completely off the scale. In doing so, Darwin situated himself in the same relationship to his Fuegian as Frankenstein to his fabricated human being. The involuntary loathing produced by his imaginary relationship to the Fuegian informs Darwin's final appeal to those still resistant to the idea that we evolved from animals:

> He who has seen a savage in his native land will not feel much shame, if forced to acknowledge that the blood of some more humble creature flows in his veins. For my own part I would as soon be descended from that . . . old baboon, who, descending from the mountains, carried away in triumph his younger comrade from a crowd of astonished dogs – as from a savage who delights to torture his enemies, offers up bloody sacrifices, practices infanticide without remorse, treats his wives like slaves, knows no decency, and is haunted by the grossest superstitions. (*Descent* 1248)

Ordinarily moved by a sense of wonder and fascination with the abundant evidence of nature's creative power, Darwin intrepidly eroded the line separating man and animal. But as he was about to offer a final drumroll celebrating the continuity among biological species he had always argued for, the figure of the Fuegian overtook his imagination and once again turned Darwin's nature into the dark and violent habitat of "savage man."

In *The Expression of Emotion in Man and Animal*, published only one year after *The Descent of Man*, Darwin tried to contain the contaminating power of this affect by reducing it to a more manageable but nonetheless visceral response. As he explains, "The term 'disgust,' in its simplest sense, means something offensive to the taste. It is curious how readily this feeling is excited by anything unusual in the appearance, odour, or nature of our food" (*Expression* 1411-12). When Darwin applied this concept to the Fuegian, however, he reanimated the negative affect that once connected his food to the savage and the savage back to his European food and by way of that tainted piece of meat to Darwin himself: "In Tierra del Fuego a native touched with his finger some cold preserved meat which I was eating at our bivouac, and plainly showed utter disgust at its softness; whilst I felt utter disgust at my food being touched by a naked savage, though his hands did not appear dirty" (*Expression* 1412). Where the Fuegian's disgust arises from food that appears to be rotten ("soft"), Darwin attributes his disgust neither to the food nor to the hand that touches it but to the figure of the "naked savage." In recalling the incident, his disgust again expands well beyond his definition of "something offensive to the taste" and becomes an altogether different affect. No doubt the feeling was originally linked to food by way of the rumor that the Fuegians ate old women when other food was scarce. But the term "disgust" cannot do justice to the enduring intensity of Darwin's initial encounter with a tribe that in living beyond the limit of the habitable world, lived under conditions where their humanity, as he understood it, had no chance of survival. Thus although he usually took delight in the idea of such extreme forms of life, he reacted very badly to this idea when it assumed human form. What began as a Fuegian greeting ritual took on aggressive energy that intensified until it spilled out in prose that objectified that loathing.

The Importance of Refusing Reparative Work

It is against this background that I'd like to try and make sense of the contemporary novel's focus on extreme forms of human life. I see the recent appearance of anomalous protagonists as an attempt to recuperate such life from the loathing that it came to embody and discharge during the colonial period. This attempt differs pointedly from the reparative work of identity politics, which shows members of excluded populations to have qualities of human subjectivity that should entitle them to a place within the ambit of public sympathy. Where identity politics argues that excluded populations can be normal too, the fiction I consider truly contemporary understands that loathsome forms of human life generate loathing because they defy exactly this translation. One cannot imagine a normal version of them. If each such form creates a category for itself, then integrating it into the sphere of normativity would call normativity itself into question in some fundamental way. Where most twentieth-century novels take up the project of endowing excluded groups with liberal selfhood, another tradition – in anticipation of the present moment – accepts the impossibility of that move. These novelists argue that loathsome forms of human life offer alternatives to liberal selfhood that other novelists have phobicized lest such monsters displace the normative protagonist, as they do in Stevenson and Wilde.

I like to think that Kafka was out to mark this difference when he dragged the human/animal distinction inside the category of the human and installed it just where we would expect to find a narrative distinguishing between normal and abnormal human beings. In *The Metamorphosis,* Kafka's protagonist goes to bed a harried salesman and family breadwinner and famously wakes up a harried cockroach and the source of family shame. At first, everyone assumes that Gregor Samsa is not himself – that his condition is, in other words, abnormal. But, no, Gregor is irreversibly on his way to being an insect associated with filth and the defilement of food. It takes but one sentence for this protagonist's biological body to slide down the scale of being from human to insect, so that the story of his short life can dwell at the stages in between, as a human consciousness settles into an insect body and strives to maintain a place within its kin group. At first, the Samsas use his room in their apartment as a closet for the shame they feel compelled to hide. After a while, they give up their fantasy that the creature in Gregor's room is an abnormal Gregor who can be either rehabilitated or confined. They begin to use his room for trash, by definition a space that belongs outside the house. At this point, we find it impossible to say whether it is the fact of being a disposable life form or his exclusion from the family that actually kills him. That Gregor looks, smells, sounds, and behaves like a giant cockroach, compounded by his tendency to wander from his room, convinces even his sister that there is no longer anything human about him. "'I won't pronounce the name of my brother in front of this monster," she avers, "and so all I say is: we have to try to get rid of it. We've done everything humanly possible to take care of it and to put up with it; I don't think anyone can blame us in the least'" (Kafka 37). This is welcome news to a family who know they can maintain their tenuous place in society by disposing of what had once been their kin.

But Kafka sees to it that his reader cannot do likewise, forcing us to acknowledge Gregor's humanity well beyond the point where a sensible human being could no longer call the cockroach human:

> The rotten apple in his back and the inflamed area around it, which were completely covered with fluffy dust, already hardly bothered him. He thought back on his family with deep emotion and love. . . . He still saw that everything outside the window was beginning to grow light. Then,

without his consent, his head sank down to the floor, and from his nostrils streamed his last weak breath. (51)

A poignant death scene, to be sure, but one nonetheless designed to put a sympathetic response well beyond our reach. After all, this protagonist is an insect, and a banged up one at that, barely distinguishable from the garbage on which he feeds. As in the case of the Fuegian, the source of the reader's disgust shifts with the family's from food that one must not eat to the one who enjoys that food. Yet the poignancy of Gregor's enduring love of family renders the object of loathing too human for us to loathe.

For several decades now, a range of intellectuals have been strangely drawn to the space between human and animal and the secret of how those human beings consigned to such a space experience life that has been reduced to slow death. Giorgio Agamben's *Homo Sacer* provides an elaborate theory of the historical emergence into centrality of "bare life," which he defines as human "life that may be killed but not sacrificed" (83), the consummate testimony to which is the Nazi concentration camp – just as it is in Foucault's early lectures on biopower. What gets lost in both accounts is not only how the Jewish people became the source of the loathing that in previous decades had been unleashed by fictional monsters, but also how such radical reclassification affects the life subjected to it. Approaching the problem with characteristic vitalism, Deleuze and Guattari resist the definition of surplus life as inherently disposable and in this sense already dead. Rather than assume that death is the fixed limit of biological life, they understand life itself as a force that circumvents that limit, not by resisting the return of any individual to matter, but by producing new permutations of an exhausted form. We might indeed attribute the attraction that neuroscience holds for some humanists and the inroads it is consequently making in humanistic inquiry to the fact that brain theory has opened a conceptual space between the moment when sensation registers on the nervous system and the moment when it becomes available to consciousness. But cognitive scientists who have garnered fame and funding for discovering ways of filling in this gap can have no more success than philosophers in providing conscious access to an experience that is by definition inaccessible to consciousness. While they have cleared this conceptual space, philosophy and neuroscience have left it to the novel to imagine what it feels like to be in one of Deleuze and Guattari's in-between states.

With this in mind, we can begin to understand the emergence of a protagonist like Kathy H. as Ishiguro's attempt to expose the twin mechanisms of sympathy and its failure – i.e., loathing – as false alternatives. "I can still see it now," says Ishiguro's Kathy H., "the shudder [Madame] seemed to be suppressing, the real dread that one of us would accidentally brush against her" (35). That shudder told Kathy that people who live in the normal world cannot help but regard her as they would a spider, not exactly a cockroach, but a variety of vermin nonetheless. Thus she knows, better than Madame does, "the real dread" that expresses itself in that shudder. Why, then, can't that knowledge set Kathy free to act on her own behalf, Ishiguro's reader wants to know (see, for example, Black). Hailsham is no different from the disciplinary institutions that produced both Madame and the novel's readership by providing its inmates with scant material with which to imagine an alternative world. And Madame is no different than Kathy in her failure to imagine an adequate alternative to organ donation, as the means of repairing the deteriorating bodies of her loved ones. Thus it is not surprising that as we acclimate to Kathy's macabre euphemisms, we also accept the limits of Hailsham academy. It would take a ruthlessly unsophisticated reader to go along with Kathy's faith in the myth that the art she produced as a child demonstrated her innate humanity and can earn her a deferral of the death that awaits her at the age of thirty-something.

It is not nearly so important that Kathy's fantasy is shattered as that of the reader's is. For although we can no longer hope that the myth of artistic originality will materialize for Kathy, who among us does not in some recess of his/her consciousness believe that to fulfill oneself is to become a special, indeed irreplaceable individual? Kathy's first direct encounter with Madame establishes the difference between Kathy's world and our own in this respect. But Kathy's second encounter with Madame exposes that difference as a fiction that depends for substance on the dehumanization that renders Kathy and her kind disposable. Despite the limitations of Kathy's education in the ways of this world, we see enough to know that the people protected by the institutions of liberal society proper are hardly better off – sick, fearful, tormented, angry, and unable to accept the finitude of individual existence. Like Kathy and Tommy, those characters representing the world of "normal" people in Never Let Me Go cannot imagine changing the way they live. They can only imagine putting off death, even if it requires – in an absolute reversal of the logic of sympathy – that other people experience mortality in their stead. Having arrived at this point, we are no longer dealing with a fictional encounter between an acquiescent human clone and a predatory class of organ recipients, for both can be seen as victims of the fantasy of individual full being. It is at this point that my argument converges with Bruce Robbins's claim that Ishiguro sees cruelty to one's closest friends and family as something that cannot be simply treated or cured, but rather as an extension of institutionalized caring that promotes the life of some at the cost of others. Rather than see Hailsham as under the discursive control of real-world class divisions and Kathy as its unwitting scribe, I want to propose another reason why Ishiguro has Kathy represent that institution in such positive terms. There's much more to it, I believe, than her ignorance or insensitivity.

Like Kafka, Ishiguro refuses to explain away the sudden intrusion within the world of the novel of what had been either outside or invisible within it. In doing so, both novelists challenge what Walter Benjamin considered the protagonist and first principle of the novel form itself: "The birthplace of the novel is the solitary individual, who is no longer able to express himself [as earlier storytellers were] by giving examples of his most important concerns, himself uncounseled, and cannot counsel others" (87). Gregor not only affects but is also affected by everyone who enters the family apartment. By thus rerouting the story's affect, he converts the family from an enclave to a hub opened up to new relationships. So, too, in her capacity as mature "carer" and narrator, Kathy H. gathers the members of her cohort into herself and disperses them according to a comprehensive network of remembering that opposes the operations of the market in human body parts. Rather than developing from childhood to completion as an adult, her tale expands with the bonds of friendship and retracts where that affect is repulsed. The narrator's self expression is consequently that of the group as a whole and, as such, creates an alternative to the community of individuals that Darwin felt compelled to protect from the Fuegian's touch.

Kathy H. begins her story after being a "carer" for eleven years as she is about to enter one of the donation centers into which her closest schoolmates, Ruth and Tommy, have already vanished. This, as Ruth put it, is "what we're *supposed* to be doing" (227), and Kathy feels the time is "about right" to fulfill her destiny (4). In accepting the teleology that produces and regulates her biological life, however, Kathy also displaces that linear plot from birth to death with another narrative form that comes closer to that of Benjamin's ideal storyteller. Finding human life especially impoverished by the culture of the novel, which makes "it possible for people to avoid the sight of the dying" (Benjamin 93), Benjamin rejects the idea that death is opposed to life. It is only near death, he contends, that an individual's "real life . . . first assumes transmissible form" and "the unforgettable emerges and imparts to everything that concerned him that authority which even the poorest wretch in dying possesses for the living around him" (94). Benjamin equates this form of "completion" (the Hailsham term for death) with the aesthetics of storytelling. "Death," he says, "is the sanction of everything that the storyteller can tell" (94).

By the time she writes that story, Kathy has assumed a relation to her biological life that resembles that which Jacques Derrida assumes on accepting his diagnosis of terminal cancer. He paradoxically assumes the position of a survivor.[4] "Survival is not simply that which remains," he claims. Quite the contrary, it is "the most intense life possible" (quoted in Fassin 82). In thus feeling that he has passed the limit of his biological life span, he also came to realize that to experience life as a survivor requires more than understanding that one's biological life is terminal. The acceptance of imminent death intensifies the experience of life for the person who can seize the moment, when, as Benjamin claims, "the unforgettable emerges" and life for the first time "assumes transmissible form" (94). Seen in this light, Kathy H. would have qualified herself to tell the story of the Hailsham children at the moment when she grasped fully the meaning of Madame's definitive shudder. In assembling the intricate network of relations in which she played but a small part, she lends that community wholeness as well as herself, in and as her story. By so doing, Kathy assumes the role of Benjamin's traditional storyteller who "imparts to everything that concerned him that authority which even the poorest wretch in dying possesses for the living around him" (Benjamin 94). In contrast to the event that authorizes that storyteller, however, Kathy's imminent dismemberment is at once real and not the least bit commonplace under cultural conditions that both require and suppress her death. The event that authorizes Kathy to "impart to everything that concerned [her] that authority which even the poorest wretch in dying possesses for the living around him" is one for which

---

[4] Fassin's groundbreaking "Ethics of Survival" first persuaded me to think of survival as an alternative relation to embodied experience. Fassin reads Derrida's reflections on his own death as shattering the distinction between "biological life" and "lived experience": "survival mixes inextricably physical life, threatened by his cancer, and existential experience expressed in his work. To survive is to be still fully alive and to live beyond death . . . in the traces left for the living" (83). I see this hope of absorption in "the living" as both ironically appropriate for Ishiguro's novel and directly opposed to the myth of *individual* immortality in and through the work of art.

there is no historical precedent and our present vocabulary seems grossly inadequate.[5]

Abandoning the fantasy of full being is not without advantages, if only because it transforms the mix of fear, disgust, and anger expressed by Madame's shudder into the pervasive sadness of Ishiguro's novel. If Madame's struggle to hang onto that fantasy perpetuates the violence of organ donation, then Kathy's abandonment of the fantasy of full being understandably produces sadness akin to mourning in those who hold it dear. In Kathy's story, the alternative to the dismal process of serial death resides in the halcyon days of Hailsham School, which structures not only the lost world of childhood but also the network that transforms her memory into a protracted diversion from and redefinition of the fate of disposability. In order to prepare them for that fate, I mean to suggest, Hailsham inadvertently provided its students with a holding environment that served them much as the playpen does a child.[6] Here, students were allowed to run in packs enforcing a kind of equality in that everyone was part of a community that maintained itself by continuously replacing its parts. Confined within the fences surrounding Hailsham, their play necessarily consisted mainly of variations on a limited number of games, forms of gossip, sexual encounters, and arts and crafts, all of which circulated individuals in clusters with shifting hierarchies. Rather than assume a leadership role or develop a practical specialization, the group learned to apply the same caretaking skills in a variety of different situations. Where Madame understood student art as the means of materializing the humanity, or inner life of individual clones, the students valued it for earning each of them tokens with which to purchase the artwork of other students in a local market. Like their play, their practice of evaluating and collecting these recycled bits of self-expression maintain their identity as a single body, one that mirrored and collectivized the repaired body of the unidentified "normal" individual who will receive their organs. This form of play presumably

---

[5] Massumi defines "the affective event" as one in which the collective anticipation of disruption becomes the disruptive event. Such an event creates a "future-past" that replaces the anticipated event with the very affect it would have caused.

[6] In providing what Winnicott describes as "the holding environment," Hailsham provides the students with something approximating this maternal environment, which reduces "the impingements to which the infant must react with resultant annihilation of personal being" ("Parent-Infant Relationship" 47). In "Primitive Emotional Development," Winnicott uses the peace associated with the play of selves to challenge the assumption that "in health the individual is always integrated, as well as living in his own body, and able to feel that the world is real" in order to suggest that we have an innate capacity to be just the reverse (150).

produced the estranged individual we encounter in Kathy's narration, one without a basis in material property, including even a body, on which to consolidate an identity. But while she lacks substance as an individual and defies our efforts to read her as a psychologically integrated whole, this narrator allows us to move fluidly and fearlessly between subject positions and across ontological divides.

The point of reading is to see our contemporary world, however briefly, through such alternative eyes – not to make us "see," as Joseph Conrad once put it, but to make us feel what it is that loathing precludes. What is the industry in human organs, after all, if not the by-product of sympathy, a mechanism for repairing the individual, and a means of materializing the fantasy of full being well past its historical lifetime? The calm and yet complicated pleasure of a re-membered Hailsham is the only antidote that Ishiguro provides to the curious mixture of anger and sadness that we feel as Kathy alternately elicits and repels our sympathetic identification. If as Claude Lévi-Strauss claims, "the hero of the novel is the novel itself" (103), then Hailsham is not only the cause and formal logic of Kathy's arrested development, it also serves as the true protagonist of *Never Let Me Go*. In order to assume this role – and it's doubtful that it will so serve for everyone – Hailsham has to perform a positive attenuation of the fantasy of full being. Hailsham's differences from the disciplinary institutions that turn out disciplined subjects like Madame – and ourselves – are neither minor nor entirely aesthetic choices. By virtue of these differences, Hailsham provides Kathy and those under her care – which includes her readers – an alternative to institutions that interpellate and discipline their subjects. For the purposes of my argument, that institution would be the novel that disciplines both protagonist and readership, as Austen does, by eliciting sympathetic responses.

With Kathy H., we survive the linear march of a protagonist toward that fullness of being that Ishiguro, like Benjamin before him, equates with death. In its place, the contemporary novel offers a holding environment where readers can momentarily abandon the anxiety that sustains modern individualism and become the diffuse, discontinuous, and relational subject that manifests itself at certain "Hailsham" moments in Kathy's narration. The contemporary novel transforms this way of being – long understood as the child's way of not yet being in the world – into a better way for those in liminal positions to survive their death as individuals, namely, as several partial selves rather than integrated identities. It cannot be coincidental that Ishiguro, Coetzee, Sebald and the other novelists I consider contemporary in the true sense have each transformed obscure, radically inhospitable places in the reader's own world into similar holding environments where we experience memorably inventive forms of this new relationship to death.

I would like to thank my efficiently studious research assistant, Ben Richardson, for his bibliographical work and editorial comments.

References

Agamben, Giorgio. *Homo Sacer: Sovereignty and bare Life.* Trans. Daniel Heller-Roazen. New York: Standford University Press, 1998.

Armstrong, Nancy. *How Novels Think: The Limits of Individualism from 1719-1900.* New York: Columbia University Press, 2005.

Austen, Jane. *Northanger Abbey, Lady Susan, The Watsons* and *Sandition.* Ed. James Kinsley and John Davie. Oxford: Oxford University Press, 2008.

Benjamin, Walter. "The Storyteller: Reflections on the Work of Nikolai Leskov." Trans. Harry Zohn. New York: Schocken, 2007. 83-110.

Black, Shameem. "Ishiguro's Inhuman Aesthetics." *Modern Fiction Studies,* 55.4 (2009): 785-807.

Cooper, Melinda. *Life as Surplus: Biotechnology and Capitalism in the Neoliberal Era.* Seattle: University of Washington Press, 2008.

Damasio, Antonio. *Self Comes to Mind: Constructing the Conscious Brain.* New York: Pantheon Books, 2010.

Darwin, Charles. *The Descent of Man, and Selection in Relation to Sex. From So Simple a Beginning: The Four Great Books of Charles Darwin.* Ed. Edward O. Wilson. New York: W. W. Norton and Company, 2006. 767-1252.

———. *The Expression of the Emotions in Man and Animals. From So Simple A Beginning: The Four Great Books of Charles Darwin.* Ed. Edward O. Wilson. New York: W. W. Norton and Company, 2006. 1255-1478.

———. *On the Origin of the Species. From So Simple a Beginning: The Four Great Books of Charles Darwin.* Ed. Edward O. Wilson. New York: W. W. Norton and Company, 2006. 441-764.

———. *The Voyage of the Beagle. From So Simple a Beginning: The Four Great Books of Charles Darwin.* Ed. Edward O. Wilson. New York: W. W. Norton and Company, 2006. 21-436.

Deleuze, Gilles and Felix Guattari. *Kafka: Toward a Minor Literature.* Trans. Terry Cochran. Minneapolis: University of Minnesota Press, 1986.

Fassin, Didier. "Ethics of Survival: A Democratic Approach to the Politics of Life." *Humanity: An International Journal of Human Rights, Humanitarianism, and Development.* 1, 1 (2012): 81-95.

Foucault, Michel. *Discipline and Punish: The Birth of the Prison.* Trans. Alan Sheridan. New York: Random House, 1998.

———. *Abnormal: Lectures at the College de France, 1974-1975.* Trans. Graham Burchell. New York: Picador, 2003.

————. *Society Must Be Defended: Lectures at the Collège de France 1975-1976.* Trans. David Macey. New York: Picador, 1997.

Ishiguro, Kazuo. *Never Let Me Go.* New York: Vintage, 2005.

Kafka, Franz. *The Metamorphosis.* Trans. Susan Bernofsky. New York: Norton, 2014.

Klein, Melanie. *The Selected Melanie Klein.* Ed. Juliette Mitchell. New York: The Free Press, 1986.

Lévi-Strauss, Claude. "From *The Origin of Table Manners.*" *Theory of the Novel: A Historical Approach.* Ed. Michael McKeon. Baltimore: Johns Hopkins University Press, 2000. 100-03.

Lewes, George Henry. *The Physiology of Common Life.* Vol. 2. New York: D. Appleton and Company, 1875.

Massumi, Brian. "The Future Birth of the Affective Fact: The Political Ontology of Threat." Ed. Melissa Gregg and Gregory J. Seigworth. Durham: Duke University Press, 2010. 52-70.

Radcliffe, Ann. *The Mysteries of Udolpho.* New York: Oxford University Press, 2008.

Robbins, Bruce. "Cruelty is Bad: Banality and Proximity in *Never Let Me Go.*" Ed. Lisa Fluet. *Novel: A Forum on Fiction* 40, 3(2007): 289-303.

Shelly, Mary. *Frankenstein, or, The Modern Prometheus: The 1818 Text.* Ed. Marilyn Butler. Oxford: Oxford University Press, 2008.

Smith, Adam. *The Theory of Moral Sentiments.* Ed. Ryan Patrick Hanley. London: Penguin, 2009. Ed. Joseph Bristow. Oxford: Oxford University Press, 2008.

Stevenson, Robert Louis. *The Strange Case of Dr. Jekyll and Mr. Hyde: And Other Tales of Terror.* New York: Penguin, 2003.

Wilde, Oscar. *The Picture of Dorian Gray.* Ed. Joseph Bristow. Oxford: Oxford University Press, 2008.

Winnicott, D. W. "Primitive Emotional Development." *Through Paediatrics to Psychoanalysis.* New York: Basic Books, 1958. 147-55.

————. "The Theory of the Parent-Infant Relationship." *The Maturational Processes and the Facilitating Environment: Studies in the Theory of Emotional Development.* New York: International Universities Press, 1965. 37-55

Delicious, Tender Chaucer:
Coleridge, Emotion and Affect

Stephanie Trigg

New studies in the history of emotion are transforming, enriching and extending current humanities scholarship. Emotional responses to literary texts have the potential to constitute an important archive for the history of feeling. The literary reception of medieval texts, especially that of Chaucer, has been mined for its potential to track changes in style and taste within textual communities over time. Using William Reddy's concept of the *emotive utterance*, this essay tests a key moment in Chaucer reception: Samuel Taylor Coleridge's discourse about the affective experience of reading Chaucer. Such analysis of the critical archive can help us understand not just the history of Chaucer reception, but also the history of feeling about medieval literature, and the literature of the past.

Studies in the history of feeling, passion and emotion can take many forms. They range from the small-scale analysis of literary or artistic works and the sensibilities they express or evoke through to broader accounts of large-scale and long-range historical change. The networked inter-disciplinary field of the *history of emotions* is similarly varied. It is interested in the history of terminology about passions, feelings, emotions; in emotional restraint and self-governance; and in the continuities and differences in emotional regimes, scripts or practices (the terminology used is very diverse), across the pre-modern, the modern and the post-modern periods (Trigg, "Introduction"). It is a field that shares affinities and methodologies with a number of diverse disciplines: cognitive psy-

Emotion, Affect, Sentiment: The Language and Aesthetics of Feeling. SPELL: Swiss Papers in English Language and Literature 30. Ed. Andreas Langlotz and Agnieszka Soltysik Monnet. Tübingen: Narr, 2014. 51-66.

chology, history, philosophy, language, literature, sociology, anthropology, and linguistics. It can also intersect productively with what is often named as the *affective turn* within cognitive, phenomenal, and cultural studies. However, it is probably fair to say that within most institutional settings, the predominant methodological orientation is historiographical. The most often cited theorists and practitioners in the history of emotions – Barbara Rosenwein, Peter and Carol Stearns, William Reddy, Thomas Dixon – are trained as historians, and while they sometimes work with "literary" sources, and are sometimes attentive to rhetorical structures and forms of expression, their own theoretical discussions tend to be directed to other historians: that is, the disciplinary default position of the field is still historical study.

In that context it is sometimes possible to discern a kind of bias against the witness of literary texts to the history of emotions. When considered in general terms, literature, drama, art, and music are all privileged sites for the exploration of emotion. As creative and imaginative forms, they open up spaces in which we may contemplate emotion, feeling, and passion without embarrassment. Indeed, works of music, art, and literature are sometimes used in clinical studies that seek to measure neurological, cognitive, or psychological affect. Yet in spite of their often very precise delineations and descriptions of feelings and passions, literary texts are sometimes sidelined as sources for the history of emotions, regarded as the expressions of specialized or élite communities or individuals, especially when that history reaches back through premodern to medieval times. Alternatively, they are seen as too self-consciously rhetorical or overtly fictional to be either truly representative or faithfully expressive of genuine feeling. It has to be said that the dominant methodologies of literary studies don't help the case here. Our characteristic love of ambivalence, uncertainty, even undecideability hardly promotes our texts as reliable or unmediated sources in the history of feeling, at least to those looking to track precise semantic changes or accurate definitions of particular emotions.

And if literature is seen as courting too much ambiguity to be a reliable witness to "real" emotions, then the discourses of literary criticism lie even further beyond the pale as potential sources for emotional histories. Even more than literature itself, criticism is heavily mediated by its own conventions, social codes, and decorum as an indirect secondary or theoretical discourse. The practice of literary criticism seems remote from broader patterns of psychic or social change; it is hardly representative of broader communal and social movements, and in its dominant modern form is often more concerned with the exercise of critical judgment and interpretation, or the shaping forces of social and cultural change than affective or emotional responses to the literary text. This broad pattern is not always even or consistent, however; and it is possible to chart distinct waves of greater and lesser intensity in emotional responses to literature, whether amongst academic, or scholarly, or "general" readers. Through most of the second half of the twentieth century, for example, the dominant critical discourse in the universities cultivated a neutral, impersonal tone that repressed, rather than celebrated, the passions. The renewed interest in a more personal tone in literary criticism in recent years reminds us of the long and uneven history of emotional expression in the critical reception of literary texts, and the different inflections – modulated by class, gender, and other cultural forces – of the reading and writing critical subject.

In this essay I suggest that the reception history of Geoffrey Chaucer offers a distinctive and symptomatic archive of feeling and thought about the past, as well as about this most intriguing medieval poet. Chaucer's reception history discloses a range of individual and shared emotions that vary dramatically from the fifteenth through to the twenty-first century, and which allow us to chart a critical and emotional lexicon quite precisely around the more or less stable core of the medieval poet's work. I say "more or less stable," because the authorship and ownership of the works we now name as Chaucer's were not always as sure as they are now; and because the history of editing Chaucer's works has produced some very different versions of his texts and narratives of his life. We have now become quite accustomed to reading this tradition in ideological terms: scholars of Middle English will think of Carolyn Dinshaw's reading of the work of E. Talbot Donaldson and D. W. Robertson (*Chaucer's Sexual Poetics*), for example; or Seth Lerer's work on the rhetorical construction of the fifteenth-century laureate Chaucer (*Chaucer and His Readers*). I am suggesting that as a kind of supplement to this work, the rich archive of Chaucer criticism (it would be the same for Shakespeare, or Homer, or Virgil, as well as other more recent writers, musicians, or artists) can also help us understand the emotional history of our critical and affective negotiations with the medieval past.

It is not just that Chaucer's own works vary so widely in tone, genre, and style, nor that the history of changing taste foregrounds different texts and different "Chaucers" in different periods, from comical, romantic, satirical, and tragic, for instance. It is crucial to remember that literary criticism has not always been practiced by the same social groups or according to the same rhetorical conventions across its history. An important part of this story, then, would be the gradual displacement of personal emotional response in favor of philological and language study as English literature moved into the university sector in the late nineteenth century, at the same time as the universities began to welcome women students. As the practices and social contexts of literary criticism change, so too do the forms and varieties of emotions that are expressed and displayed.

My central example of the way reception studies can meet the study of the history of emotions is a tiny fragment of Chaucerian response from a famous and influential poet-critic, Samuel Taylor Coleridge. In 1835, the year after Coleridge's death, his nephew and son-in-law, Henry Nelson Coleridge, published his *Specimens of the Table Talk of Samuel Taylor Coleridge*, a collection of his uncle's conversational discourse on various topics of literature, philosophy, and other matters. Somewhat less formal than his *Biographia Literaria*, Coleridge's *Table Talk* is frequently mined for its opinions on various topics that are then lifted out and cited in different contexts. His short discussion of Geoffrey Chaucer is a good example of this tendency; it is discussed far more often in the traditions of Chaucer reception than Coleridge criticism.

The extract in question is dated 15 March 1834:

> I take unceasing delight in Chaucer. His manly cheerfulness is especially delicious to me in my old age. How exquisitely tender he is, and yet how perfectly free from the least touch of sickly melancholy or morbid drooping! The sympathy of the poet with the subjects of his poetry is particularly remarkable in Shakespeare and Chaucer; but what the first effects by a strong act of imagination and mental metamorphosis, the last does without any effort, merely by the inborn kindly joyousness of his nature. How well we seem to know Chaucer! How absolutely nothing do we know of Shakespeare! (Coburn 466)

This is not part of a larger discussion of Chaucer or medieval poetry. The "entry" for this date begins here. The paragraph that follows is a discussion of Chaucer's poetics including a few suggestions about how to regularize his meter and modernize his vocabulary, before Coleridge turns to discuss Shakespeare, Beaumont, Fletcher, and Herrick. There is no obvious connection to the "talk" that precedes or follows it on other days, nor any record of Coleridge's interlocutors on this occasion.

The conventions of the "table talk" genre frame these remarks as if they were an accurate record of the poet's thoughts and discourse over dinner or in other company, though they must have been mediated, revised, and polished to some degree by their editor. This discussion of Chaucer is particularly conversational and personal, far more than some of the more philosophical topics treated in the collection. Already this shows us that literature, or medieval literature, or at least the poetry of Chaucer seems to license a different form of emotional discourse.

The simplest way to read this paragraph is as one side of a casual, though not unconsidered, conversation. The commentary on Coleridge's *Table Talk* often draws attention less flatteringly to the poet's reputation for long conversational monologues, sometimes to the frustration of his hearers and interlocutors. Indeed, Henry Nelson Coleridge goes to some pains in his introduction to defend his uncle from such charges. Nothing is recorded about the immediate context of these remarks about Chaucer. If they were part of a conversation, the voices of any other participants are silenced, and the discussion of Chaucer is absorbed into the continuous stream of Coleridge's opinions, collected and recorded over many years.

When they appear as part of the long archive of *Chaucer* criticism, on the other hand, Coleridge's remarks are lifted out decisively from the context that celebrates *his* collected works and thoughts, and placed into a different, much longer chronological stream of Chaucerian reception. This is a deep, rich, and varied record of opinions and feelings about Chaucer, from the earliest fifteenth-century attempts to complete and supplement *The Canterbury Tales* and the long history of adaptations and translations of his work; through the interplay of personal, private, and public statements about his poetry; and into the less personal, more formal conventions of modern, academic, and pedagogical discourse. In this context, even though it is so short, Coleridge's paragraph on Chaucer carries a disproportionate amount of symbolic capital: as the words of one poetic master about another; as words of high praise that have the added virtue for Chaucerians of comparing Chaucer quite favorably to Shakespeare; and as words that model a deeply personal affective and emotional response to Chaucer, as someone we feel we can come to know on quite intimate terms (Trigg, *Congenial Souls*). This is already a very influential mode in Chaucer criticism by this period.

The standard way to read extracts cited out of context in this manner is through the history of taste, through changing fashions in medievalism, the readerly construction of different images and representations of Chaucer and his poetry; even different relationships with Chaucer, and ideological assumptions about what literature does, and is for. Such reception studies are nevertheless usually positioned as a kind of secondary adjunct to literary interpretation.

However, these responses to literary texts have the further potential to contribute to the broader history of feeling. The long history of reception of a poet like Chaucer, for example, that ranges from the medieval period through to the present, can be read as an important, focused, historical narrative archive for the history of emotions. It is not just that this archive can help us track changing patterns of affective, emotional response in literary criticism; it can also help us understand the changing rhetorical and expressive language in which literature is read and discussed, and the changing ways readers have responded emotionally to the literature of the past.

The very act of writing literary criticism may thus be analyzed as an indicative component of the social and cultural habitus, in Pierre Bourdieu's sense of that term (52-65). Such readings encourage greater attention to the social context of literary response as well as criticism's structures of feeling. Literary criticism and response may have become the specialist product of the literate classes, but in the case of Chaucer this is still part of a continuous history of feeling about medieval literature and the medieval past, a history that operates according to its own internal logics and patterns of influence.

Reading and studying reception history is usually practiced in a very abstracted way: the most typical form of assembling the Chaucerian archive is to extract descriptions and characterizations of the work or author in question and to anthologize them historically, as in Eleanor Hammond's *Chaucer: A Bibliographical Manual*, Caroline Spurgeon's *Five Hundred Years of Chaucer Criticism and Allusion*, D. S. Brewer's two volumes in the *Critical Heritage* series, or J. A. Burrow's *Geoffrey Chaucer: A Critical Anthology*. Chaucer's reception history is thus constituted as a precisely dated archive. Typically, in such anthologies, extracts from reviews, criticism proper, introductions to translations and commentaries, diaries and other forms are gathered and put into sequence with little regard to their textual or social context. This is the form in which Coleridge's remarks on Chaucer usually appear. While this is itself a distinctive form of critical practice, it is also profitable to slow down and examine these references and allusions to Chaucer in closer detail to analyze their emotional and affective import.

Monique Scheer has recently shown how Bourdieu's understanding of the "habitus" can be used to shape an understanding of emotions as themselves a form of practice. In contrast to studies that insist on the ontological priority of affect, or that try to untangle the competing claims of mind, body, brain, and language, Scheer emphasizes "the mutual embeddedness of minds, bodies, and social relations in order to historicize the body and its contributions to the learned experience of emotion" (199). She avoids the word "affect," citing Ruth Leys' critique of this concept when it is used to force an artificial division between mind and body.

Scheer's approach, rejecting the Cartesian opposition between mind and body, seems particularly useful for this study. We may thus work with the highly individualized texts of literary expression and response, but read them in their own broader social contexts: the texts, bodies, objects, and practices of everyday life. Bourdieu's habitus does not *constrain* emotion, but provides a framework, an orientation for feeling. For Scheer, "[e]motions can thus be viewed as acts executed by a mindful body, as cultural practices" (205). As she explains:

> the habits of the mindful body are executed outside of consciousness and rely on social scripts from historically situated fields. That is to say, a distinction between incorporated society and the parts of the body generating emotion is hard to make. [...] [t]he feeling self executes emotions, and experiences them in varying degrees and proportions, as inside and outside, subjective and objective, depending on the situation. (207)

This method of reading can help us make sense, for example, of the way we read medieval bodily gestures and other emotional practices such as weeping, and the response to them, both in literary fictions themselves, and in the textual, editorial, and critical reception of such moments (Trigg, "Langland's Tears").

In the context of literary criticism, however, practice theory encourages us to think about the social context in which such discourse is practiced. How are the author roles of scribe, editor, copyist, translator, typesetter, printer, publisher, critic, reader, and reviewer differentiated from each other at different times? In what social contexts and with what social expectations and assumptions is Chaucer's work read and discussed? Chaucer's reception history is of particular interest, it must be admitted, if only because the long patterns of his reception help us track changes in the construction of authorship and its reception from the medieval period through to the postmodern.

To sketch out the broad parameters of this reception history we could do worse than quote Stephen Knight, who in 1986 deftly summed up the main trends of critical response to the medieval poet:

> Chaucer's near-contemporaries admired the technical dexterity and wide scope of his poetry, because an author was then seen as a socially responsible craftsman ("maker" is the Middle English for poet), but when writers

came to be conceived of as sophisticated renaissance individuals, Chaucer was only seen as a surprisingly learned precursor. Later, among the constrained self-concepts associated with the emergent bourgeois state, readers found an almost noble savagery in Chaucer, ranging in its direction from the vulgarity relished by Dryden and Pope to Coleridge's "manly cheerfulness." Some nineteenth century ideologues heard in him a patriotic voice from "Merry Old England"; a less reductive re-reading linked with the mainline sociocultural tradition of the novel and when Kittredge disseminated the model of Chaucer as a wisely passive observer of humankind, he only brought to a head a dominant attitude of his period. That is still the most widespread reception of the texts, but the special social world of the academy has generated some new and even more conservative versions. The "new criticism" found Chaucer a master poetic ironist, making wit and euphony a sufficient response to the world. An even more potent ivory tower was constructed by the allegorical school, who deployed their quasi-monastic learning to find in the texts consistent reference to sin and salvation. (1)

It would be possible to update this, now, to take account of more recent developments in feminist, Marxist, postmodernist, performativity, reception, and medievalist theory, for example. There are other more detailed summaries of Chaucerian reception, but this gives a good survey that is unusually alert to the social, institutional, and political contexts in which Chaucer criticism is practiced. Knight is less interested in embodied, emotional responses here than charting the ideological history of Chaucer criticism.

A different kind of summary comes from Corinne Saunders, in her more detailed account of nineteenth-century responses to Chaucer:

In the nineteenth century, realism and the power to inspire sentiment were seen as Chaucer's great qualities: Crabbe (*Tales*, preface, 1812) writes of Chaucer's "powerful appeal to the heart and affections"; Hazlitt (*Lectures on the English Poets*, 1818) of the "severe activity of mind" that leads to Chaucer's reality of sentiment, particularly pathos; Coleridge (1834) of "How exquisitely tender he is" – and how knowable by contrast to Shakespeare; Leigh Hunt of how his images are "copied from the life" (1844). Englishness was crucial to understandings of Chaucer: for Ruskin (*Lectures on Art*, 1870), Chaucer's was "the most perfect type of a true English mind in its best possible temper," combining beauty, jest and the danger of degenerate humour! Arnold ("The Study of Poetry," 1880) offered a learned discussion of Chaucer in terms of his French and Italian, and placed him as "a genuine source of joy and strength, which is flowing still for us and will flow always"; he admired his humanity, his plenty, his "truth of substance" and especially his fluidity. For Arnold, praise of Chaucer needed to be qualified:

"he lacks the high seriousness of the great classics, and therewith an important part of their virtue," yet "He has poetic truth of substance, though he
has not high poetic seriousness, and corresponding to his truth of substance
he has an exquisite virtue of style and manner. With him is born our real
poetry." (7-8)

Saunders' citations focus our attention on the distinctive, descriptive
rhetoric used by these commentators, all writing in the same century.
Her account is slower and richer than Knight's, as part of a longer and
more leisurely narrative. It offers a more comprehensive window onto
the world of "sentiment": the world constructed by nineteenth-century
literary men and their reading of Chaucer, and conditioned by a range of
social, cultural, and gendered expectations. What Knight loses in detail,
he makes up for in the boldness of his ideological and social analysis,
brief and suggestive though it is. My point in comparing these two accounts, which both foreground key phrases from Coleridge's *Table Talk*,
is that the very act of citation inevitably produces a distinctive critical
frame that itself is a form of social and cultural practice. There are many
different ways of writing the reception history of Chaucer, contingent
on scale, and the reader's interest in ideology, rhetoric, questions of influence, originality, and so forth. Knight and Saunders both focus on
the different versions of "Chaucer" that are produced by these critical
discourses, not the emotional *relationship* between poet and reader that
emerges in more painstaking, detailed readings of critical practice.

Coleridge's discussion of Chaucer encourages us to explore some of
these ideas, and tease out the emotional work performed by his remarks.
The first three sentences set the tone, and establish the form of social-
ized, conversational discourse at work in Coleridge's discussion of
Chaucer; and indeed I will focus just on these three. In the context of
the reported speech of the "table talk" genre, we are invited, I think, to
hear a warmly personal, even confessional tone in these words:

> I take unceasing delight in Chaucer. His manly cheerfulness is especially de-
> licious to me in my old age. How exquisitely tender he is, and yet how per-
> fectly free from the least touch of sickly melancholy or morbid drooping!
> (Coburn 466)

Coleridge affirms the perpetual pleasure of "Chaucer," in a way that
helps to construct the twinned ideas of the timeless value and appeal of
the canonical author, and the capacity of such an author's name to stand
in for all his works. In the words of Michel Foucault, the author's name
is "the principle of thrift in the proliferation of meaning" (146). Later in

this paragraph, Coleridge compares Chaucer to Shakespeare: in doing so, he lifts both writers out of their own centuries and their own distinctive writerly genres to contrast the apparent intimate familiarity of Chaucer against the apparent mystery of Shakespeare's character. This is personal, comparative author-centric criticism of the kind hardly acceptable in conventions of modern academic pedagogy and professional practice, yet such comparisons are still the bread-and-butter, as it were, of modern "table talk": in book clubs, dinner party conversation, and general conversation about what we like and do not like about certain books and certain authors.

Coleridge's discourse moves back and forth between the discourses of subjective pleasure and emotion ("I take unceasing delight," "delicious to me in my old age"); and descriptive evaluation ("manly cheerfulness," "exquisitely tender," "perfectly free from the least touch of sickly melancholy or morbid drooping!"). He also uses the powerful rhetorical form of the *exclamatio*: "How exquisitely tender he is!"

What kind of language is this? I suggest that these expressions of emotion can be read as a species of "emotional utterance," in the sense that William Reddy uses that term, in *The Navigation of Feeling*:

> The startling features of emotional utterances that take the form of first-person, present-tense emotion claims warrant designating such utterances as constituting a form of speech that is neither descriptive nor performative. I propose that we call such utterances "emotives." (104)

Reddy's idea of "emotional utterances" or "emotives" draws attention to the role of language in simultaneously expressing and describing emotions (104-105), and is thus very well suited for literary criticism, though that is not Reddy's concern. For Reddy, emotives are similar to performatives (and differ from constatives) in that emotives do things to the world:

> Emotives are translations into words about, into "descriptions" of, the on-going translation tasks that currently occupy attention as well as of the other such tasks that remain in the queue, overflowing its current capacities. Emotives are influenced directly by, and alter, what they "refer" to. Thus, emotives are similar to performatives (and differ from constatives) in that emotives do things to the world. Emotives are themselves instruments for directly changing, building, hiding, intensifying emotions, instruments that may be more or less successful. (105)

Reddy's emphasis on emotives as translations of feeling has widespread application, especially in literary studies and practice theory, far wider than his initial focus on first-person, present-tense expression would seem to suggest. Coleridge's language, in his discussion of Chaucer, serves many comparable rhetorical and social functions. Like Reddy's emotives, it gives further shape to the speaker's own "aggregated self": the subject-in-process who both utters and is shaped by emotive discourse as he responds to the earlier poet; it shapes a community of readers who silently accede to Coleridge's judgments and feelings about Chaucer in the abstracted context of his table talk; and it models a personal, emotional and affective relationship with Chaucer that will be deeply influential in subsequent centuries.

The distinction between "emotional" and "affective" response is worth pausing over. While I do not think "affects" are always clearly distinguishable from "emotions," I use the adjective "affective" to draw attention to that aspect of Coleridge's language that describes the things that *happen to him* when he reads Chaucer. Coleridge *takes* "unceasing delight" in Chaucer, for example, while "[h]is manly cheerfulness *is especially delicious to me* in my old age." These are things that happen to him when he reads Chaucer at a particular time in his life, when Chaucer appears "tender" in comparison to his own age. Coleridge does not foreground his own somatic response, but his language is nevertheless sensory and embodied as well as emotional, describing the effects of Chaucer's works upon him.

For students of medievalism and Chaucer reception, it is significant that Coleridge does not refer to any particular Chaucer text. If we think about this in practical terms, it is probably not the entirety of Chaucer's works that produces these affects on Coleridge, but either selected works or the generalized properties of Chaucer as "author." When Coleridge appeals to the idea of Chaucer's tenderness, and manly cheerfulness, this composite Chaucer is a mix of his narrative voices as love poet, nature poet and the presiding genial spirit of *The Canterbury Tales*. There is little sense here of Chaucer's medieval author-functions as translator or *compilator*, for example. By the early nineteenth century, "Chaucer" had clearly been absorbed into the modern authorial economy, the owner and origin of all his works, with the potential to be compared with Shakespeare and other writers.

Further clues to the nature of this authorial economy are found in the single exclamation: "How exquisitely tender he is . . . !" As we will see, the language of emotional response is closely linked with the language of somatic, or tactile experience. As in all exclamations, there is a strong degree of performativity here. In the younger Coleridge's collection, the older "Coleridge" – for we are negotiating two author-functions here – performs for perpetuity a sense of surprise at this perennial capacity of "Chaucer" to impress with his tenderness. Any original context for this conversation, and any original or historical audience are displaced by an inclusive, self-conscious appeal to subsequent readers to agree with Coleridge's assessment. This becomes an enabling and productive practice in modern criticism: the personalized expression of a critical evaluation that is offered to other readers with an implicit invitation to agree.

The association of Chaucer with tenderness may evoke the love-sick, nature-loving narrator of the early dream visions, or the small boy murdered in *The Prioress's Tale*, or female victims of fate and narrative twists such as Criseyde, Griselda, or Emily. But the word itself also repays further examination, as it is often used by Chaucer. "Tender" is borrowed into English from French in the early thirteenth century, and is derived from Latin *tenerem* (the accusative form of *tener*), meaning "soft, delicate, of tender age" (*OED* definition 3). In English it also comes to mean "kind, affectionate, loving" while the meaning "having the delicacy of youth, immature" is attested from the early fourteenth century. Chaucer seems "tender" to Coleridge in the latter's old age. While Coleridge may be echoing Chaucer's own use of the word, the cumulative effect is to suggest Chaucer's own perpetual youthfulness. This idea of the naïve and tender poet is sustained by the commonly perceived childishness or simplicity of the medieval period. The emotional utterance – "how tender he is" – works to establish a temporal and emotional affinity between Chaucer's perpetual and youthful tenderness and Coleridge's old age.

Chaucer uses the word "tender" many times, often in the phrase, "tendre herte" (Burnley 156). It is repeatedly used in *The Merchant's Tale* to describe the young bride, May ("Hir fresshe beautee and hir age tendre," 356; "Whan tendre youthe hath wedded stoupyng age," 494; "He rubbeth hire aboute hir tendre face," 582). Chaucer draws a strong contrast between ageing patriarchal sexual desire and the young virgin's powerlessness.

There is another sense of "tender" that is also relevant to Coleridge's exclamation. The word is already used in the medieval period of food that is soft, juicy, and easily consumed. January's attitude to bridal meat is expressed most tellingly when Chaucer has him debating the virtues of marrying a younger woman. "And bet than old boef is the tendre veel," he tells his friends (176).

Consciously or not, Coleridge pairs this association with Chaucer's "delicious" (and "manly") cheerfulness. The language of consumption in literary criticism is not unique to Coleridge. We have become familiar with the imagery of "devouring" literature, for example, or of "savoring" favorite passages. Coleridge's enthusiastic characterization of Chaucer and the fiction or recollection of literary talk over a meal gives particular social form to this intellectual and critical practice, and bespeaks a number of implicit assumptions about the relationship between text and food on the one hand, and reader and consumer on the other. The medieval poet is brought into the present through the act of consuming the tender meat of his poetry. The discursive genre of "table talk" thus offers a doubled, or at least, layered model of the relationship between thinking and feeling. As one in a series of speeches, Coleridge's account of Chaucer appears abstracted from its putative social context of discussion at dinner. It appears disembodied, dehistoricized and neutral, ripe for anthologizing in the context of Chaucer criticism. Yet the comestible language ("delicious," "tender") cannot help but return us to the idea of the body that consumes and tastes food as well as a mind that experiences the emotions of reading poetry. Coleridge's language reminds us how difficult it is to separate emotional from mental processes and social practices. I have written elsewhere about the persistence of the idea of the communal Chaucer, in which the act of criticism is often likened to the idea of talking, eating, and drinking with Chaucer at the Tabard Inn on his way to Canterbury. Even in this one-sided account of Coleridge's "table talk" we can read traces of these strong social associations.

We may also pair Chaucer's use of "tender" with Coleridge's use of the adjective elsewhere. In his *Biographia Literaria Vol. 1*, for example, he describes how a friend introduces him to the sonnets of "Mr Bowles":

> It was a double pleasure to me, and still remains a *tender* recollection, that I should have received from a friend so revered the first knowledge of a poet, by whose works, year after year, I was so enthusiastically delighted and inspired. (9, my emphasis)

Here, the word "tender" evokes the memory of reading another poet who, like Chaucer, continues to delight over many years. In the same passage he describes the salutary effects of

> the genial influence of a style of poetry, *so tender and yet so manly*, so natural and real, and yet so dignified and harmonious, as the sonnets and other early poems of Mr. Bowles. (10, my emphasis)

These lines are instructive for our present concerns as Coleridge here contrasts the idea of "tenderness" with manliness, as he does in his discussion of Chaucer.

Moreover, when Chaucer is "perfectly free from the least touch of sickly melancholy or morbid drooping" it sounds very similar to Coleridge's comparison, at this point in the *Biographia*, with his own somewhat morbid speculations about metaphysics, theological controversy, free will, and predestination from which Bowles' poetry and "an accidental introduction to an amiable family" seem to have saved him. Chaucer's tenderness is a corrective, in many different ways, to Coleridge's own tendencies to both ageing and melancholy.

The difficulties of finding the perfect balance of tenderness and manliness is further apparent from a contrasting discussion of Spenser in Coleridge's *Literary Remains*, Vol.1:

> Lastly, the great and prevailing character of Spenser's mind is fancy under the conditions of the imagination, as an ever present but not always active power. He has an imaginative fancy, but he has not imagination, in kind or degree, as Shakespeare and Milton have; the boldest effort of his powers in this way is the character of Talus. Add to this a *feminine tenderness and almost maidenly purity of feeling*, and above all, a deep moral earnestness which produces a believing sympathy and acquiescence in the reader, and you have a tolerably adequate view of Spenser's intellectual being. (97, my emphasis)

Coleridge's association of tenderness with femininity and maidenly purity here is telling, especially as it is firmly contrasted with and corrected by Chaucer's "manly cheerfulness."

We could draw out further semantic, historical, and psychological associations of Coleridge's critical vocabulary, but I hope I have begun to thicken our understanding of the textual and social habitus in which Coleridge's reading is performed. We can read the rhetoric of criticism as a form of social and emotional practice, by focusing on the associations of vocabulary and critical assumptions and practices on display. Lines that are often quoted in the bloodless context of citation history are performed in their own rich (if putative) social context, and trail their own semantic and critical associations, when they are considered as emotional performances.

The reception history of Chaucer is not just "opinions" about Chaucer, then, but "feelings" about him and his poetry. The same may also be said for Coleridge. Such analysis and such critical archives can help us understand not just the history of Chaucer reception, but also the history of feeling about medieval literature and the literature of the past.

References

Benson, Larry D., ed. *The Riverside Chaucer.* Boston: Houghton Mifflin, 1987.

Bourdieu, Pierre. *The Logic of Practice.* Trans. Richard Nice. Stanford: Stanford University Press, 1990.

Brewer, Derek S., ed. *Chaucer, the Critical Heritage.* 2 vols. London and Boston: Routledge and Kegan Paul, 1978.

Burnley, J. D. *Chaucer's Language and the Philosophers' Tradition.* Cambridge: D. S. Brewer; Totowa, New Jersey: Rowman and Littlefield, 1979.

Burrow, J. A. *Geoffrey Chaucer: A Critical Anthology.* Baltimore: Penguin, 1969.

Coburn, Kathleen and B. Winer, eds. *The Collected Works of Samuel Taylor Coleridge, Volume 14: Table Talk.* 2 vols. Princeton: Princeton University Press, 1990.

Coleridge, Samuel Taylor. *Biographia Literaria.* Vol 1. Intro. Arthur Symons. London: Dent; New York: E. P. Dutton, 1939.

Coleridge, Samuel Taylor. *The Literary Remains of Samuel Taylor Coleridge Collected and Edited by Henry Nelson Coleridge.* 4 vols. London: William Pickering, 1836-1839.

Dinshaw, Carolyn. *Chaucer's Sexual Poetics.* Madison, Wisconsin: University of Wisconsin Press, 1989.

Dixon, Thomas. *From Passions to Emotion: The Creation of a Secular Psychology.* Cambridge: Cambridge University Press, 2003.

Foucault, Michel. "What Is an Author?" *Textual Strategies; Perspectives In Post-Structuralist Criticism.* Ed. J. V. Harari. Ithaca, New York: Cornell University Press, 1979.

Hammond, Eleanor Prescott. *Chaucer: A Bibliographical Manual.* New York: P. Smith, 1933.

Knight, Stephen. *Geoffrey Chaucer.* Oxford and New York: Blackwell, 1986.

Lerer, Seth. *Chaucer and His Readers: Imagining Authors in Late-Medieval England.* Princeton: Princeton University Press, 1993.

Leys, Ruth. "The Turn to Affect: A Critique." *Critical Inquiry* 38 (2011): 434-72.

Reddy, William. *The Navigation of Feeling: A Framework for the History of Emotions.* Cambridge: Cambridge University Press, 2001.

Rosenwein, Barbara. *Emotional Communities in the Middle Ages.* Ithaca, New York: Cornell University Press, 2006.

Saunders, Corinne, ed. *Chaucer.* Oxford and Malden: Blackwell, 2001.

Scheer, Monique. "Are Emotions a Kind of Practice (And is That What Makes Them Have a History?): A Bourdieuian Approach to Understanding Emotion." *History and Theory* 51 (2012): 193-220.

Spurgeon, Caroline. *Five Hundred Years of Chaucer Criticism and Allusion, 1357-1900*. New York: Russell and Russell; Cambridge: Cambridge University Press, 1925.

Stearns, Peter N. and Carol Z. Stearns. "Emotionology: Clarifying the History of Emotions and Emotional Standards." *The American Historical Review* 90 (1985): 813-36.

Trigg, Stephanie. *Congenial Souls: Reading Chaucer from Medieval to Postmodern*. Minneapolis: University of Minnesota Press, 2002.

——. "Langland's Tears: Poetry, Emotion, and Mouvance." *Yearbook of Langland Studies* 26 (2012): 27-48.

——. "Introduction: Emotional Histories – Beyond the Personalization of the Past and the Abstraction of Affect Theory." *Exemplaria* 26.1 (2014): 3-15.

Impoliteness and Emotions
in a Cross-Cultural Perspective

Jonathan Culpeper, Gila Schauer, Leyla Marti,
Meilian Mei and Minna Nevala

This study investigates the emotions one experiences when one participates in impolite discourses. Specifically, it addresses the question of
whether different cultures experience different emotions in the light of
discourses deemed impolite. We begin by discussing the nature of impoliteness, pointing out that key concepts such as *face* and *sociality rights*
seem to be closely connected to particular emotions. We discuss the role
of cognition in the mediation of emotion, arguing that it is essential in
the explanation of impoliteness, and indeed cultural variation. We analyse 500 reports of impoliteness events generated by undergraduates
based in England, Finland, Germany, Turkey and China. We extract
emotion labels from our data and classify them into emotion groups.
Our results suggest that there is less cultural variation at higher level
emotion categories, but more at lower level. For example, our Chinese
and Turkish data suggests that our informants contrast with the other
datasets in experiencing sadness to a greater degree.

1. Introduction

Navigating the field of impoliteness research is daunting. There is no
agreed definition of *politeness* or *impoliteness* (Bargiela-Chiappini; Locher
and Bousfield 3). Even the terms that can be used for such notions are
controversial (why not use *civility* instead of *politeness*, or *rudeness* instead
of *impoliteness*?). In fact, in this paper we use the term impoliteness as a

Emotion, Affect, Sentiment: The Language and Aesthetics of Feeling. SPELL: Swiss Papers
in English Language and Literature 30. Ed. Andreas Langlotz and Agnieszka Soltysik Monnet. Tübingen: Narr, 2014. 67-88.

cover term. (Im)politeness clearly involves particular behaviours, but it cannot be reduced to a fixed list of linguistic forms or behaviours that are guaranteed to have polite or impolite meanings on all occasions (perhaps something that might be more associated with etiquette manuals). Consider that the expression *thank you* could be said in such a way and in such a context that its meaning could be construed as impolite (e.g. sarcastic). Deciding on whether *thank you* is polite or impolite involves more than simply decoding semantic meanings; it involves inferring interpersonal meanings in context. More specifically, impoliteness refers to behaviours, verbal or non-verbal, which evoke particular (mental) attitudes. The idea that politeness is subjective and evaluative is fairly frequently stated in the politeness literature (e.g. Eelen; Watts; Spencer-Oatey, "(Im)Politeness"; Ruhi). (Im)politeness concerns behaviours which evoke impoliteness attitudes, or, more specifically, judgements that a behaviour is unexpected, unacceptable and/or unwanted. Such attitudes can be evoked in any participant; even a speaker of something impolite may judge their own behaviour to be impolite. However, speakers or producers of impoliteness-evoking-behaviours do not suffer the same emotional consequences as the other participants. A particular characteristic – perhaps the defining characteristic – of impoliteness is that it also causes (usually strong) emotional reactions in those other participants whose impoliteness attitudes have been evoked. This is possibly the major point of difference from politeness. As Blitvich (69) points out, with reference to Kienpointner (41): "we tend to associate impoliteness, but not necessarily politeness, with true emotions." Linguistic impoliteness work is not only geared towards exacerbating negatively valenced emotions, but intimately associated with them. The main objective in this essay is to discover whether there is cultural variation in the emotions that are experienced – or, more accurately, reported – during impoliteness events. This objective extends the work presented in Culpeper (*Impoliteness*) and Culpeper, Marti, Nevala, Mei and Schauer. We need to stress at this early juncture that referring to the "English" or "German" data or labelling a table with the word "Finnish" or "Chinese" should be recognised as a shorthand for the specific set of undergraduate informants born and bred in that particular nation. Each national dataset will not reflect all the cultural diversity within national boundaries, though it may well give hints about wider cultural norms that can be followed up in further research.

In the next section, we will begin by conducting a general survey of impoliteness and emotions. Given the importance of the concepts of *face* and *sociality rights* in relation to impoliteness, in the first part of this survey we describe how emotions are connected to these concepts. In the second part of this survey, we will elaborate on the workings of impoliteness in context, especially cultural context. Here, we note the importance of the notion of cognitive appraisal in accounting for the role of context, and especially how both sarcasm and banter work. Furthermore, we will point out the role of cognition in explaining cultural variation in emotion. The aim of the following section is to set up some of the background on emotions for our empirical work. More specifically, we introduce Shaver, Schwartz, Kirson and O'Connor's influential study on categories of emotion. We also discuss cross-cultural issues. In the final major section of this paper, we report our empirical work based on impoliteness events recorded by undergraduates in England, Finland, Germany, Turkey and China. We begin by briefly describing our data collection method, and then elaborate on how we classified emotions in our impoliteness data. We note the particular problems we encountered on the basis of cultural variation in the experience of emotion, and also issues to do with the translation of emotion labels. Finally, we present and discuss our results.

2. Impoliteness and Emotions

2.1. Impoliteness Concepts and Functions: The Role of Emotion

Influential politeness and impoliteness frameworks make much of the notion of *face* (e.g. Brown and Levinson; Bousfield; Culpeper "Towards an Anatomy"). In English, the term face is perhaps most commonly used in the idiom *losing face*, meaning that one's public image suffers some damage, often resulting in emotional reactions, such as embarrassment. In academic writings, most scholars draw on Goffman's (5) definition of face: "the positive social value a person effectively claims for himself by the line others assume he has taken during a particular contact. Face is an image of self-delineated in terms of approved social attributes." Note that when you lose face you feel bad about how you are seen in other people's eyes. Face concerns vary in sensitivity. For example, some people might not be particularly bothered by an insult targeting their appearance, but much more so by the insult targeting their partner. As argued in Culpeper (*Impoliteness* 26), "we can hypothesize the self as a schema consisting of layers of components varying in emotional importance with the most highly-charged closest to the cen-

tre, and this is thus where potentially the most face-sensitive components lie."

Goffman notes the emotional consequences of face loss at various
points:

> If events establish a face for him [sic] that is better than he might have ex-
> pected, he is likely to "feel good"; if his ordinary expectations are not filled,
> one expects that he will "feel bad" or "feel hurt." (6)

> He may become embarrassed and chagrined; he may become shamefaced.
> (8)

> It is plain that emotions play a part in the cycles of response, as when an-
> guish is expressed because of what one has done to another's face, or anger
> because of what has been done to one's own. (23)

The key emotions here are: hurt, embarrassment, shame, anguish (possibly related to guilt) and anger. Hurtful communication has been the
subject of research (e.g. Feeney; Leary, Springer, Negel, Ansell and Evans; Vangelisti "Messages that Hurt," "Making Sense," "Communicating
Hurt"; Young). Here, it is generally understood that "[p]eople feel hurt
when someone else says or does something that they perceive emotionally injured them or when they perceive someone's failure to say or do
something emotionally injures them" (Vangelisti, "Communicating
Hurt" 139). People experience "a combination of sadness at having
been emotionally wounded and fear of being vulnerable to harm" (Vangelisti, "Communicating Hurt" 123). Some researchers have looked
again at face and facework in the context of emotions, particularly
shame and embarrassment (e.g. Samra-Fredericks; Gerholm).

Other researchers, notably Spencer-Oatey (*Culturally Speaking*), have
argued that the notion of face does not adequately cover all cases of
(im)politeness, and that we also need to factor in *sociality rights*, which
might be thought of as social "oughts" – authoritative standards of behaviour held by a community, involving positive or negative evaluations
of behaviour as being consistent or otherwise with those standards. For
example, failing to respond to a greeting might imply that the target cares little for the person who greeted, thus threatening their face, but it
also flouts social norms of reciprocity whereby one greeting is met by
another. Such flouts are more likely to result in frustration or anger.
There is a link here with moral emotions. Haidt (853) defines moral
emotions as "those emotions that are linked to the interests or welfare
either of society as a whole or at least of persons other than the judge or

agent." Moral emotions can be positive or negative (gratitude would be an example of a positive moral emotion, and an insult would be an example of a negative emotion). The more negative moral emotions are: anger, disgust, contempt, embarrassment, shame and guilt. Haidt (855; see also Rozin, Lowery, Imada and Haidt) divides these into two groups: (1) anger, disgust and contempt which consist of "other-condemning" emotions, and (2) embarrassment, shame and guilt which consist of "self-conscious" emotions. Culpeper (*Impoliteness* 61-65) argues that violations of sociality rights are more likely to be accompanied by other-condemning emotions (e.g. anger, disgust and contempt), whilst violations of face are more likely to be accompanied by self-conscious emotions (e.g. embarrassment and shame).

2.2. Impoliteness, Emotions and Context: The Role of Cognition[1]

Losing face or flouting a sociality right is certainly not hotwired to particular emotions. Emotions are considered by many scholars to be evoked as part of people's cognitive appraisal of situations. This view is contrary to the Darwinian perspective in which displays of emotion are reflexes of physiological states (see, for example, Darwin), and to its extension in evolutionary social psychology where expressions of emotion are seen as genetically predetermined (see, for example, Morris). Consider the fact that people can be angry, yet control that anger and not display signs of aggression. This kind of example is not easily accounted for without factoring in cognition. In the field of aggression studies, Anderson and Bushman (see also Anderson, Deuser and De-Neve) develop a "general aggression model" to explain how emotions are treated. Their model has three internal states: cognitions, emotional affect and (physical or perceived) arousal, all of which feed into the experience of emotion. These states are triggered not just by a stimulus, such as a gun or a swearword, but also by a person with specific characteristics in a particular context. Importantly, these internal states are not hotwired to behaviours. They are appraised, in other words, the person judges what happened, why it happened, how angry he or she feels, what actions to take, and so on. This appraisal can be more thoughtful or more impulsive. A model of this kind better accounts for the complexities of social interaction. Specifically with regard to impoliteness, we need to factor in cognitive appraisal, otherwise banter, for example,

---

[1] This section is based on material presented in Culpeper (*Impoliteness*).

would not exist. Banter is mock impoliteness: using the conventional words and behaviours of impoliteness but doing so in a context where they are understood (cognitively appraised) not to be genuinely offensive (e.g. saying *Come here you bastard* to a friend).

Appraisal of this kind can only happen if emotions are represented in our minds. There is indeed ample support for this idea. Since at least the 1980s cognitive models have assumed that emotions can be represented in our minds (e.g. Ortony, Clore and Collins). Indeed, there is empirical evidence that emotions are represented in a mental schema, a complex bundle of generic knowledge (e.g. Conway and Bekerian). An excellent description of what all this might mean is produced by Russell (his term "script" is roughly equivalent to our term "schema"):

> Although we often speak of an emotion as a thing, a more apt description is a sequence of subevents. In other words, the features that constitute emotion concepts describe the subevents that make up the emotion: causes, beliefs, feelings, the physiological changes, desires, and overt actions, and vocal and facial expressions. These subevents, described by the concept features, are ordered in a casual sequence – in much the same way that actions are ordered in a playwright's script. To know the sense of a term like anger, fear or jealousy is to know a script for that emotion. [. . .] Few or no features of the script are necessary; rather, the more features present, the closer the resemblance and the more appropriate the script label. (39)

Emotions interact with information about situations and their norms, and all this information is represented in an emotion schema in memory. Moreover, people are aware of norms about the appropriateness of emotions in particular situations. For example, the emotional state of happiness, with related displays of laughing and smiling, are not appropriate at a funeral. Or, to take an impoliteness example, insults and threats displaying the emotional state of anger, would not be appropriate at a wedding. People cognitively appraise the situation and regulate their emotion displayed accordingly.

A number of studies have attempted to discover both the structure and contents of emotion concepts. A major and influential study is offered by Shaver, Schwartz, Kirson and O'Connor. These researchers compiled a list of 135 emotion names and then asked 100 North American subjects to sort them into groups on the basis of similarity, and then these results were put through a statistical cluster analysis. The resulting clusters emerged as a tree-like hierarchy of groups, with a basic level in the middle and superordinate categories above and subordinate categories below. This structure echoed work on prototypes, which are con-

ceived of as similar to schemata and other generic mental representations. Eleanor Rosch and her colleagues (e.g. Rosch "Natural Categories," "Principles"; Rosch, Mervis, Gray, Johnson and Boyes-Braem)
also found three levels in their work: superordinate (e.g. furniture), basic
(e.g. chair) and subordinate (e.g. kitchen chair). At the highest superordinate level, the only distinction that emerged was a very generic,
though important, one between positive and negative emotions. Obviously, impoliteness is associated with the latter. The basic level was
comprised of love, joy anger, sadness, fear and, more weakly, surprise.
Table 1 displays the three negative emotions, anger, sadness and fear,
and the subordinate groups which comprise them, along with the specific emotion names that comprise those subordinate groups. Note that
some labels appear at more than one level. Sadness was an emotion
name supplied by the North American subjects. Its statistical centrality
to the subordinate group, calculated on the basis of its co-occurrence
with other items in the group, led to it being chosen as label for that
subordinate group. Basic level labels were chosen on the basis of both
their statistical centrality and the labels used in the emotion literature.
Sadness is not only statistically central at a basic level but also widely
used in the emotion literature. It should be remembered, then, that labels from subordinate level through basic to superordinate are progres-
sively more technical.

The basic emotional concepts of sadness and anger, and to a lesser
extent fear, intuitively seem particularly relevant to impoliteness events.
At the subordinate level the most relevant categories seem to be neglect
and suffering, and disgust, rage, exasperation and irritation. Indeed, the
relevance of these categories has been demonstrated in Culpeper (*Impoliteness*), at least as far as British data is concerned.

A further study reported by Shaver, Schwartz, Kirson and O'Connor
revealed the wider prototype or schema of which the emotion concepts
are a part. In other words, they were investigating the nature of what we
described as a script above, with reference to Russell. They did this by
listing 120 accounts of emotional experiences, and then using six coders
to identify features of these accounts, some of which obviously involved
impoliteness, as illustrated here:

> I called him a jerk. I yelled at him. I said (excuse me, please) "fuck you" and
> called him "shit head." I also try to tell him he was wrong to act the way he
> was over no big deal. I hit and kicked and cursed him repeatedly.
> (1073)

Table 1: Negative emotion concepts (data drawn from Shaver, Schwartz, Kirson and O'Connor)

Superordinate	Basic	Subordinate	Emotion names
Negative	Fear	Nervousness	anxiety, nervousness, tenseness, uneasiness, apprehension, worry, distress, dread
		Horror	alarm, shock, fear, fright, horror, terror, panic, hysteria, mortification
	Sadness	Sympathy	pity, sympathy
		Neglect	alienation, isolation, neglect, loneliness, rejection, homesickness, defeat, ejection, insecurity, embarrassment, humiliation, insult
		Shame	guilt, shame, regret, remorse
		Disappointment	dismay, disappointment, displeasure
		Sadness	depression, despair, hopelessness, gloom, glumness, sadness, unhappiness, grief, sorrow, woe, misery, melancholy
		Suffering	agony, suffering, hurt, anguish
	Anger	Torment	torment
		Envy	envy, jealousy
		Disgust	disgust, revulsion, contempt
		Rage	anger, rage, outrage, fury, wrath, hostility, ferocity, bitterness, hate, loathing, scorn, spite, vengefulness, dislike, resentment
		Exasperation	exasperation, frustration
		Irritation	aggravation, irritation, agitation, annoyance, grouchiness, grumpiness

The schemata for all five basic emotions contained three features: situational antecedents, behavioural responses and self-control procedures. We briefly elaborate the situational antecedents of the three most important basic level emotional concepts for impoliteness, as in doing so we etch in the kind of contexts surrounding the experience of impoliteness. Fear antecedents relate to the individual's lack of power or control, particularly in certain situations (e.g. "loss of control or competence," "possibility of loss or failure," "being in a novel, unfamiliar situation"). Sadness antecedents relate to the realisation that an undesirable outcome has occurred, which may include, similar to fear, the discovery that one is relatively powerless (e.g. "an undesirable outcome; getting what was not wanted: a negative surprise," "loss of a valued relationship; separation," "rejection, exclusion, disapproval," "not getting what was wanted, wished for, striven for, etc."). Anger antecedents involve the judgement that something/someone has interfered with one's plans or goals by reducing power, violating expectations, interrupting, etc., and that interference is illegitimate, not what ought to be (e.g. "reversal or sudden loss of power, status, or respect; insult," "violation of an expectation; things not working out as planned," "frustration or interruption of a goal-directed activity," "real or threatened physical or psychological pain," "judgement that the situation is illegitimate, wrong, unfair, contrary to what ought to be").

3. Emotions and Cultural Variation

Approaches to emotion emanating from cognitive psychology have been criticised for a variety of reasons. A key problem concerns the fact that cognitive models are based on language data. It is worth quoting Wierzbicka's articulation of the problem:

> According to Izard and Buechler (1980:168), the fundamental emotions are (1) interest, (2) joy, (3) surprise, (4) sadness, (5) anger, (6) disgust, (7) contempt, (8) fear, (9) shame/shyness, and (10) guilt. I experience a certain unease when reading claims of this kind. If lists such as the one above are supposed to enumerate universal human emotions, how is it that these emotions are all so neatly identified by means of English words? For example, Polish does not have a word corresponding exactly to the English word disgust. What if the psychologists working on the "fundamental human emotions" happened to be native speakers of Polish rather than English? Would it still have occurred to them to include "disgust" on their list? And Australian Aboriginal language Gidjingali does not seem to distinguish lexically "fear" from "shame," subsuming feelings kindred to those identified by the English words fear and shame under one lexical item (Hiatt 1978:185). If the researchers happened to be native speakers of Gidjingali rather than English, would it still have occurred to them to claim that fear and shame are both fundamental human emotions, discrete and clearly separated from each other? English terms of emotion constitute a folk taxonomy, not an objective, culture-free analytical framework, so obviously we cannot assume that English words such as disgust, fear, or shame are clues to universal human concepts, or to basic psychological realities.
> ("Human Emotions" 584)

As we saw with Shaver, Schwartz, Kirson and O'Connor, the source for their content model was language, and more specifically English, and even more specifically, North American English as used by their student informants. Researchers have even suggested that the prototype structure with three levels does not hold up in a broader perspective. Majid for example, surveying the role of language in emotion research states that:

> some languages lack superordinate terms for emotion or have a term that embraces other psychological states as well; many cultures use high levels of somatic vocabulary to describe affective feelings; and that even "basic" feeling states such as "anger" and "fear" are frequently conflated under a single term. (381)

The question to what extent our native language influences our view of the world, and thus also our perception and feelings, has been debated for several decades now, largely as a consequence of Sapir and Whorf's ideas about linguistic relativity and linguistic determinism. Edward Sapir, quoted in Whorf (134), argued that "[w]e see and hear and otherwise experience very largely as we do because the language habits of our community predispose certain choices of interpretation." Researchers using prototype frameworks for emotion research follow the tradition of the weak version of linguistic relativity and determinism, which means that concepts can be translated into other languages and that different languages may have words for similar concepts that describe very similar experiences. Other researchers, such as Wierzbicka ("Human Emotions," *Emotions Across Languages and Cultures*) and Hurtado De Mendoza, Fernández-Dols, Parrott and Carrera argue that emotional concepts should be researched in considerable detail to examine potential differences in the equivalence of the two terms or in the nuances of the terms.

Whilst the issue of language variation remains a serious methodological issue in trying to understand the nature of emotion concepts, we should not let that mislead us into thinking that cognitive psychologists were unaware of cultural variation. Shaver, Schwartz, Kirson and O'Connor explicitly point out that the contents of emotion concepts are culturally sensitive. Interestingly, they argue that it is at the subordinate level that cross-cultural variation is likely, because it is here that context is reflected, but that it is less likely at higher levels (1083). For subordinate-level distinctions, the context in which the emotion arose is important in explaining differences (1069). In fact, some particular subordinate-level emotions seem to be more culturally sensitive than others. A case in point is the line between the emotions of embarrassment and shame:

> In Western cultures, shame is elicited by the appraisal that there is something wrong or defective with one's core self. [. . .] Embarrassment, in contrast, is said to be elicited by appraisals that one's social identity or persona within an interaction is damaged or threatened, [. . .] at times because of events beyond one's control. In many non-western societies, however, any appraisal that one has violated cultural standards of behaviour in front of other people or that one is at high risk of such violations (as when one is around one's superiors) triggers a self-conscious emotion that combines shame and embarrassment. (Haidt 860)

The point can perhaps be illustrated by the case of Jacintha Saldanha, the nurse who committed suicide shortly after falling for a prank call in which two radio presenters pretended to be Queen Elizabeth and Prince Charles enquiring after the health of the Duchess of Cambridge. Saldanha had spent the first 35 years of her life in Mangalore, India, and the last ten working in London. Many British people were puzzled that she had taken her own life. Falling for a prank call was embarrassing maybe, but hardly a reason for such drastic action (assuming that mental health issues did not play a part). But this is a very British cultural perspective. As Wierzbicka (*Emotions Across Languages and Cultures* 112) reminds us: "[e]mbarrassment is one of the most important emotion concepts in the modern Anglo world." It is conceivable that Saldanha's emotional landscape was rather different, being based on different experiences, with the consequence that for her this incident was at least in part a matter of shame. (For more on the cultural aspects of shame and guilt, see Wallbott and Scherer).

Note here that the idea that different cultural experiences result in different prototypes or schemata is entirely compatible with the theory. Fredric Bartlett's early pioneering work in schema theory was partly designed to explore cultural differences in interpretation (see also the experiment by Steffensen, Joag-Dev and Andersen), and schema theory is used today in the context of cross-cultural pragmatics (e.g. Scollon and Scollon). Problems have come about because people sometimes assume that the results of a study based on one typically English-speaking cultural group can be applied to other cultural groups.

4. An Empirical Study of Reports of Impoliteness Events Across Five Cultures

4.1. Data Collection

Naturally-occurring impoliteness is relatively rare in everyday contexts and thus difficult to collect for analysis, and experimentally induced impoliteness is fraught with ethical problems. Consequently, we decided to use the diary or fieldnotes method. Our inspiration here is Spencer-Oatey ("Managing Rapport"). In this study students were asked to record "rapport sensitive" incidents, that is, "incidents involving social interactions that they [the student informants] found to be particularly noticeable in some way, in terms of their relationship with the other person(s)" (533-534). We devised a report form that was more detailed and focused than Spencer-Oatey's, not least with respect to the fact that we are only interested in negative behaviours and emotions. One aspect of our design was to avoid mentioning a label that described the kind of behaviour we are interested in – labels such as "impolite," "rude," "abusive," "aggressive" – because the choice of a particular label may have biased our results. Thus, we asked informants to report conversations that had a particular *effect* on them – conversations "in which someone said something to you which made *you* feel bad." A box extending a little less than half a page was provided for reports. Unlike Spencer-Oatey ("Managing Rapport"), we also asked informants to reflect on their reported conversations in a number of specific ways. In order to gain information about emotions that might have been experienced, we asked two questions: (1) "We know you felt 'bad,' but describe your feelings?" and (2) "Why did this particular behaviour make you feel bad?" Boxes allowing for a few lines of text were supplied for responses.

Spencer-Oatey's ("Managing Rapport") analysis was based on 59 report forms; we will analyse 100 report forms per "national" dataset, Chinese, English, Finnish, German and Turkish (i.e. 500 in total). In the remainder of this paper the labels Chinese, English, and so on indicate the country from which the informants originated. With respect to language varieties, our study involved Mandarin Chinese, British English and German German. Table 2 displays the social profile of our informants.

Table 2: The social profile of our data sets

		English	*Chinese*	*Finish*	*German*	*Turkish*
Age	*18-29*	98	100	99	99	100
	30-59	2	0	1	1	0
Gender	*Female*	79	67	89	73	64
	Male	21	33	11	27	36

As can be seen, the profile of each national dataset is broadly similar. However, a limitation of our work is that our results are dominated by the perceptions not only of young students but also students who are female.

For the non-England-based informants, the questionnaires were translated into the participants' native languages. The students completed the questionnaires in their native language, reporting incidents that had happened to them with fellow native speakers of their language. Finally, all questionnaires were transcribed into electronic files, all non-English data were also translated into English. From these data we extracted the emotion descriptors or labels. Some informants only supplied one emotion label, whereas others sometimes supplied a number of labels representing mixed emotions. To take account of this in our quantitative work, we weighted our scores: if a label is the only emotion reported, it was given "1"; if it is one of several, it was given "0.5."

4.2. Classifying Emotions Across Cultures

As mentioned above, we used Shaver, Schwartz, Kirson and O'Connor's prototype framework to analyse the emotion labels provided by our participants in the five languages investigated. Since our main aim is not to provide a detailed analysis of the universality of emotion labels in different languages, but rather to try and see if impoliteness experiences result in different negative emotions in five different languages and cultures (which means that we are not interested in the wider range of emotions often investigated in prototype emotion research, such as emotions that could be assigned to the basic categories of love and joy), we considered the prototype framework a suitable instrument for our research. However, we are, of course, aware that there could be differences in the meaning of certain emotion labels in the different languages. Hurtado De Mendoza, Fernández-Dols, Parrott and Carrera, for example, discuss differences in the English emotion label *shame* and the presumed Spanish equivalent *vergüenza*. Therefore, we decided to follow a multiple step analysis procedure to address potential differences and to ensure that we were comparing similar emotions across the five languages.

First, the translated emotion labels of all languages were assigned to Shaver, Schwartz, Kirson and O'Connor's basic and subordinate emotion categories. In the second step, the native speaker analyst who was responsible for the individual language reviewed the resulting model that represented the classification of the emotion labels for their language to check if the assigned basic and subordinate categories provided a good fit for the emotions described by their participants. For the majority of the cases, Shaver, Schwartz, Kirson and O'Connor's model provided a clear and acceptable fit for the basic categories. This finding thus supports previous research on emotion universals that suggested that at least some emotions labels are similar in a variety of different languages and cultures (e.g. Hupka, Lenton and Hutchinson, but note that this study relied on dictionaries).

In some cases, the emotion labels used by the participants to describe their feelings seemed to entail more than one basic emotion category. For example, the German *lächerlich gemacht* translated as "ridiculed" in English seemed to include aspects of two basic categories, anger and sadness. As the description of the participants using this emotion label in German suggested that the dominant emotion was sadness, we assigned *lächerlich gemacht* to the basic emotion sadness rather than anger. This approach was also followed in all other cases, where a close reading of the context provided by the participants in their reports enabled us to assign emotion labels to one of the basic and subordinate categories.

In other cases, we classified one English emotion label as representing two different subordinate emotions but the same basic emotion. For example, the Finnish expressions *vituttaa* and *ottaa päähän* were both translated as "pissed off" in English, but based on the context provided in the participants' reports assigned to different subordinate categories of anger, namely, rage and irritation.

Following the individual analysis of the emotion labels done by each of us individually, we then, in a third step, discussed the fit of individual emotion labels given by Shaver, Schwartz, Kirson and O'Connor that did not seem to represent the data in our native languages. One emotion, represented in the German and Chinese data, did not fit any of the basic categories of Shaver, Schwartz, Kirson and O'Connor's framework. This is the emotion that is described by the German adjective *unangenehm*, which was translated into English as "unpleasant," "uncomfortable" or "awkward" depending on the context of the participants' report. It does not easily fit any of the basic categories anger, sadness or fear. As the Chinese word for "uncomfortable" also did not fit any of the three basic categories, we decided to introduce a new category called *unpleasant* to the framework.

We think that this multiple step approach helps to ensure that differences in the perception of emotion labels are addressed. Also, multilingual projects such as ours can provide useful additions to existing frameworks and thereby help address the potential language bias of frameworks that have been developed based solely on the English language.

4.3. Impoliteness and Emotions in England, Finland, Germany, Turkey and China

In this section, we highlight some of the interesting patterns in that data. Figure 1 displays the basic emotion groups for the five nation data sets.

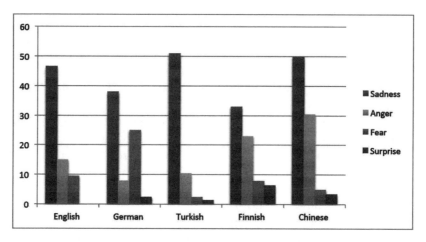

Figure 1: Basic emotion groups for five nation groups (the numbers represent scores; see section 4.1)

Sadness seems to be a particular feature of the Turkish group, far exceeding any other emotion. Anger is strongest for the Chinese group. The German group seems distinctive in having the least anger but the most fear. Nevertheless, a generally striking facet of this Figure is the similarities amongst the five nation data sets, not the differences (statistical testing of those differences is not possible, because of the scoring method used). All groups are dominated by sadness, anger follows some distance behind, and then the other groups fear and surprise are quite minor, except fear in the German data. This similarity supports Shaver, Schwartz, Kirson and O'Connor's claim that basic level emotion categories are less susceptible to cultural variation. The fact that the basic level emotion category of sadness is the most prominent in all datasets is noteworthy, as this particular group encompasses nearly all of the emotions named by Goffman as accompanying the loss of face (including hurt, embarrassment, shame and anguish). The one other emotion that Goffman mentioned was anger, and this, of course, is the second most prevalent group. This emotion is most likely to be triggered by violations of sociality rights.

In order to reveal possible cultural variation we need to look more closely at the detail, and this means looking at the subordinate emotion groups. Table 3 displays the subordinate emotion groups for the five nation groups in rank order. This table also displays the most frequent emotion label within each of the subordinate groups that it displays.

It should be remembered at this point that the names of the subordinate emotion groups – neglect, shame, suffering, rage, and so on – were not invented by Shaver, Schwartz, Kirson and O'Connor to represent the semantic characteristics of the whole subordinate group. This is partly because, unlike basic level labels, they are real labels that were used by informants. Sometimes this works quite well (e.g. the subordinate group surprise is represented by the most dominant label "surprised"). Other times the fit of the label is awkward. The subordinate group neglect, for example, represents quite a diverse set of emotion labels, whilst the subordinate group shame represents emotion labels that include "embarrassed," and, as we saw in section 3, that emotion can be separate from shame.

Nevertheless, Table 3 does reveal some intriguing results. One can detect somewhat more similarity between the English, German and Finnish groups, compared with the Turkish and Chinese. All three have neglect in first or second position and shame in second or third. Anger features in the English and Finnish lists, and we should remember that for the German data the new category "unpleasant and awkward" in-

Table 3: Subordinate emotion groups for five nation groups in rank order (only groups scoring above 5 are included; the item in italics is the most frequent emotion label in that group; after the slash the original language label is supplied)

English	German	Turkish	Finnish	Chinese
Neglect (20) *(humiliated)*	Unpleasant and Awkward (21.5) *(unpleasant/ unangenehm)*	Sadness (30) *([feeling] bad / kötü hissetmek)*	Neglect (14.5) *(not appreciated / aliarvostettu, arvoton)*	Sadness (26.5) *(unhappy / 郁闷)*
Shame (16) *(embarrassed)*	Neglect (11.5) *(ridiculed / lächerlich gemacht)*	Suffering (16.5) *(offended / kirilmak)*	Irritation (14.5) *(annoyed / ärsyyntynyt)*	Rage (19.5) *(angry / 生气)*
Suffering (9.5) *(hurt)*	Shame (10.5) *(embarrassed / peinlich [berührt])*	Rage (8.5) *(angry / kizmak)*	Shame (11) *(embarrassed / nolostunut)*	Suffering (14) *(hurt / 受伤)*
Rage (8) *(angry)*		Neglect (8) *(humiliated / küçük düsürülmek)*	Rage (10) *(angry / vihainen)*	Irritation (11.5) *(annoyed / 恼火)*
Irritation (6.5) *(annoyed)*			Surprise (7) *(surprised / yllättynyt)*	Shame (5.5) *(embarrassed / 难堪)*

corporates anger. In contrast, the Turkish and Chinese groups feature the group sadness in strong first position. Geographically, of course, England, Germany and Finland are relatively close together, whereas Turkey is further to the East and China even further. But why sadness? A clue is given in Spencer-Oatey ("Conceptualising 'the Relational' in Pragmatics"). This study investigated Chinese / British workplace communication, deploying similar analyses of emotion labels to the ones being undertaken in this essay. Spencer-Oatey comments that for the Chinese sadness is "even more strongly linked to team issues; for example, lack of consultation, failure to carry out what had been agreed, lack of commitment from a team member, lack of mutual understanding, and a distant attitude of other team members" ("Conceptualising 'the Relational' in Pragmatics" 3572). Such issues involve violations of sociality rights. In another study (Culpeper, Marti, Nevala, Mei and Schauer), which analysed the same data, we demonstrated that violations of sociality rights dominated the Chinese data in particular, probably because of the importance of group relations in Chinese cultures. The intriguing conclusion one might draw then is that when Chinese informants experience impoliteness events which violate sociality rights, instead of predominantly experiencing anger or irritation, as would be the typical reaction of English informants (Culpeper, *Impoliteness* 62-65), they more often experience sadness. The difference is important: anger aligns with other-condemning emotions, whereas sadness aligns with self-conscious emotions.

It is intriguing to briefly note that the subordinate group of shame, containing "embarrassed" as its most dominant label, appears highest in the rank order for the English data, more specifically, in second position. This accords with points we made earlier about embarrassment seeming to be a particular feature of English culture.

5. Conclusion

At the beginning of this essay we emphasised the more general point that emotions are linked to contexts, including cultures, through cognition. In discourse, emotions can be experienced or displayed – or withheld – by those producing impoliteness, as well as those receiving it, not to mention third parties. The phenomenon of banter is an interesting case in point; the "normal" reaction to impoliteness, and emotional stimulus, is withheld.

Impoliteness and emotions are intimately connected, and more so than politeness. Goffman had argued that such notions as face are strongly linked to the emotions of embarrassment, hurt and anger. Our results suggest that he was right. Sometimes impoliteness involves violations of sociality rights. Culpeper (*Impoliteness*) has suggested on the basis of his English data that such violations are strongly linked to anger. In this essay, we show evidence that may conflict with that. Instead of feeling angry about such violations, if we can extrapolate from our data set, it seems that the Chinese in particular may feel sadness, a sense of being let down by a behaviour that should not be.

Of course, we must remember that we used retrospective reports of emotions, not on-line emotional experiences. There are issues about the role of language in mapping emotion, not to mention problems with translating emotions labels. Finally, we need to acknowledge that our study has been limited by the fact that we only looked at reports from 500 undergraduates in five nations, not a cross-section of people; it does not reflect the cultural diversity in a nation.

References

Anderson, Craig A. and Brad J. Bushman. "Human Aggression." *Annual Review of Psychology* 53 (2002): 27-51.

——, William E. Deuser and Kristina M. DeNeve. "Hot Temperatures, Hostile Affect, Hostile Cognition, and Arousal: Tests of a General Model of Affective Aggression." *Personality and Social Psychology Bulletin* 21 (1995): 434-448.

Bargiela-Chiappini, Francesca. "Face and Politeness: New (Insights) for Old (Concepts)." *Journal of Pragmatics* 35.10-11 (2003): 1453-1469.

Bartlett, Frederic C. *Remembering: A Study in Experimental and Social Psychology.* Cambridge: Cambridge University Press, 1995 [1932].

Blitvich, Pilar Garcés-Conejos. "A Genre Approach to the Study of Impoliteness." *International Review of Pragmatics* 2 (2010): 46-94.

Bousfield, Derek. *Impoliteness in Interaction.* Philadelphia and Amsterdam: John Benjamins, 2008.

Brown, Penelope and Stephen C. Levinson. *Politeness: Some Universals in Language Usage.* Cambridge: Cambridge University Press, 1987.

Conway, Martin A. and Debra A. Bekerian. "Situational Knowledge and Emotions." *Cognition and Emotion* 1 (1987): 145-191.

Culpeper, Jonathan. "Towards an Anatomy of Impoliteness." *Journal of Pragmatics* 25 (1996): 349-367.

——. *Impoliteness: Using Language to Cause Offence.* Cambridge: Cambridge University Press, 2011.

——, Leyla Marti, Minna Nevala, Meilian Mei and Gila Schauer. "Cross-Cultural Variation in the Perception of Impoliteness: A Study of Impoliteness Events Reported by Students in England, China, Finland, Germany and Turkey." *Intercultural Pragmatics* 7.4 (2010): 597-624.

Darwin, Charles R. *Origin of Species.* London: John Murray, 1872.

Eelen, Gino. *A Critique of Politeness Theories.* Manchester: St. Jerome Publishing, 2001.

Feeney, Judith A. "Hurt Feelings in Couple Relationships: Towards Integrative Models of the Negative Effects of Hurtful Events." *Journal of Social and Personal Relationships* 21 (2004): 487-508.

Gerholm, Tove. "Children's Development of Facework Practices – An Emotional Endeavour." *Journal of Pragmatics* 43.13 (2011): 3099-3110.

Goffman, Erving. *Interactional Ritual: Essays on Face-to-Face Behavior.* Garden City, New York: Anchor Books, 1967.

Haidt, Jonathan. "The Moral Emotion." *Handbook of Affective Sciences.* Ed. Richard J. Davidson, Klaus R. Scherer and H. Hill Goldsmith. Oxford: Oxford University Press, 2003. 852-870.

Hupka, Ralph B., Alison P. Lenton and Keith A. Hutchinson. "Universal Development of Emotion Categories in Natural Language." *Journal of Personality and Social Psychology* 77.2 (1999): 247-278.

Hurtado De Mendoza, Alejandra, José Miguel Fernández-Dols, W. Gerrod Parrott and Pilar Carrera. "Emotion Terms, Category Structure, and the Problem of Translation: The Case of Shame and vergüenza." *Cognition and Emotion* 24.4 (2010): 661-680.

Kienpointner, Manfred. "Cortesía, emociones y argumentación." *Cortesía y conversación: de lo escrito a lo oral. III Coloquio Internacional del Programa EDICE.* Ed. Antonio Briz, Antonio Hidalgo, Marta Abelda, Josefa Contreras and Nieves Hernández Flores. València: Universitat de València, 2008. 25-52.

Leary, Mark R., Carrie Springer, Laura Negel, Emily Ansell and Kelly Evans. "The Causes, Phenomenology, and Consequences of Hurt Feelings." *Journal of Personality and Social Psychology* 74 (1998): 1225-1237.

Locher, Miriam A. and Derek Bousfield. "Introduction: Impoliteness and Power in Language." *Impoliteness in Language: Studies on its Interplay with Power in Theory and Practice.* Ed. Derek Bousfield and Miriam A. Locher. Berlin and New York: Mouton de Gruyter, 2008. 1-13.

Majid, Asifa. "The Role of Language in the Science of Emotion." *Emotion Review* 4.4 (2012): 380-381.

Morris, Desmond J. *The Naked Ape.* London: Bantam Books, 1967.

Ortony, Andrew, Gerald Clore and Allan Collins. *The Cognitive Structure of the Emotions.* Cambridge and New York: Cambridge University Press, 1988.

Rosch, Eleanor. "Natural categories." *Cognitive Psychology* 4 (1973): 328-350.

——. "Principles of Categorization." *Cognition and Categorization.* Ed. Eleanor Rosch and Barbara B. Lloyd. New Jersey and London: Lawrence Erlbaum, 1978. 27-48.

——, Carolyn B. Mervis, Wayne D. Gray, David M. Johnson and Penny Boyes-Braem. "Basic Objects in Natural Categories." *Cognitive Psychology* 8 (1976): 382-439.

Rozin, Paul, Laura Lowery, Sumio Imada and Jonathan Haidt. "The CAD Triad Hypothesis: A Mapping Between Three Moral Emotions (Contempt, Anger, Disgust) and Three Moral Codes (Community,

Autonomy, Divinity)." *Journal of Personality and Social Psychology* 76.4 (1999): 574-586.

Ruhi, Şükriye. "Intentionality, Communicative Intentions and the Implication of Politeness." *Intercultural Pragmatics* 5.3 (2008): 287-314.

Russell, James A. "In Defense of a Prototype Approach to Emotion Concepts." *Journal of Personality and Social Psychology* 60.1 (1991): 37-47.

Samra-Federicks, Dalvir. "Ethnomethodology and the Moral Accountability of Interaction: Navigating the Conceptual Terrain of 'Face and Face-Work'." *Journal of Pragmatics* 42.8 (2010): 2147-2157.

Scollon, Ronald and Suzanne Scollon. *Intercultural Communication: A Discourse Approach*. Oxford: Blackwell, 1995.

Shaver, Phillip, Judith Schwartz, Donald Kirson and Cary O'Connor. "Emotion Knowledge: Further Exploration of a Prototype Approach." *Journal of Personality and Social Psychology* 52.6 (1987): 1061-1086.

Spencer-Oatey, Helen D. M. "Conceptualising 'the Relational' in Pragmatics: Insights from Metapragmatic Emotion and (Im)politeness Comments." *Journal of Pragmatics* 43.14 (2011): 3565-3578.

———. "Managing Rapport in Talk: Using Rapport Sensitive Incidents to Explore the Motivational Concerns Underlying the Management of Relations." *Journal of Pragmatics* 34.5 (2002): 529-545.

———. "(Im)Politeness, Face and Perceptions of Rapport: Unpackaging their Bases and Interrelationships." *Journal of Politeness Research: Language, Behaviour, Culture* 1.1 (2005): 95-119.

———. *Culturally Speaking: Managing Rapport through Talk across Cultures (2nd ed.)*. London and New York: Continuum, 2008.

Steffensen, Margaret S., Chitra Joag-Dev and Richard C. Andersen. "A Cross-Cultural Perspective on Reading Comprehension." *Reading Research Quarterly* 15 (1979): 10-29.

Vangelisti, Anita L. "Messages that Hurt." *The Dark Side of Interpersonal Communication*. Ed. William R. Cupach and Brian H. Spitzberg. New Jersey and London: Lawrence Erlbaum, 1994. 53-82.

———. "Making Sense of Hurtful Interactions in Close Relationships: When Hurt Feelings Create Distance." *Attribution, Communication Behavior, and Close Relationships*. Ed. Valerie L. Manusov and John H. Harvey. New York: Cambridge University Press, 2001. 38-58.

———. "Communicating Hurt." *The Dark Side of Interpersonal Communication*. 2nd ed. Ed. Brian H. Spitzberg and William R. Cupach. New Jersey and London: Lawrence Erlbaum, 2007. 121-142.

Wallbott, Harald G. and Klaus R. Scherer. "Cultural Determinants in Experiencing Shame and Guilt." *Self-Conscious Emotions: The Psychology of Shame, Guilt, Embarrassment and Pride.* Ed. June Price Tangney and Kurt W. Fischer. New York: Guilford Press, 1995. 465-487.

Watts, Richard J. *Politeness.* Cambridge: Cambridge University Press, 2003.

Whorf, Benjamin Lee. "The Relation of Habitual Thought and Behaviour to Language." *Language, Thought and Reality: Selected Readings of Benjamin Lee Whorf.* Ed. John B. Carroll. Cambridge, Massachusetts: MIT Press, 1956 [1939].

Wierzbicka, Anna. "Human Emotions: Universals or Culture-Specific?" *American Anthropologist* 88.3 (1986): 584-594.

———. *Emotions Across Languages and Cultures: Diversity and Universals.* Cambridge: Cambridge University Press, 1999.

Young, Stacy L. "Factors that Influence Recipients' Appraisals of Hurtful Communication." *Journal of Social and Personal Relationships* 21 (2004): 291-303.

Feeling Dredeful: Fear and Therapy
in *The Scale of Perfection*

Daniel McCann

Fear, as understood by medieval medicine, is a dangerous and potentially lethal passion of the soul that ought to be avoided. Yet while both academic medical texts and vernacular regimens of health stress the dangers of fear, medieval theology holds a very different opinion. As popular devotional materials and complex theological treatises make clear, fear is uniquely suited to promote the ultimate health of the soul – its *salus* and union with God. This paper will explore how medieval theology reconfigures fear as a passion of the soul that edifies and promotes health. Focusing upon the connection between emotion, medicine and religious literature in late-medieval England, the paper will explore *drede* – or fear – and its therapeutic uses in Walter Hilton's *The Scale of Perfection*. This text is remarkable not simply for its widespread dissemination, but also for its sophisticated comments regarding drede's utility. It identifies drede as a means of altering the soul in specific and highly desirable ways, as an initial means of returning the soul to God by promoting the key virtue of *kenosis* or *mekenesse* within the very construction of the soul itself.

Introduction

> Hys sorwful hert gan faste faynte
> And his spirites wexen dede;
> The blod was fled for pure drede
> Doun to hys herte, to make hym warm—
> For wel hyt feld the herte had harm.   (Chaucer ll.488-92)

Emotion, Affect, Sentiment: The Language and Aesthetics of Feeling. SPELL: Swiss Papers in English Language and Literature 30. Ed. Andreas Langlotz and Agnieszka Soltysik Monnet. Tübingen: Narr, 2014. 89-107.

The Man in Black is feeling seriously unwell. The symptoms and cause
of his illness are listed by Chaucer: "pure drede" has overcome the character. Drede, or fear, is dangerous due to the cardiac and pneumatological changes it causes. It weakens the pulse, cools the body, contracts the
heart, and hinders the circulation of vital spirit and blood to a potentially
fatal extent. Its effects cause a humoral imbalance that Chaucer, blend-
ing medical knowledge with poetic purpose, evokes in the description of
the character's skin pigmentation – he turns green "[a]nd pale, for ther
noo blood ys sene / In no maner lym of hys" (ll.498-499).[1] Though poetic, such a description is wholly consistent with medieval medical understanding. Drede, according to the period's key medical compendia
the *Articella* and *Pantegni*, was a passion of the soul that should be
avoided. Both these Latin compendia deal with the physiological consequences of fear – variously termed *timor* or *metus*; drede being the Middle
English equivalent.[2]

In contrast to medical literature, medieval devotional and religious
materials express a very different opinion. These sorts of texts view fear
more positively, rendering it as a tool of emotional/spiritual cleansing
that can enable union with God. Walter Hilton's *Scale of Perfection* (circa.
late1380s) is an excellent Middle English example of one such text.
Unlike the medical literature of the time, the *Scale* renders drede not as
something to be avoided but as an instrument that can purify the heart,
cleanse the soul, and encourage humility. As I shall argue in this essay,
the *Scale* identifies drede as the cure for mankind's emotional pathology
– as a therapy that enables purity of heart, humility, and "reformynge in
feelynge" (2.557).[3] But, before examining the *Scale*'s use of drede, I shall
provide some context by discussing the understanding of fear within
medieval medical and religious literature.

---

[1] The breadth of Chaucer's scientific knowledge has been documented well; for an overview see Glending Olson's "Geoffrey Chaucer." I am grateful to Professor Vincent
Gillespie for drawing my attention to the complexities of this passage and for his insightful comments on an earlier draft; see his "Dead Still/Still Dead." Also, Professor
Peregrine Horden has illuminated the medical significance of this passage in his "A
Non-Natural Environment" and has been generous with advice. Additional thanks are
owed to Professor John Thompson (Director of the Institute for Collaborative Research
in the Humanities, Queen's University Belfast), and Professor Malcolm Andrew for
reading earlier versions of this article. Finally, thanks are owed to the Leverhulme Trust
for funding my research.

[2] I was able to find a number of synonyms in the Middle English Dictionary that share
in the meaning, such as *aue, eie, ferde, ferdeleik, ferdnesse, ferdship, ferfulli, frai, gastli, gastnesse,
hidour, radnesse, reuli*, and *ugginge*.

[3] Henceforth quoted as *Scale* with book and line number.

Reforming Feelings

It is unity, not division, that defines the medieval understanding of the human being. Body and soul are subtly blended into an interconnected system with changes in one aspect causing changes in others. As the emotions are one such aspect, they are of considerable importance, a fact made clear in the medical compendia mentioned above. The *Isagoge ad Techne Galiene* of Johannitius classifies them as one of the *res non naturales*, or "non-natural things" (Wallis 146). These form a category of six factors which determine health, such as the "air and the environment, eating and drinking, exercise and baths, sleep, coitus, and the 'passions/accidents of the soul'" (Horden, "Religion as Medicine" 143). The last factor refers to the emotions and presents them as variable states that the soul is subject to, and that have a direct physiological impact. Specifically, they cause the body's natural heat and energy to contract or diffuse (Wallis 146). Thus the experience of the passions is both psychological and physiological, causing specific changes in the movement and quality of the body's various fluids.

Constantine of Africa's translation of the *Pantegni* provides more detail. It establishes a connection between the passions and the internal movement of vital spirit to or from the heart – the organ responsible for its generation. Joy (*gaudium*) and anger (*ira*) are centrifugal and cause vital spirit to move from the heart to the body's extremities; distress (*tristitia*) and fear (*timor*) are centripetal, causing vital spirit to retreat to the heart (Harvey 25). Joy and distress work slowly, while anger and fear work rapidly. The medical consequences are far-reaching. If vital spirit rushes out from the heart, the organ weakens while the body's extremities overheat and desiccate. Conversely, if it rushes to the heart, the extremities cool and become deficient in vital spirit. In both cases humoral imbalance occurs thus increasing the likelihood of disease (Rawcliffe, "The Concept of Health" 330). By extension this will impact upon the subsequent production quality of natural, vital, and animal spirits.[4] Compounding all this is the danger of habituation. The natural reciprocity between the passions and their somatic consequences causes certain forms of feeling, and certain physiological states, to become habituated and potentially permanent (Harvey 19). As some of these states are conducive to disease or characterised by high morbidity, the dangers posed by certain passions are clear.

---

[4] For a survey of the medical significance of emotions and theological engagements with them, see Knuuttila, *Emotions* 214-15.

Fear, given its rapid and potentially fatal effects upon the body, is in many ways the most dangerous. It is for this reason that these medical compendia recommend its opposite – moderate joy – as the passion most conducive to good health. Similar recommendations are found in medical regimen texts aimed at a more general audience; these were often in high demand after occurrences of the plague (Bonfield 241). For instance, the Middle English translation of the *Secretum Secretorum* emphasises the therapeutic significance of joy, extolling its readers to be "mery and glad . . . and beholde delitable bokes" (Manzalaoui 59). In the same way, John Lydgate's *Dietary* stresses the importance of "a glad hert," because "care-a-way is a good medycyne" (ll. 62-65). A clear consensus emerges: fear is dangerous and ought to be avoided, and the other passions of the soul must be regulated to ensure good health.

While this is the case for medical knowledge, medieval theology views fear as something positive – as a passion of the soul that can lead to God. This is all the more remarkable given the close relationship between science, medicine and theology during the period.[5] The medieval definition of health demonstrates this most clearly: the Latin *salus* is a complex concept encompassing both health and salvation. Yet, despite the overlap, there is a considerable gulf between the medical and theological understanding of fear – negative in the former and positive in the latter. The precise reasons for this dichotomy lie beyond the scope of this essay. It is clear, however, that fear shifts dramatically in its significance. It moves from being an aetiology for various psychosomatic problems towards a tool or instrument of treatment for mankind's postlapsarian state of illness.

Unsurprisingly, this positive attitude towards fear is inherited from the Bible and early Church writings. Both the Old and New Testament frequently mention fear. It is to be reserved only for God (Jeremiah 5:22, Isaiah 8:12-13), an experience that initially brings wisdom (Psalms 111:10, Proverbs 9:10, Job 28:28), but ultimately cleansing and spiritual perfection (2 Corinthians 7:1). Such utility is explored and extended by key thinkers in patristic theology. For Clement of Alexandria fear is central to an advanced Christian life. Each person begins by fearing God's Law and His punishment, characterised as the fear of a slave or *timor servillis*. From there, the person progresses to the fear of sin and the reverential fear of God's awesome nature, characterised as the fear of a son

---

[5] For an overview of the interaction between theology and medicine during the period see Peter Biller and Joseph Ziegler. For more detail on the scientific aspects of theology see A. J. Minnis, and A. B. Scott 197-212.

towards his father or *timor filialis* (Clement of Alexandria 2.12). St. Basil, Gregory of Nyssa and Gregory of Nazianzus develop its programmatic utility further. They combine Christian anthropology and Platonic psychology to render fear as a means of perfecting the soul: it helps restore the soul's divine image, cleanse it from sin and further mitigate the disastrous consequences of the Fall (Basil 889-1,052; Gregory of Nazianzus 813-51; Gregory of Nyssa 2.320). Fear becomes an instrument of therapy, a tool for cleansing the soul and restoring its original state of operation. In this sense, it is a restorative treatment that returns the soul to a state of order. Ultimately, this would result in the soul being restored so much to God as to share in His being – a deifying process termed *theosis* (Knuuttila, *Emotions* 128). Fear is thus a process as much as a passion, facilitating better moral behaviour and an increasingly intimate relationship with God.

During the twelfth and thirteenth centuries these patristic discussions receive fresh philosophical and methodological interest. The understanding of the soul's programmatic ascent, and the role the passions play in that process, is reinvigorated due to the widespread dissemination of the medical compendia mentioned above, and the translation of Avicenna's works on the soul. Such knowledge allows the abstract aspects of Christian mystical and spiritual experience, and the preparatory benefits attributed to fear, to become conceptually grounded within intricate medical frameworks. New understandings of the soul's relation to the body arise and provide clearer ways of articulating the precise psychosomatic mechanisms by which, and through which, the soul is cleansed and brought closer to God (Knuuttila, *Emotions* 178). Treatises such as William of St Thierry's *On the Nature of the Body and the Soul*, Hugh of St Victor's *The Union of Body and Spirit*, and Alcher of Clairvaux's *The Sprit and Body*, are all sophisticated examples of the fusion of medical and theological knowledge. They contend that the vital and animal spirits are the medium through which the body and the soul are subtly interconnected. They are the point of contact between the corporeal and the incorporeal, and so play a pivotal role in the operation of the body, the cognitive faculties and, by extension, the higher powers of the soul. Crucially, the quality and nature of these spirits are themselves affected by the humors and, more broadly, the regulation of the nonnaturals:

Each spirit, whether it be animal, vital, or natural, although all their substance is from the subtle parts of the humours, yet has its own complexion
by reason of the proportion of the quantities of the subtlety of the humours, and of the form of the mingling.

(Avicenna, *De medicinis cordialibus*, quoted in Harvey 25)

Given such interconnection, there exists the tantalising possibility of
manipulating the soul through manipulating its basest aspect – the
body's pneumatological system. Medieval theology, therefore, embraces
contemporary medical knowledge to construct a methodology for the
proximal treatment of the soul. As the heart is the organ which generates vital spirit, and the passions of the soul are physiologically constituted by the movement of vital spirit, the instrumental value of fear begins to become apparent. Careful modulations of it cause predictable
cardiac and pneumatological changes. These changes will in turn alter
the quality of the body's vital and animal spirit, refining them, and thus
refining the operation of the soul and its higher powers – changes which
can become habituated through frequency. Such refinement is essential
for advanced access to God. As St Bernard notes, "the heart must be
cleansed if the soul is to see God" (89). In his influential *Speculum Naturale*, Vincent of Beauvais emphasises the connection between the vital
spirit and God, noting that within the soul "God is there as a [principle
of] life, that is, he vivifies the soul . . . is inside [the soul], for he is united
with it and poured into it" (quoted in Caciola 282). Unity with God,
according to such medically informed theology, requires a pneumatological transplant – the gradual refinement and eventual replacement
of vital spirit with the Holy Spirit. Fear, due to its psychosomatic effects,
works to purify the heart and the vital spirit, thereby facilitating the possibility of divine contact.

Its utility in theosis, though very much at the initial stages, becomes
increasingly clarified. Later writers, such as John Blund, John of La Rochelle, and Isaac of Stella, offer increasingly sophisticated engagements
with Avicenna's faculty psychology. Their works offer new taxonomies
for the soul and its powers, and address its disordered state following
the Fall. They contend that the concupiscible and irascible powers in the
soul contain specific emotional responses and states, and schematise
them into opposite pairs. Fear's utility rises even higher here, as the passion becomes directly connected to the irascible power of the soul and
can therefore play a key role in restoring its prelapsarian functional order. It can do so because one of the key motive acts of the irascible
power is humility or "poverty of spirit" or *paupertas spiritus* (John Blund
20.25-21.7; 25.4; John of La Rochelle, *Summa de anima* II.107.50-91, and

his *Tractatus de divisione multiplici potentiarum animae* 143.205; Isaac of Stella 153-77). Such humility is the foundation of *kenosis* – the Christian ideal of "self-emptying" exemplified by Christ that must precede any theotic union with God. Another key motive act, penitence or *paenitentia*, is also evoked by fear. As a direct part of the soul's irascible power, fear therefore facilitates the emergence of an emotional complex within the soul, enabling states that constitute "various forms of the flight from evil" and are vital for an advanced Christian life (Knuuttila, "Emotion" 435). While it is still a dangerous passion, fear nevertheless becomes rendered as a preparatory treatment – one of the initial steps in the soul's programmatic reformation that can help further theosis. In this sense medieval theology draws from medical knowledge to render fear as therapeutic if correctly directed and controlled.

All these theological texts are primarily theoretical in nature; others are more practical. Just as medieval regimen texts distil academic medical knowledge into mnemonic guidance for healthy living, medieval manuals of meditation, contemplation, pastoral care and catechetical instruction are themselves distillations of advanced theological materials. Such texts are practical guides for those embarking on the initial to advanced stages of Christian life and function as regimens of the soul designed to promote its ultimate *salus*. In later medieval England a wealth of these texts can be found. Due to the labours of medieval scholars such as John Blund, Robert Grosseteste and Roger Bacon, advanced speculation on the soul's ascent developed in Paris finds a home in Oxford, and becomes part of the innovative and "increasingly forensic pastoral care of the thirteenth- and fourteenth-centuries" in England (Gillespie, "Thy Will Be Done" 101). I shall now turn to one Middle English example that clearly sets out drede's importance for bringing the soul closer to God – Walter Hilton's *The Scale of Perfection*.

Regimens of the Soul

Directed to a "goostli suster in Jhesu Crist," the *Scale* is a didactic text from the fourteenth century designed to help its reader advance in his or her spiritual life. It consists of two books which differ in terms of length and complexity, and were probably written at different points in Walter Hilton's religious life and career.[6] Despite these modest differences, both books deal with a central issue: the gradual reformation and restoration of the soul to the image and likeness of God; a process consisting of two interrelated stages. The first is the most uncomplicated and is termed the reforming in faith; the second is much more complex and difficult and is termed the reforming in feeling and faith. A central feature of the *Scale* is thus a marked interest in the psychological and emotional disposition of its intended recipient. The text's discussion of "affecciouns," "feelynges," and "mekenesse" is a clear sign that its spiritual advice is directly concerned with how best to govern and regulate the passions and powers of the soul.[7] To a large extent, therefore, the text can be considered as a regimen of the soul: the *Scale*, like the medical regimen texts mentioned earlier, offers practical advice on how to promote "goostli hele" (1.1233).

Achieving such a state of health requires not just sacramental and liturgical observance, but also the programmatic experience of precise emotional states designed to alter the soul. This reforming in feeling and faith is a long-term goal that requires constant effort, yet it all begins with a key passion of the soul – drede. It is through drede that the benefits of an advanced Christian life can be realised: it purifies the heart and soul, encourages a Christ-like humility, and – should grace be granted – facilitates a much closer relationship with God. However, before the text extols the benefits of drede to the reader, it makes it very clear why it is needed in the first place: the soul is sick and damaged almost beyond repair. The precise cause of the soul's affliction is simple – original sin, or "synne." It is due to such synne that the soul is "wel foule disfigured and forschapen with wrecchidnesse" (1.2418-9) and "forschapen fro the kyndeli schap of the ymage of Crist" (1.2587-8). Synne thus occludes and defaces the image of God in the soul. Yet it also goes much further, and through it mankind is "forschapen like to a beest; with

---

[6] For an overview of Hilton's life and career, see John H. P. Clark. For a richer understanding of the text's influence and use in a variety of pastoral contexts, see Gillespie's "Idols and Images," also Jeremy Catto's "1349–1412."

[7] These terms possess a wider semantic range and, broadly speaking, cover a multitude of interconnected cognitive and perceptual processes within the mind.

whiche beestli clothis we alle aren born, and umbilapped and disfigured from oure kyndeli schaap" (1.2426-7). In this sense, synne is much more than an abstract theological concept, and instead operates like a leprous disease: synne is debilitating and deforming, it corrupts the soul's order and nature, and blights the body through deforming the soul (Rawcliffe, *Leprosy* 71-3). Hilton foregrounds this sense of a complete pathology by noting not just how synne occludes the image of God in the soul, but also how it compromises its functional order:

> For thou schalt undirsronde that a soule hath two parties. The toon is called the sensualite; that is the fleschli feelynge bi the fyve outeward wittes, the whiche is comoun to man and to beest. Up the whiche sensualite, whanne it is unskilfulli and unordynateli rulid, is maad the image of synne, as I have bifore seid, for than is the sensualite synne, whanne it is not rulid aftir resoun. (2.658-62)

Synne causes deformity through disarray: its presence subverts the natural hierarchy within the soul, causing the lesser sensuality to run amok and strive for control. The soul's rational part, which "schulde be maister and sovereyne, and that is propirli the ymage of God" (2.664) is thus compromised and unable to properly govern this lower part. The result is a soul ruled not by reason, but rather disordered desire. The overall results of this deformity are a state of defective cognition and an emotional pathology – the soul no longer loves virtue, but instead delights in improper pursuits and is divided against itself. There are now "two lawes in a soule" (2.499) – God in the reason and synne in the sensuality – which are opposed and keep the soul in a state of perpetual inner conflict. In its original state the soul was "the moste worthi creature that evere God made" (2.686) and so "schulde noo thinge loven and liken but oonli God" (2.688-9). After synne, however, it has become so contorted and deformed that it "cheseth his reste and his blisse in a passynge delite of an ertheli thinge" (2.694-5). The internal operation and order of the soul has become compromised to the point that it desires the wrong things: its affective power is now wholly disordered and misdirected, so much so that an emotional pathology blights the soul. In short it loves itself, not God.

Hilton makes the disastrous consequences of this affective disorder quite clear. He asserts that synne is "a fals mysruled love unto thisilf. Oute of this love cometh al maner of synnes bi sevene ryveres, the whiche aren thise: pride, envie, ire, accedie, coveitise, glotony, and leccherie" (1.1556-8). From self-love comes a host of additional sins. Thus, a "mysruled" affection is a vicious circle that exists as the foundation, cause and consequence of all further damage to the soul. It is little wonder then that the text places such emphasis on reforming the feelings and re-aligning the affections towards God. The soul's deformity and sickness through synne are what the text seeks to remedy, and it provides a two-tiered process for doing just that. The first stage is the reforming in faith which "mai lighteli be geten" (2.466), as it comes from the saving work of Christ's Passion. It requires simply faith in Christ and the Church and receiving the sacraments. However, while this mitigates the disastrous consequences of synne, the affective and cognitive deformity still persists. It is the second stage, the reforming in feeling and faith, that addresses the remaining problems. Unlike the first, this stage "mai not lightli be geten, but thorugh longe traveile and mykil bisynesse" (2.857-58). Treating the affective disorder of the soul is a long-term process which begins with the programmatic experience of a specific passion of the soul – drede.

Over the course of the text, the reader is encouraged to appreciate drede's complexity and utility. It must, like all the passions of the soul, be directed towards its proper object – God. From the very outset of the text a contrast is established between the self-focused and self-loving "dredis of alle ertheli thynges" (1.21) and the correct drede of God; with the stipulation that an advanced spiritual life requires the reader to become "as it were deed to alle ertheli loves and dredes" (1.7-8). The distinction between them is not affective but rather object-orientated. As a passion of the soul, drede operates within the same psychosomatic parameters as set down by medieval medicine; what differs, and what is key here, is the focus of that drede. When directed towards earthly/non-spiritual matters it is part of those "fleschli desires and veyne dredes, that risen oute of thi herte thorugh corrupcioun of thi fleschli kynde" (1.7-8). Such drede is a species of pride and self-love – and all love must be reserved for God alone. Drede of God, therefore, is by its very nature self-less, as the passion's object is not the self but instead wholly another.

The text, drawing from those theological materials mentioned earlier, makes the further distinction between *timor servillis* and *timor filialis*. It notes that, initially, the drede of God takes the form of "drede as a thral" (2.3319). This is the "fear of slaves," of those who "dreden Him as man" (2.1991-2) and "thenken thanne that God is wrooth with hem as a man schulde be yif thei hadden trespaced agens hym" (2.1993-5). Only later, after much effort and grace, may the person progress to the more advanced "fear of sons." It is a state consisting of a different relationship to God, in which the person "maketh him His freend bi trewe acord, and therfore as to a trewe frend that pleseth Hym with love, not serveth Him bi drede as a thral" (2.3318-9).

The text, however, does not rest here, but offers a sustained metaphorical treatment of drede that emphasises its instrumental potential in reforming the soul. Sin which arises from self-love – the "stirynges of pride, envie, veynglorie, or ony othir" (1.2560-1) – can be stopped and contained if confronted with drede:

> Agenstonde it, and folwe hit not neither in word ne in deede, as moche as thou mai, but as he riseth smyte him doun agen; and so schalt thou slee it with the swerd of drede of God, that it schal not dere thee.   (1.2557-60)

Endowed here with a martial force, drede is a potent passion of the soul that acts as a targeted treatment for synne. Such a metaphorical rendering is wholly consistent with contemporary medical knowledge, as the forceful, violent and potentially dangerous aspects of drede are encapsulated with this image of a sword. Yet it is also highly precise. Drede does not run rampant, but targets synne and strikes it down alone. Within the context of this metaphorical presentation, therefore, there is the implicit idea of surgical precision and directed therapy: drede of God works curatively by removing only sins. A more domestic metaphor reinforces this function. In a passage which compares the reader's soul to a house for God to live in, Hilton states that "thou schalt cast oute of thyn herte alle siche synnes, and swepe thi soule clene with the besome of the drede of God" (1.1407-09). Drede is likened to a broom that cleanses and purifies by removing corruption from heart and soul. This metaphor, in particular, conveys a crucial point: drede purifies the heart. Drede can do this because it directly and precisely targets the sins arising from self-love; sins which the text asserts come from a specific place:

> Badde thoughtes and unclene affeccions comen oute of the herte, the whiche filen a man, as oure Lord seith. Thei owthere bynemen the liyf of the soule bi deedli synne, or ellis thei feble the soule and maketh it seek, yef thei ben venial. (1.2500-02)

Such a statement distils complex medical knowledge and theological speculation into accessible advice. It highlights in succinct form that many of the soul's problems stem from its basest aspect – the heart, or seat of the soul. While synne damages the soul in specific ways, its pernicious effects are total. The whole soul is damaged by synne, from its highest affective and cognitive powers to its lowest cardiac and pneumatological aspect. Purifying the heart, therefore, is a matter of some urgency. If left unchecked, synne will continue to contaminate and infect the soul, and so the text offers practical solutions to achieve purity or *clennesse*. While Christ's Passion and the sacraments are the most important forms of initial treatment, it is drede which takes the cleansing process further. Like a sword, it will cut out those sins and contaminating affections, and so purify the heart. Since "her is moche pride hid in the grounde of thyn herte, as a fox daareth in his den" (1.1824-5), the reader must "gete clennesse of herte bi distroynge of synne" (1.637-8). Drede specifically targets these sins – it is instrumental in enabling purity of heart.

Clennesse is vitally important for those wishing to join with God in theosis. As the text makes clear via a Biblical quotation, it is not only a state to aspire to but also a condition to be met – "Blissid be the clene of herte, for thei schullen see God" (1.346-47).[8] The goal of seeing God, therefore, first requires purification: "the more clene and sotil that the soule ys maad . . . the scharpere sight it hath and the myghtiere love of the Godhede of Jhesu" (2.2201-203). Drede helps realise this goal, as it purifies the basest aspect of the soul – the heart and its vital spirit – and makes it more suitable for God. Yet, such purification is only the initial therapeutic function of drede; at this stage it treats the symptoms of the deformed soul, not the cause. There is another level to its healing work that is more expressly concerned with effecting changes in the soul, with reforming it:

> [W]hat that thou feelist, seest, or smellest or savours, withouten in thi bodili wittes, or withinne in ymagynynge or feelynge in thi resoun or knowynge: brynge hit al withynne the trowthe and rulis of Hooli Chirche and caste it al in the morter of mekenesse and breke it smal with the pestel of drede of God. (1.619-23)

The totality of perceptual, cognitive, and psychological being must be submitted not just to the rules of the Church, but also to the reforming power of drede. Its therapeutic instrumentality is brought to the fore here by use of a sophisticated medical metaphor. It is likened to a pestle, to a common tool used to prepare medicinal ingredients. Such a rendering conveys how drede functions therapeutically: it is an instrument of reformation, as the pestle works by grinding down what it touches. In this sense, drede functions literally to reform the deformed psychology of the reader – it grinds it down into a "pouder" that can then be burnt "in the fier of desire, and offre it soo to thi Lord Jesu Crist" (1.623-4).

---

[8] A similar quotation from the Beatitudes occurs in 2.569-71.

However, it can only carry out this reforming work when used with another instrument – the mortar of mekenesse. Only when drede is combined with the virtue of humility – or mekenesse – can it take the deformed soul and reform it into something acceptable to God. Both are complimentary; the pestle of drede only works when used with the mortar of mekenesse.

The metaphorical context conveys this sense of interconnected function: they are instruments of reformation that must be used together to achieve their therapeutic effect. Drede, therefore, cannot be separated from mekenesse – both must be used to reform the soul. The course of treatment is clear. Only drede removes the damaging pride that blights the soul, and thereby encourages the virtue of humility. As the text asserts, "for but yif a soule be first smyten doun fro the heighte of itsilf bi drede . . . it is not able to suffre the schynynges of goostli light" (2.1586-9). Without drede there can be no humility – no mekenesse – and without mekenesse the soul can never move closer to God:

> Upon whom schal My spirit reste? And He answereth Himsilf and seith: upon noon but upon the meke, poverli and contrite in herte and dredynge My wordes. Thanne yif thou wolt have the spirit of God rulynge thyn herte, have mekenesse and dreede of Hym. (1.528-31)

An over-arching condition is set: only those who achieve the precise emotional states specified in the Beatitudes are worthy to have God inhabit their hearts. Drede and mekenesse are forever connected, yet they differ in terms of their therapeutic function. With drede, the sins arising from self-love are treated and purged from the heart; with mekenesse, self-love is targeted. Purifying the heart is one thing, and an initial stage at that; joining with God in theotic union is quite another. To achieve such a state, the soul must undergo a further and more radical treatment carried out by mekenesse:

> The trewe sunne of rightwisenesse, that is, oure Lord Jhesu, schal springe to yow that dreden Him; that is, to meke soulis that meke hemself undir her even Cristene bi knowynge of here owen wrecchidnesse, and casten hemsilf doun undir God bi noghtynge of hemsilf in here owen substaunce thorugh reverente drede and goostli biholding of Him lastandli, for that is perfight mekenesse. (2.1593-97)[9]

---

[9] This is another Biblical quotation that Hilton is explicating, specifically of Isaiah 66.1-2.

Treatment now moves from purification to reformation. The
"noghtynge" of the soul, a process of kenotic self-emptying, must be
undertaken by those wishing to unite with God. It is the very essence of
mekenesse, and it is dependent upon drede. The passage stresses their
interdependence and interconnection – only the "reverente drede" of
God can engender a mekenesse in the soul which empties it of self-love
and self-absorption. In this sense the text distils advanced theological
materials which, as mentioned earlier, make an explicit connection between fear and humility. As fear belongs to the irascible power, and
humility – or poverty of spirit – is localised to the contrary disposition of
the irascible power, drede and mekenesse thus reside within the same
system. By using drede, the soul can be manipulated or influenced in
specific ways – it can be purified in a pneumatological sense, and then
treated and partially reformed through the mekenesse that drede engen-
ders. The *Scale* foregrounds the reforming power of this course of emotional therapy. From the outset, the reader is encouraged to "turne
thyne herte with thy body principali to God, and schape thee withinne
to His likenesse bi mekenesse" (1.14-15), to "breke thisilf in mekenesse"
(1.627), and to "be first reformed bi fulhed of mekenesse and charitee to
the liknesse of Jhesu in His manhede" (1.2607-9). Mekenesse is understood to reshape and remodel, to alter the soul in the best possible way.
It is "soothfast and medicynable" (2.1151-52), as it "maken good acord
in the harpe of thi soule" (2.1145-46) – it takes the deformed and disordered soul and brings it back into a state of harmony. Specifically,
mekenesse realigns the soul's affective power towards its proper object,
replacing self-love with love of God:

> Mekenesse seith, I am nought, I have nought. Love seith, I coveite nought
> but oon, and that is Jhesu . . . The lasse thou felist that thou art or that thu
> hast of thisilf thorugh mekenesse, the more thou coveiteste for to have of
> Jhesu in desire of love.   (2.1143-9)

The "noghtynge" of the soul is as much a process of affective restructuring as it is of self-emptying. It is a course of treatment that removes
the "fals mysruled love unto thisilf" (1.1556) which is the cause and
consequence of synne. In its place a profound love of God emerges that
works to remedy the soul's principal deformity – its misaligned affective
power. By loving God rather than itself, the soul is brought back to its
proper order with its affective power disciplined and re-directed towards
its creator. Such a restructuring of the soul will also work to eliminate
sin and beget virtue. As the cause of all sin is self-love, replacing it with
love of God will cause the "ground of synne" (1.1514) to be "stoppid

and distroied, and the springe mai be dried" (1.2185-86), and the soul will pursue virtue instead of vice. The role mekenesse plays in ensuring the health of the soul is therefore considerable, so much so that the text asserts that "as mykil as thu hast of mekenesse, so mykil haste thou of charité, of pacience, and of othere vertues" (1.452-53). Yet, despite its benefits, such a process is long and difficult.

Initially, mekenesse is engendered through the rational power of the soul; only later, God's grace permitting, will it work through the affective power: "there is two maner of mekenesse. Oon is had bi wirkynge of resoun. Anothir is feelt bi special gifte of love. But bothe aren of love" (2.2569-70). At this stage not only will the soul find virtue pleasant instead of arduous, it will also be ready to come towards the highest level of reformation possible – the reforming in feeling. Such an achievement is, however, wholly conditional upon mekenesse: "he that hath not trewe mekenesse ne ful herteli bisynes mai not come to the reformynge in feelynge" (2.1090-91). From drede comes such mekenesse, and from such mekenesse an intense love of God. It is an emotional trajectory consistent with the higher *timor filialis*. This advanced state of fear generates an emotional complex of humility and love that allows the soul to become more like Jesus, to reflect better the image of God, and begin to return to its original state of perfection. It is, if properly controlled and directed, a therapeutic feeling that can reform the soul.

Conclusion

In a poetic manner, Chaucer's description of the Man in Black with which the essay began offers a perfect example of how dangerous drede can be. Not only has drede caused circulatory problems and a general humoral imbalance, but it has also cost the character the use of his wits – he "had wel nygh lost hys mynde" (1.511). This passion of the soul affects the whole person, from the operation of the internal organs and the pneumatological system, to the perceptual and cognitive capacities of the soul. The fiction, therefore, conveys the well-attested medical fact of drede's extreme potency. Yet, as the new, medically-informed theological works on the soul made clear, such power also carries great potential. For these works on the soul and its powers, fear is a useful instrument of therapy that, if properly used and directed, can treat the soul in specific and desirable ways. On the most physical level, it affects the heart and vital spirit, subsequently altering the production quality of

animal spirit and thus refining the operation of the soul. On the most
rarefied and spiritual level, fear directly engages with a specific power of
the soul, and can be used to promote kenotic and penitential states
within its irascible power. It is, in all senses, preparatory, as fear can be
used to prepare body and soul for the possibility of Divine contact.
Herein lies its chief utility – while it is a dangerous passion, its ability to
encourage humility within the soul is too great a potential to overlook.
Emerging from such advanced theological texts are more focused, practical ones designed for spiritual progression and development – applied
regimens of the soul. Hilton's *Scale* is one such text, as it offers the
reader accessible advice and programmatic guidance to help the soul on
its journey towards God, towards "goostli hele." It emphasises drede as
crucial in reforming the deformed soul: this passion does not simply
purify the heart, but also destroys sin and promotes the key virtue of
mekenesse. Drede thus reshapes the soul away from self-love to love of
God alone. It is a text, therefore, that draws from a range of theological
works that employ medical knowledge to aid Fallen humanity: a text that
combines literature, theology and medicine to demonstrate that feeling
dredeful can be the best thing for you.

References

Avicenna. *De Medicinis Cordialibus. Liber De Anima Seu Sextus De Naturalibus IV-V.* Ed. S. Van Riet. Leiden: Brill, 1972: 187-210.

Basil the Great. *Regulae Fusius Tractatae. Patrologiae Cursus Completus, Series Graeca.* Ed J. P. Migne. Volume 31. Paris: Garnier Frères, 1857-66: 889-1052.

Bernard of Clairvaux. *On Conversion. Bernard of Clairvaux Selected Works.* Trans. G. R. Evans. New York: Paulist Press, 1987: 68-98.

Biller, Peter and Joseph Ziegler, eds. *Religion and Medicine in the Middle Ages.* Woodbridge: York Medieval Press and The Boydell Press, 2001.

Blund, John. *Tractatus De Anima.* Eds. D. A. Callus and R. W. Hunt. London: Oxford University Press, 1974.

Bonfield, Christopher Alan. "The Regimen Sanitatis and its Dissemination in England, c.1348-1550." Unpublished doctoral dissertation: University of East Anglia, 2006.

Caciola, Nancy. "Mystics, Demoniacs, and the Physiology of Spirit Possession in Medieval Europe." *Comparative Studies in Society and History* 42/2 (2000): 268-306.

Catto, Jeremy. "1349–1412: Culture and History." *The Cambridge Companion to Medieval English Mysticism.* Eds. Vincent Gillespie and Samuel Fanous. Cambridge: Cambridge University Press, 2011. 113-33.

Chaucer, Geoffrey. *The Book of the Duchess. The Riverside Chaucer. 3rd Edition.* Ed. Larry D. Benson. Oxford: Oxford University Press, 1988.

Clark, John H. P. and Rosemary Dorward, trans. *Walter Hilton: The Scale of Perfection.* Mahwah, New Jersey: Paulist Press, 1991.

Clement of Alexandria. *The Stromata or Miscellanies. The Ante-Nicene Fathers. Volume 2.* Eds. A. Robert and J. Donaldson. Grand Rapids, Michigan: Eerdmans, 1967.

Gillespie, Vincent. "'Thy Will Be Done': Piers Plowman and the Pater Noster." *Middle English Religious Texts and Their Transmission: Essays in Honour of Ian Doyle.* Ed. Alastair J. Minnis. Cambridge: Cambridge University Press 1994: 95-119.

——. "Dead Still/Still Dead." *The Medieval Journal* 1.1 (2011): 53-78.

——. "Idols and Images: Pastoral Adaptations of *The Scale of Perfection.*" *Langland, the Mystics and the Medieval English Religious Tradition: Essays in Honour of S. S. Hussey.* Ed. Helen Phillips. Cambridge: Cambridge University Press, 1990. 97-123.

Gregory of Nazianzus. *Adversus Iram. Patrologiae Cursus Completus, Series Graeca.* Ed. J. P. Migne. Volume 37. Paris: Garnier Frères, 1857-66: 813-51.

Gregory of Nyssa. *Life of Moses.* Eds. A. Malherbe and E. Ferguson. New York: Paulist Press, 1978.

Harvey, Ruth. *The Inward Wits: Psychological Theory in the Middle Ages and the Renaissance. Warburg Institute Surveys VI.* London: Warburg Institute, 1975.

Hilton, Walter. *The Scale of Perfection.* Ed. Thomas H. Bestul. Kalamazoo, Michigan: Medieval Institute Publications, 2000.

Horden, Peregrine. "Religion as Medicine: Music in Medieval Hospitals." *Religion and Medicine in the Middle Ages.* Eds. Peter Biller and Joseph Ziegler. York: The University of York, 2001. 135-154.

——. "A Non-Natural Environment: Medicine Without Doctors and the Medieval European Hospital." *The Medieval Hospital and Medical Practice.* Ed. Barbara S. Bowers. Aldershot: Ashgate, 2007. 133-145.

Isaac of Stella. "Epistola De Anima." *Three Treatises on Man: A Cistercian Anthropology.* Ed. Bernard McGinn. Kalamazoo, Michigan: Cistercian Publications, 1977. 153-77.

John of La Rochelle. *Summa De Anima.* Ed. J. G. Bougerol. Paris: Vrin, 1995.

——. *Tractatus De Divisione Multiplici Potentiarum Animae.* Ed. P. Michaud-Quantin. Paris: Vrin, 1964.

Knuuttila, Simo. "Emotion." *The Cambridge History of Medieval Philosophy. Volume One.* Ed. Robert Pasnau. Cambridge: Cambridge University Press, 2010. 428-40.

——. *Emotions in Ancient and Medieval Philosophy.* Oxford: Oxford University Press, 2004.

Lydgate, John. *The Minor Poems of John Lydgate.* Ed. H. N. MacCracken. EETS o.s. 192. London: Oxford University Press, 1934.

Manzalaoui, A., ed. *Secretum Secretorum: Nine English Versions.* EETS o.s. 276. London: Oxford University Press, 1977.

Minnis, A. J. and A. B. Scott, eds. *Medieval Literary Theory and Criticism c.1100-c.1375: The Commentary Tradition.* Oxford: Oxford University Press, 1988.

Olson, Glending. "Geoffrey Chaucer." *The Cambridge History of Medieval English Literature.* Ed. David Wallace. Cambridge: Cambridge University Press, 1999. 566-88.

Rawcliffe, Carole. "The Concept of Health in Late Medieval Society." *Le interazioni fra economia e ambiente biologico nell'Europa preindustriale secc. XIII-XVIII.* Florence: Florence University Press, 2010. 321-38.

———. *Leprosy in Medieval England*. Woodbridge: Boydell and Brewer, 2006.

Vincent of Beauvais. *Speculum Naturale*. Graz, Austria: Akademische Druck- und Verlagsanstalt, 1965.

Wallis, Faith, ed. *Medieval Medicine: A Reader*. Toronto: University of Toronto Press, 2010.

The Affectionate Author: Family Love as Rhetorical Device in Eighteenth-Century Conduct Books for Young Women

Elizabeth Kukorelly

Eighteenth-century conduct manuals for young women did all they could to obtain their readers' compliance with the conduct rules they laid down; one way in which they did this was to deploy familial affection as a rhetorical device. Although at first glance this may seem to be an expression of companionate family love, a closer look shows how affection is systematically exchanged for obedience, and thus serves to maintain hierarchical power difference. Nevertheless, the use of an affectionate rhetoric can be read as evidence of limited emancipation for young women, since rather than commanded to obey, they are enjoined to comply with, the conduct rules laid down in the texts. The love of parents for their children was considered to be entirely natural, and natural parental love was seen to obtain in return, not filial love, but respect and gratitude. Eighteenth-century conduct books transform affection into advice through the work of writing; girls are expected to transform gratitude into good conduct through the work of reading. The respective labours of writing and reading make the raw materials of affection and gratitude into exchangeable commodities: books on the print market, and young women on the marriage market. In this essay, I look at how a group of epistolary familial conduct books, each of which is posited as being written from an affectionate family member to a daughter or a niece, uses love in order to obtain good conduct.

Emotion, Affect, Sentiment: The Language and Aesthetics of Feeling. SPELL: Swiss Papers in English Language and Literature 30. Ed. Andreas Langlotz and Agnieszka Soltysik Monnet. Tübingen: Narr, 2014. 109-123.

With what joy should I see my dearest girl shine forth a bright example of
everything that is amiable and praiseworthy! – And how sweet would be the
reflection that I had, in any degree, contributed to make her so! –My heart
expands with the affecting thought, and pours forth in this adieu the most
ardent wishes for your perfection! – If the tender solicitude express'd for
your welfare by this "labour of love" can engage your gratitude, you will always remember how deeply your conduct interests the happiness of
                    Your most affectionate Aunt.   (Chapone II: 229-230)

When Hester Chapone ends her *Letters on the Improvement of the Mind* with
this outpouring of familial love, she bears witness to a cultural moment
that was convinced that texts could influence their readers. One way
conduct books for young women endeavoured to maximize their influence was by deploying words of affection. Chapone hopes her niece will
become "a bright example of everything that is amiable and praiseworthy" because her aunt's "labour of love" will "engage [her] gratitude."
Striving for readers' compliance, familial epistolary conduct books gently
ease them into a state of beloved bliss at the centre of affectionate sociability. Affection is used as a rhetorical device aimed at obtaining the
unconditional obedience of young women.

The use of familial love in this context is aligned with contemporary
ideas on how it functioned and what it could obtain. The love of parents
for their children was considered to be entirely natural, and natural parental love was seen to obtain in return, not filial love, but respect and
gratitude. Eighteenth-century conduct books transform affection into
advice through the work of writing; girls are expected to transform
gratitude into good conduct through the work of reading. The respective labours of writing and reading make the raw materials of affection
and gratitude into exchangeable commodities: books on the print market, and young women on the marriage market. This gives young
women some power over their own value, in what is surely a reforma-
tory and emancipating move. The act of deploying love as rhetoric implies that young women need to be enjoined to comply, instead of
commanded to obey. Furthermore, if conduct books attempt to discipline young women, by resorting to persuasion rather than compulsion,
their writers implicitly recognize that they are, to quote John Locke, in
charge of "the right direction of [their] conduct to true happiness" (*Essay* 246; bk. II, ch. 21, sect. 53). Although it has become commonplace
to dispute Lawrence Stone's progressive family historiography (from
authoritarian and unloving before the eighteenth century to egalitarian
and loving thereafter) there is certainly an evolution of familial relations

towards greater freedom for children from parental control.[1] Conduct books for adolescent girls may be part of this evolution. In this essay, I will show how they use familial love in a transactional affective paradigm to obtain the good conduct of daughters and nieces. Though this transaction upholds the power differential between older and younger family members, it bears witness to greater latitude for young women, if not to choose to misbehave, at least to envisage choice as an option. I will examine how eighteenth-century moral philosophers and novelists describe parental affection and foster the idea of the family as a sentimental unit built on love and respect, before turning to a small corpus of epistolary conduct manuals for young women, purportedly written by family members, as I explore how their authors deployed affection as part of their persuasive arsenal.

Familial affection, especially parental love, was deemed by many moral philosophers of the eighteenth century to be entirely natural since human offspring required lengthy and sustained care to bring them to maturity; children reciprocated with duty, gratitude and reverence. John Locke, the Earl of Shaftesbury, Francis Hutcheson, David Hume, Adam Smith and Thomas Reid were all convinced of this.[2] The Scottish Enlightenment philosophers viewed parental love as natural, yet described it in their writing as a social event validated by the community, at times a community of genteel consumers of culture.[3] Hutcheson – the earliest of the four – is convinced that parents have a "fond disinterested affection" for their children and describes a family as "an amiable society" which "nature has constituted" as a "permanent relation" (188). Hume states that "the relation of blood produces the strongest tie the

---

[1] Margaret Ezell notes the high degree of control that seventeenth-century mothers and fathers had over their children's lives (34), citing Robert Filmer (139) and Mary More's unprinted essay "The Woman's Right" (139, 152). This was undoubtedly on the wane in the next century, though it would be fallacious to assert that parent-child hierarchy was abolished; even a radical thinker such as Mary Wollstonecraft stopped short of claiming that this was desirable, although she went far in stipulating a more egalitarian version of the family. As Eileen Botting has shown, Wollstonecraft wished to rid the family of "patriarchal hierarchies" but "retain[ed] its affectionate tutelary environment, its benevolent parental hierarchy" (157).

[2] For Locke "Parents [are] wisely ordain'd by nature to love their children" (*Some Thoughts Concerning Education* 103). Shaftesbury puts "parental Kindness, Zeal for Posterity, Concern for the Propagation and Nurture of the Young" at the head of his list of "natural Affection," claiming that such feelings are as "*proper* and *natural*" as "for the Stomach to digest, the Lungs to breathe" (II, 78).

[3] The production of sentiment in and by sociability has been shown by John Mullan in *Sentiment and Sociability*, and Eileen Botting also discusses this in *Family Feuds* (137).

mind is capable of in the love of parents to their children, and a lesser degree of the same affection, as the relation lessens"; this "strongest tie" rather than felt by parents, is a function of the imaginative capacity of the mind, and "it must be from the force and liveliness of conception" that the love is derived (228, 229). Later he writes: "We blame a father for neglecting his child. Why? because it shews a want of natural affection, which is the duty of every parent," showing parental neglect to be subject to a communal tribunal ("We blame") that judges paternal value (307).

Further into the century, the role of community affirmation becomes more focussed, and happy families are an edifying spectacle. In his *Theory of Moral Sentiments*, Adam Smith spends some time rehearsing the by now familiar notion that parental love is natural (199) whilst children reciprocate with duty. Both are culpable when deficient: "A parent without parental tenderness, a child devoid of all filial reverence, appear monsters, the objects not of hatred only, but of horror" (323). In opposition to this monstrous spectacle is "that cordial satisfaction, that delicious sympathy, that confidential openness and ease," described earlier in the work as a scene of affectionate familial bliss:

> With what pleasure do we look upon a family, through the whole of which reign mutual love and esteem, where the parents and children are companions for one another, without any other difference than what is made by respectful affection on the one side, and kind indulgence on the other; where freedom and fondness, mutual raillery and mutual kindness, shew that no opposition of interest divides the brothers, nor any rivalship of favours sets the sisters at variance, and where every thing presents us with the idea of peace, cheerfulness, harmony and contentment? (53)

In this tableau, hierarchical difference between parents and children is attenuated by a sense of companionship, though it perdures in the opposition of respect (by children) and indulgence (by parents).

Thomas Reid begins his chapter on "the particular Benevolent Affections" by stating that parents and children are linked by what "we commonly call *natural* affection" (III, 141). His discussion is quickly drawn in a representational direction, as a succession of tableaux are presented to illustrate parental love:

> How common is it to see a young woman, in the gayest period of life, who has spent her days in mirth, and her nights in profound sleep, without solicitude or care, all at once transformed into the careful, the solicitous, the watchful nurse of her dear infant: doing nothing by day but gazing upon it,

and serving it in the meanest offices; by night, depriving herself of sound sleep for months, that it may lie safe in her arms. (III, 143)

Reid moves to the animal kingdom:

> How pleasant it is to see the family economy of a pair of little birds in rearing their tender offspring; the conjugal affection and fidelity of the parents; their cheerful toil and industry in providing food to their family; their sagacity in concealing their habitation; the arts they use, often at the peril of their own lives, to decoy hawks, and other enemies, from their dwelling place, and the affliction they feel when some unlucky boy has robbed them of the dear pledges of their affection, and frustrated all their hopes of their rising family. (155-56)

Like Smith, Reid engages his readers to look on with delight at this sentimental scene. He makes explicit the importance of representation for his enterprise: "When these [parental] affections are exerted according to their intention, under the discretion of wisdom and prudence, the economy of such a family is a most delightful spectacle, and furnishes the most agreeable and affecting subjects, to the pencil of the painter, and the pen of the orator and poet" (145). Real-life affection produces a representation that in turn influences real lives, as the fiction is described as an "affecting subject."

Happy families are central to the discourse of sentimental affection, and they are described quite specifically as spectacle. Samuel Richardson uses this tactic on a number of occasions: memorable in *Clarissa*, when Lovelace imagines "seeing" and "behold[ing]" captive Clarissa breastfeeding twin boys (706), and perfectly forgettable in *Pamela*'s sequel, when the eponymous heroine writes to her old friend Miss Darnford:

> imagine you see me seated, surrounded with the joy and the hope of my future prospects, as well as my present comforts. Miss Goodwin, imagine you see, on my right hand, sitting on a velvet stool, because she is eldest, and a Miss; Billy on my left, in a little cane elbow-chair, because he is eldest, and a good boy; my Davers, and my sparkling-ey'd Pamela, with my Charley between them, on little silken cushions, at my feet, hand-in-hand, their pleased eyes looking up to my more delighted ones; and my sweet-natured promising Jemmy, in my lap; the nurses and the cradle just behind us, and the nursery maids delightedly pursuing some useful needle-work for the dear charmers of my heart – All as hush and as still as silence itself, as the pretty creatures generally are, when their little, watchful eyes see my lips beginning to open: . . . and yet all my boys are as lively as so many birds: while my

> Pamela is cheerful, easy, soft, gentle, always smiling, but modest and harm-
> less as a dove. (590-591)

Reader attention in both cases is drawn to the act of seeing as we are imaginatively transported to the family scene, becoming supplementary spectators to narrated intimacy and affection.[4] In *La Nouvelle Héloise* Rousseau makes clear the spectacular value of good parenting: "the picture of well-being and felicity touches the human heart, which hungers for such images" (939, my translation), each of which is a "laughing tableau" that "spreads in the soul of its spectators a secret charm that grows without cease" (941, my translation). This prepares us to correctly read Julie's maternal affection. Her sentiments for her children are communicated to those who watch her without "the intermediary of words"; "Her eyes became entirely fixed on her three children, and her heart, ravished in delicious ecstasy, animated her charming face with the most touching tokens of motherly tenderness" (955, my translation). As observer, St. Preux is a useful narrative device through which readers are voyeuristically privy to the endless good parenting that goes on in the house at Clarens. A naturally occurring urge that is nonetheless systematically elevated to a moral imperative in the fiction of the period, good parenting is seen to reward its propagators (the parents feel good) and its objects (the children turn out well), as well as its spectators, who sentimentally partake in the family warmth that it creates.

If Stone's theory of the companionate family is not verifiable in historical fact, it is omnipresent in eighteenth-century discourse. Joanne Bailey argues: "while there is no firm evidence to argue that affection between parents and children was growing during the eighteenth century, as Stone asserted, there is evidence that the depth of parental emotional intensity was increasingly the focus of attention in conveying the tensions and ideals of elite parenting" (211). Affectionate parents are described in various genres and with various purported functions, often in the form of tableaux held up to the gaze of readers who are evidently meant to aspire to and enact the roles that they find there.[5] The "emo-

---

[4] The use of birds to depict families seems to have been common in the period. Sarah Fielding publishes a long passage from Edward Moore's "The Sparrow and the Dove" (from his *Fables for the Female Sex*) in *The Governess*, in which a mother dove and her offspring welcome the father back to the nest. In Fielding this scene becomes a spectacle as it is played out before a gathering of birds who are keen to find which of them is the happiest; the doves, of course, win hands down (233-236).

[5] In *La Fibre Littéraire*, Alexandre Wenger shows how the tableau was considered to be an efficacious literary form, as it precipitated an "epiphany of sensibility" and "per-

tional intensity" on show in these discursive productions certainly
served to focus attention on the ideals (if not always the tensions) of
"elite parenting."

The conduct book genre participates in this discursive landscape
though its textual thrust is rarely the tableau. Example tends to take the
form of anecdote, and shares the page with precept and letter; together
these forms make a bid to ensure reader compliance. The different textual forms position the reader variously: anecdotes partake in the casuist
tradition, and give readers the chance to witness good and bad behaviour as practice, and to experimentally cast themselves into the situations that are depicted.[6] Precept concentrates its authority through the
use of the imperative mode, or by using aphorisms to proclaim incon-
trovertible truths. The epistolary creates proximity between writer and
reader, who is addressed with solicitous affection, and elevated to the
status of privileged addressee. The letter form also contributes authenticity and announces "a natural writing, spontaneous, impulsive, a fresh
and immediate projection of sentiment" (McKeon 56, Wenger 163, my
translation). Finally, the letter form encodes the possibility of a reply, a
way of involving the reader as an active participant in the construction
of meaning. As a textual form, the epistolary is conversational and
transactional and a peculiarly efficacious way of positioning the reader
to be improved: addressed as if personally by a sincere and spontaneous
author, she is given an, albeit illusory, right of reply. However, epistolary
conduct books serve not only to cement the family with sentiment, but
also to maintain the hierarchical power differential that made families
into the proper components of the nation.[7] Daniel M. Gross considers
emotion as historically and socially produced in an "economy of scar-
city" in order to explain "the role that rhetoric plays in routinizing
communication and delineating the channels of social power" (126, 14);
familial affection in conduct books plays such a role.

---

suaded by a narrative composition founded not on discursive reasoning, but on the
solicitation of the imagination" (123, 126, my translation).

[6] In *The Practice of Everyday Life*, Michel de Certeau finds in stories "the decorative con-
tainers of a narrativity for everyday practices" (70). The "primary role of the story" is
that it "opens a legitimate *theater* for practical *actions*" (125); which is consistent with that
which it adopts in the conduct book. De Certeau states that "narrated reality constantly
tells us what must be believed, what must be done"; in turn, "social life multiplies the
gestures and modes of behavior *(im)printed* by narrative models" (186).

[7] For an extended discussion of the family as foundational to national wellbeing, see
Botting (11, 59, 155, 195).

The conduct books I discuss are presented as letters from family members to young women in need of instruction. Two are from mothers, Sarah Pennington's *An Unfortunate Mother's Advice to her Absent Daughters* (1761) and Charles Allen's *The Polite Lady* (1775). One is from a father, John Gregory's *A Father's Legacy to his Daughters* (1774). One is from an uncle, Wetenhall Wilkes's *A Letter of Genteel and Moral Advice to a Young Lady* (1743), one is from an aunt, Hester Chapone's *Letters on the Improvement of the Mind* (1773), and one is from a sort-of aunt, John Hill's *The Conduct of a Married Life* (1753). Three are verifiably written to real family members (Pennington, Gregory and Chapone), one is probably written to such (Wilkes), and the last two are fictional discursive constructions (Allen and Hill).[8] The focus of my analysis will be on the exchange of love and obedience as the labour of writing and reading transforms them into good advice and good conduct. First, though, it is useful to note an important aspect of epistolary familial conduct books: the way they posit the book as a replacement for the writer who is necessarily absent, and their related struggle to transcend the particularity of private epistolarity to address a general readership. These characteristics enable the advice manuals to situate their efficaciousness at the cusp of the private and the public as published but purportedly authentic letters.[9] Written from the privacy of familial relations, the manuals are made public through publication, but they re-enter private lives in acts of intimate reading; they become public once again, as the young woman reader displays her good conduct in her bid to get the best possible husband. This end-result is made clear, for example, in the quotation with which I began this essay: Chapone's niece will best reward her aunt by "shin[ing] forth" in public as a "bright example" of good female conduct.

While in most of the texts the addressee's reception of the letters is left undescribed, *The Polite Lady* is unique in the corpus in that it is a correspondence: Sophy's letters back to her mother, Portia, are included in the book, and she expresses delight in receiving, and promises obedience to, maternal instruction. Affection is seen to acquire obedience and respect: the mother extends the former to her daughter, the daughter reciprocates with the latter, and the power differential between hierarchically positioned individuals is maintained. However, providing a

---

[8] The two male-authored conduct books that ventriloquize the advice of women were published anonymously (Allen) and pseudonymously (Hill).

[9] This resonates strongly with Michael McKeon's theory in *The Secret History of Domesticity* that one characteristic of the move towards modernity was publishing the private (see chapter two, 49-109).

voice for the daughter gives her a textual and moral existence that assumes that she needs to be persuaded to comply, rather than commanded to obey.

Perhaps it is appropriate that the text that least expresses the exchange of affection for obedience is Pennington's. A banished woman, struggling to maintain social personality under aspersions of adultery, Lady Sarah is the writer with the least power to undergird her position as authoritative purveyor of conduct advice; this may be why she uses the least expressions of affection, and if the book stipulates obedience, it is located outside the mother-daughter relationship, and is to a future husband (59, 63, 65, 67), to God (12, 14), or to both (70). Writing a *Legacy*, so addressing his daughters from beyond the grave, Gregory implies that their obedience will be motivated by his late affection for them: "You will all remember your father's fondness, when perhaps every other circumstance relating to him is forgotten. This remembrance, I hope, will induce you to give a serious attention to the advices I am now going to leave with you" (4-5). Gregory appeals to his daughters for their attention; he does not command them to obey. These are the two writers – the only historically real parents in the present corpus – whose absence from their daughters is most permanent: they are truly spectral parents.[10] Gregory, though, unlike Pennington, is able to tie compliance to affection as he can rely on his daughters' having once experienced paternal fondness. Wilkes and Chapone are avuncular writers; their expectation of obedience is not strong. Nevertheless, both tie this expectation to love. Wilkes makes the link: "be but persuaded of my tender Affection to you, and then my Cautions will become agreeable" (80). Closing her first letter, Chapone uses the rhetoric of sentimental affect:

> Adieu, my beloved Niece! If the feelings of your heart, whilst you read my letters, correspond with those of mine, whilst I write them, I shall not be without the advantage of your partial affection, to give weight to my advice; for believe me, my own dear girl, my heart and eyes overflow with tenderness. (30)

The production and reception of advice is located in the heart. The overflowing eyes are a legible signifier of true sentiment stored to overflowing in the heart; they underline the authenticity of the emotion (Goring 48). The emotion that is felt by the aunt and expressed by her

---

[10] Spectral in the sense given by Marilyn Francus in *Monstrous Motherhood*: physically absent but somehow present, the texts being "compensatory for both mother [or father] and child" (173).

tears is extended to the niece, who should reciprocate with affection *and* obedience, as she is invited to "give weight to [Chapone's] advice."

In *The Polite Lady*, we have the most explicit illustration of how affection is exchanged for obedience. Although in *The Conduct of a Married Life* we get a sort of ghostly reader presence at the beginning of the second and third letters, where the writer refers to the addressee's oral assent to the advice that is given (8, 22), she disappears thereafter. Chapone, Gregory, Pennington and Wilkes never mention their reader's reactions, although they repeatedly invite proper reception. *The Polite Lady* thus stages a correspondence, with ten out of forty letters written by the daughter, an exchange that presents general readers with a model for reading, and despite that fact that the hierarchical power differential is blatantly expressed as a function of access to emotion, the daughter's access to expression casts her as one to whom appeals for good conduct must be made. Twenty-one of the mother's letters end with expressions of affection (4, 6, 9, 13, 16, 19, 23, 27, 30, 32, 36, 44, 68, 167, 183, 199, 221, 239, 250, 273, 275), whereas the daughter never expresses affection: all her letters end with expressions of duty, obedience, and obligation (11, 24, 33, 38, 69, 76, 98, 122, 157, 202). The absence of the daughter's written assurances of affection do not mean that daughters cannot love their mothers. Yet in this discursive setting, filial love yields to hierarchical difference. This is emphasized by the fact that in nine out of ten letters from the daughter, she precedes her final salutation to her mother with her regards to the rest of her family, each of which reads more or less as follows: "Please to offer my duty to my papa, and my kind love to my brothers and sisters" (11; similar formulations at 24, 33, 69, 76, 122, 157, 202). It is clear that love is something that daughters can offer to their peers (siblings), but not to their superiors (parents), recalling the power structure in Adam Smith's tableau of the happy family.

This is upheld when one looks further into the text. In all but two letters, Sophy expresses obligation to her mother, often explicitly linked to assurance that she will follow her mother's advice: "I am greatly obliged to you for the good advice and directions you have given me, and will endeavour to conduct myself accordingly" (68). The daughter is in debt to her mother for the work of advice and she is worried that she can never pay her back: "How shall I ever repay the obligations you are daily laying upon me! I never can; nor do you expect it. The only return, I know that you desire, is, that I should, at last, become a virtuous and accomplished woman" (32). The daughter identifies the sort of work she must perform to pay her debt: the labour of reading will produce the good conduct needed to repay her mother, who answers, in the same transactional vein:

> Do not make yourself uneasy, my Dear, because you can never repay the favours I have done you. I am repaid already. I enjoy as much pleasure in bestowing them, as you can possibly do in receiving them; and if I should have the additional happiness to see you become a polite and virtuous woman, I shall be doubly rewarded. (34)

Different things (love, pleasure, duty, good behaviour) are transformed by labour into items that can be exchanged and consumed. In *The Culture of Sensibility*, G. J. Barker Benfield quotes Norbert Elias to show how the "the growth of demands for unified mobile means of exchange" in the eighteenth century enabled people to take consumer pleasure in their own private feelings (80, 83).[11] The private emotions of parental affection and filial gratitude become exchangeable once they have become mixed with the reciprocal labours of writing and reading.

Sentimental expressions of love and joy mask the more pragmatic motivation for the deployment of affection. Having received news about Sophy's improvement Portia writes:

> To say I was glad on this occasion, is flat and unmeaning; I was over-joyed; I felt an emotion of pleasure known only to those who have a daughter of their own whom they love with the same warmth of affection. Go on, my dear Sophy, thus to encrease the happiness of your mother . . . by making yourself a complete mistress of your needle. (30)

Hyperbolic, even bathetic, the rhetoric is also sentimental, as the mother's satisfaction with her daughter's advancement is located in a positive emotion felt in the heart, and in describing her joy she reaches limits of expression, a stylistic feature frequently found in sentimental fiction. The mother repeatedly expresses her intense positive emotions at her daughter's continuing and expanding good conduct:

> I believe, you have such a tender regard for my happiness, that, when once you know how greatly it depends on your good behaviour, you will never lessen it by a contrary conduct. And now, after this flow of parental affection, I come to give you my best advice with regard to the choice of your friends. (39)

---

[11] Barker Benfield cites *Power and Civility*, pp. 78-85.

The relation between "parental affection" and good conduct is made evident as the former – described as a "flow" – not only propels the ensuing good advice, but somehow produces it as an extension of its own existence. Parental affection produces good advice; good advice deployed on a "flow of parental affection" produces obedient good conduct; good conduct secures parental happiness, which in turn reinvigorates parental affection. Portia makes this productive dynamic clear:

> My dear Sophy, How shall I express the joy I received from the perusal of your last letter! How happy am I in having a daughter, who, at an age, when most young ladies imagine they can think and act for themselves, is so humble and dutiful, as to undertake nothing without the permission and advice of her mother! But can't I conceal my joy within my own breast? Or, if it must have vent, can't I be satisfied with imparting it to others? Why tell it to my daughter? Why, my Dear, I tell it to you for two reasons: both because I like to think of you, and talk to you, and also because I am persuaded it will be an additional motive to your persevering in the same virtuous course. For, I believe, you have such a tender regard for my happiness, that, when once you know how greatly it depends on your good behaviour, you will never lessen it by a contrary conduct.   (38-39)

The virtuous circle of love (transformed into and made manifest as good advice) buying obedience (transformed into and made manifest as good conduct), is, one suspects, infinite, as one Polite Lady breeds another through the exchange of letters, and perhaps many more, as the exchange is publicized throughout the nation.[12] In the end, the exchange of letters has lasted something over ten years, from when Sophy first goes to boarding school and learns to read and then write, to when she spends time in "the world" (i.e. London) with an aunt and cousins. It peters off without telling us if she makes a successful marriage, so we are not able to assess if Sophy has been able to capitalize on her mother's affectionate investment.

By giving Sophy a voice *The Polite Lady* plays on two fronts. The fact of giving the daughter the right to reply to her mother promotes mutual companionate sociability as the cement of happy families; ultimately, though, as she is never shown to disagree with her mother, *The Polite Lady* does not really move in the emancipatory direction that Mary Wollstonecraft longed for in family relations some decades later. In *A Vindication of the Rights of Woman*, Wollstonecraft deplores the tyranny

---

[12] *The Polite Lady* was a fairly popular conduct manual, with eight editions between 1760 and 1798 indicated in the *English Short Title Catalogue*, including two in Dublin and one in Philadelphia that were probably pirated, a strong signal of print-market success.

and abjection that habitually characterized relations between parents and children. When Sophy explicitly eschews reason in favour of blind obedience, stating: "I think myself bound in duty to obey all your orders, whether I understand the reasonableness of them or not" (36-37), she promotes what Wollstonecraft calls "the absurd duty . . . of obeying a parent only on account of his being a parent," an attitude that "shackles the mind, and prepares it for a slavish submission to any power but reason" (235-6). Perhaps the move to publish a correspondence rather than a one-sided series of letters was a better way of preserving parental hegemony; indeed, as readers are exposed to Sophy's abject compliance, they might find it difficult to project alternative, less docile responses. Giving an actual voice to the daughter, rather than the possibility of response to the reader, is a way of closing off the emancipatory potential of the epistolary advice manual. Yet when Sophy writes her answers and other readers no longer have to perform the work of reading, they may instead close the conduct book in disgust, exclaiming against such "slavish submission" (Wollstonecraft 236).

References

Allen, Charles. *The Polite Lady; or, a Course of Female Education. In a Series of Letters from a Mother to Her Daughter.* London: T. Carnan and F. Newberry, 1775.

Bailey, Joanne. "Reassessing parenting in eighteenth-century England." *The Family in Early Modern England.* Ed. Helen Berry and Elizabeth Foyster. Cambridge, New York and Melbourne: Cambridge University Press, 2007.

Barker Benfield, G. J. *The Culture of Sensibility: Sex and Society in Eighteenth-Century Britain.* Chicago and London: The University of Chicago Press, 1992.

Botting, Eileen Hunt. *Family Feuds: Wollstonecraft, Burke and Rousseau on the Transformation of the Family.* Albany: State University of New York Press, 2006.

Chapone, Hester. *Letters on the Improvement of the Mind, Addressed to a Young Lady.* London: H. Hughs, 1773. 2 vols.

Cooper, Anthony Ashley, Third Earl of Shaftesbury. *Characteristics of Men, Manners, Opinions, Times.* 1711. New York and Hildesheim: Georg Olms Verlag, 1978.

De Certeau, Michel. *The Practice of Everyday Life.* Berkeley and Los Angeles: University of California Press, 1984.

Elias, Norbert. *The Civilizing Process.* Vol. 2: *Power and Civility.* New York: Pantheon, 1982.

Ezell, Margaret J. M. *The Patriarch's Wife: Literary Evidence and the History of the Family.* Chapel Hill and London: The University of North Carolina Press, 1987.

Fielding, Sarah. *The Governess; or Little Female Academy.* London: Printed for the Author, 1749.

Francus, Marilyn. *Monstrous Motherhood: Eighteenth-Century Culture and the Ideology of Domesticity.* Baltimore: Johns Hopkins University Press, 2012.

Goring, Paul. *The Rhetoric of Sensibility in Eighteenth-Century Culture.* Cambridge: Cambridge University Press, 2005.

Gregory, John. *A Father's Legacy to His Daughters.* 2nd ed. London: W. Strahan, 1774.

Gross, Daniel M. *The Secret History of Emotion: From Aristotle's "Rhetoric" to Modern Brain Science.* Chicago and London: The University of Chicago Press, 2006.

Hill, John. *The Conduct of a Married Life. Laid down in a Series of Letters, Written by the Honourable Juliana-Susannah Seymour, to a Young Lady, her Relation, Lately Married.* London: R. Baldwin, 1753.

Hume, David. *A Treatise of Human Nature. A Critical Edition.* Ed. David Fate Norton and Mary-J. Norton. Vol. 1: Texts. Oxford: Clarendon Press, 2007.

Hutcheson, Francis. *A System of Moral Philosophy.* Glasgow: R. and A. Foulis, 1755. Vol. 2.

Locke, John. *An Essay Concerning Human Understanding.* 1690. London and New York: Penguin Books, 1998.

———. *Some Thoughts Concerning Education.* 1693. Oxford: Oxford University Press, 1989.

McKeon, Michael. *The Secret History of Domesticity: Public, Private, and the Division of Knowledge.* Baltimore: The Johns Hopkins University Press, 2005.

Mullan, John. *Sentiment and Sociability: The Language of Feeling in the Eighteenth Century.* Oxford: Oxford University Press, 1988

Pennington, Lady Sarah. *An Unfortunate Mother's Advice to Her Absent Daughters.* London: S. Chandler, 1761.

Reid, Thomas. *Essays on the Intellectual and Active Powers of Men.* 1788. Dublin: P. Byrne and J. Milliken, 1790. Volume 3.

Richardson, Samuel. *Clarissa, Or the History of a Young Lady.* 1748. London and New York: Penguin Books, 1985.

———. *Pamela in Her Exalted Condition.* 1742. Cambridge, New York, Melbourne, etc.: Cambridge University Press, 2012.

Rousseau, Jean-Jacques. *Julie, ou la Nouvelle Héloise.* 1761. In *Oeuvres Complètes.* Ed. Raymon Trousson and Frédéric Eigeldinger. Vol. 15. Geneva: Slatkine, and Paris: Champion, 2012.

Smith, Adam. *The Theory of Moral Sentiments.* 1759. New York: Prometheus Books, 2000.

Stone, Lawrence. *The Family, Sex and Marriage in England 1500-1800.* London and New York: Penguin Books, 1990.

Wenger, Alexandre. *La Fibre Littéraire. Le Discours Médical sur la Lecture au XVIIIe Siècle.* Geneva: Droz, 2007.

Wilkes, Wetenhall. *A Letter of Genteel and Moral Advice to a Young Lady.* 2nd ed. Dublin: Oliver Nelson, 1741.

Wollstonecraft, Mary. *A Vindication of the Rights of Woman,* 1792, and *A Vindication of the Rights of Men,* 1790. Oxford: Oxford University Press, 2008.

Exuberant Energies: Affect in *Vathek*, *Zofloya* and *The Giaour*

Enit Karafili Steiner

This essay discusses affectivity in three Romantic texts: William Beckford's *Vathek* (1787), Charlotte Dacre's *Zofloya; or, The Moor: A Romance of the Fifteenth Century* (1806) and Lord Byron's *The Giaour, a Fragment of a Turkish Tale* (1813). These texts have in common a symbiosis of Gothic tenor and Oriental features and it is by virtue of this conflation that I discuss them together. The essay considers the ways in which this synergy bears on the representations of the emotions, whereby the emphasis lies on the emotions' political and aesthetic significance at the turn of the eighteenth century. I argue that the affect dynamics of the protagonists of these works embodies a vehement defiance of inherited institutions, in particular the family and the domestic fiction that promoted its social centrality. More importantly, because this defiance expresses itself through an exuberance of visceral and less sociable emotions, one can read the conjunction of the Gothic and Oriental as an aesthetic enclave which resists the social integration and disciplining propagated in the domestic realism that dominated British eighteenth- and nineteenth-century literature.

Due to their Oriental representations, William Beckford's *Vathek* (1787), Charlotte Dacre's *Zofloya* (1806) and Byron's *The Giaour* (1813), have been affiliated with the Oriental tale that rose to prominence in the eighteenth century after Antoine Galland's translation of *Les mille et une*

Emotion, Affect, Sentiment: The Language and Aesthetics of Feeling. SPELL: Swiss Papers in English Language and Literature 30. Ed. Andreas Langlotz and Agnieszka Soltysik Monnet. Tübingen: Narr, 2014. 125-142.

nuits (1704-1708).[1] Already upon its publication in Britain, *Vathek* was praised in almost synonymous terms with *The Arabian Nights*, which had "attracted every reader by the splendour of their descriptions, and the magic of their enchantments before we learnt that they exhibited a faithful copy of eastern manners, and oriental conversations" (*Critical Review* 38). The reviewer of *The Giaour*, too, commended Byron for achieving originality while preserving the "Oriental costume [. . .] with admirable fidelity" (*Edinburgh Review* 299, 308). Not surprisingly, more often than not, *Vathek* and *The Giaour* have been read in response to Edward Said's contention that the West saw the Orient at best as alien and "if not patently inferior to, then in need of corrective study by the West" (Said 41). Said deemed works like Beckford's *Vathek* or Byron's Turkish Tales, which capitalized on a fascination with Oriental themes mingled with Gothic "visions of barbaric splendour and cruelty" (118), to be particularly complex. Indeed, Charlotte Dacre's novel *Zofloya* takes this mixture of "barbaric splendour and cruelty" to sublime extremes, by depicting Zofloya, the Satanic agent of the story, as a "majestic and solemnly beautiful" Moor whose appearance can only be "acknowledged with sensations awful and indescribable" (Dacre 158). It is by virtue of this conflation of Gothic and Oriental elements that I discuss these three texts together. My main interest concerns the ways in which such a conflation bears on the representation of the emotions. I claim that in *Vathek*, *Zofloya* and *The Giaour*, emotions are fraught with political and aesthetic significance, whereby aesthetics encompasses the literal meaning derived from sensory life as well as the moral sense with which the eighteenth century coupled it (Eagleton 106). Thus, the emphasis lies on the perception of British writers and readers of their own society, culture and history rather than their misconceptions of the East.

My analysis rests on two premises: first, in order to preserve the eighteenth-century breadth of the concept, "emotions" are understood as a manifold of associations such as "sentiments," "affections" and "passions." As Thomas Dixon shows in *From Passions to Emotions*, it was only in the first half of the nineteenth century that "emotion" came to

---

[1] Galland's *Les mille et une nuits*, rendered into English as *The Arabian Nights Entertainments*, was popularized by the Grub Street writers in England among the bourgeois public with a thrice-weekly serialization in 445 instalments from 1723-6 in the *London News*. By 1800, more than twenty different editions of the *Arabian Nights* existed and were avidly read (Makdisi and Nussbaum 14-15).

connote a distinctly psychological category (Dixon 2).[2] Before this narrowing of the concept occurred, "emotions," "sentiments" and "passions" appeared in eighteenth-century philosophical tracts that capture the implications of these phenomena in a process of imaginary intersubjective identification called "sympathy." Adam Smith's interweaving of these terms in his *Theory of Moral Sentiments* (1759), as he sets out to define "sympathy" in the first chapter of the book, is telling:

> In every passion of which the mind of man is susceptible, the emotions of the by-stander always correspond to what, by bringing the case home to himself, he imagines, should be the sentiments of the sufferer. (Smith 4-5)

In this passage as well as throughout his *Theory of Moral Sentiments*, Smith mobilizes the words "passion," "emotions" and "sentiments" to demonstrate the moral ties that organize intersubjective relations and civil society.

The second premise of my analysis is based on Paul Stenner's evaluation of emotions as phenomena that cut across body, mind and culture. Accordingly, I am mindful of psychological reductionism (also regretted by Dixon) and approach emotionality as a set of experiences that depend on the social, biological and psychic life that occasion human emotions (Stenner 8-9). As such, emotionality consists of a range of human responses that are generated from and move within the interplay of social, psychic and organic forms of order.

I. Emotions and Disintegration

The most influential event that affected the late-eighteenth century social order in Britain was the French Revolution. I believe it is also the event that informs the emotional management of *Vathek*, *Zofloya* and *The Giaour*, whose Gothic tone is steeped in the revolutionary energy that preceded and followed this historical turmoil. The connection between the Gothic and the French Revolution was most famously made by the Marquis de Sade, who declared Gothic fictions to be "the necessary fruit of the revolutionary tremors felt by the whole of Europe"

---

[2] The OED describes emotion as "an agitation of mind; an excited mental state" and subsequently "any strong mental or instinctive feeling, as pleasure, grief, hope, fear, etc., deriving especially from one's circumstances, mood, or relationship with others." Sentiment is closely related to emotion since it can stand for "intellectual or emotional perception" as well as "a sensation or physical feeling."

(Sade 49). However, considering that the rise of the Gothic genre precedes the French Revolution (Miles 42-43), William Hazlitt's assessment
seems more convincing:

> It is not to be wondered, if, amidst the tumult of events crowded into this
> period, our literature has partaken of the *disorder* of the time; if our prose
> has run mad, and our poetry grown childish. Among those few persons
> who "have kept the even tenor of their way," the author of Evelina, Cecilia,
> and Camilla, holds a distinguished place. Mrs. Radcliffe's "enchantments
> drear" and mouldering castles, derived a part of their interest, we suppose,
> from the supposed tottering state of all old structures at the time.
>
> (*Edinburgh Review* 335, emphasis added)

Unlike de Sade, who saw the Revolution as giving birth rather straight-
forwardly to the genre, Hazlitt seems invested in understanding the collective social psyche of the writers and readers of Gothic fiction. Radcliffe published her first novel *The Castles of Athlin and Dunbayne* in 1789,
twenty-five years after Walpole's *Castle of Otranto* (1764). Throughout
these years of gestation, the steady increase of tales of terror about remote ages and places suggests that the writing and reading of such fiction channelled revolutionary energies before these openly broke out in
neighbouring France. Hazlitt refers to the "disorder of the time" as a
socio-historical energy that permeated all layers of contemporary human
life. Having been defined by Samuel Johnson as "force, influence,
spirit," the word energy lends itself to conceive of the "disorder" that
links the Gothic and the French Revolution in intersecting rather than
sequential terms (Johnson 699). Indeed, Stephen Greenblatt reminds us
that, although hard to define, energy, called in the Greek rhetorical tradition *energia,* was characterized as a stirring of the mind and bore social
and historical significance (Greenblatt 6). We can speak of social energy
where a certain range of repetitions are reproduced and circulated within
a variety of receptive communities. This is the case in the three texts
discussed here: they produce a set of repetitions that exploit the contemporary aesthetic *energia* derived from scenes of emotional outbursts,
or, as the reviewer of *The Giaour* put it, of "the darker passions and more
gloomy emotions from which the energy and the terrors of poetry are
chiefly derived" (*Edinburgh Review* 309).

Hazlitt suggests that such taste became so popular because the
Gothic couched in the language of sensations the anxiety of a civilization that perceived itself as being in decline. As an aesthetic and socio-
historical energy before, during and in the aftermath of the Revolution,
the Gothic was marked by a tendency to make the old structures that

Hazlitt mentions unambiguously old by removing them in time and space. Medieval and Catholic settings provided diverse communities of readers with a safe distance to contemplate the excess of their estrangement with their own past. This removal became more imprecise, and consequently more estranging, when Gothic and Oriental elements converged. Together, the Gothic and Oriental figured an amplified version of an archaic Other that was at the same time close and far away from home. As Gary Kelly rightly puts it, such figures of the Other stood not only for the danger emanating from the enemy without, but also from the enemy within (Kelly 3).

Beckford's *Vathek*, Dacre's *Zofloya* and Byron's *The Giaour* describe threats from within and without. In these texts, the challenge from outside is Orientalized and thus exoticized: the Caliph Vathek becomes obsessed with a mysterious Indian who alluringly promises him access to the treasures of the pre-Adamite sultans; Dacre's female protagonist Victoria is haunted in her dreams by the Moor Zofloya, who orchestrates the poisoning of her husband; the love prospects between the Giaour, the nameless Byronic hero, and Leila are shattered by the Muslim Hassan, Leila's master and executioner. However, as sensational and menacing as these Orientalized presences are, they only amplify imminent threats that linger within. These inner threats take the shape of exuberant affective drives which all three works link to the domestic particularities in which they originate. Long before the exotic Other (the mysterious Indian, Zofloya or Hassan) enters the scene, the main characters gestate strong emotions that are rooted in their familial history. I will go on to argue that the connection between emotions and domestic relations has political ramifications, but, before doing so, it is important to dwell a little longer on the depictions of family in the three works.

Family history features in the genealogical expositions that initiate the stories of *Vathek* and *Zofloya*. Vathek is not introduced simply as an individual but as the last link in a long chain of Caliphs: Vathek is the grandson of Haroun al Raschid. Dacre's protagonist Victoria as the daughter of Marchese di Loredani descends from a noble Venetian family. With such name-dropping – Haroun al Raschid is mentioned in the *Arabian Nights* and Loredan was the Doge of Venice from 1501-1521 – both narratives draw attention to ancestry and the intergenerational transmission of power and privileges. This gains further significance in light of *Vathek*'s and *Zofloya*'s tragic endings that erase the successors of long-standing houses of rulers. If in *Vathek* and *Zofloya* the family appears in a "tottering state" (to use Hazlitt's wording) and steering toward destruction, in *The Giaour* we are left with its ubiquitous dissolu-

tion. Due to the fragmentary form of Byron's "snake poem," the protagonist's genealogy is lost with other fragments of the story that unite
the Western male character with the Eastern Leila and Hassan. Here,
the very absence of any sense of familial history turns the Giaour into a
ghost. The "Advertisement" of the poem reveals that the protagonist is
a young Venetian (Richardson 182), however, the poem not only persistently blurs the traces of his origin, but also builds up an aura of im-
penetrable solitude that isolates the Giaour both from his native culture
and that of the foreign land he treads. His "memory is but the tomb"
and his life a "sleep without the dream/ of what I was, and would be
still" (Richardson 210: 1000, 997).[3] The erasure of familial belonging is
complete toward the end of the poem, where the Giaour is told to have
"pass'd – nor of his name and race/ Hath left a token or a trace"
(Richardson 219: 1329-30).

I want to suggest that the emphatic presence or absence of the family betrays a deep-seated suspicion of domestic affections. Suspicion of
domestic bonds in eighteenth-century Gothic fiction is not uncharacter-
istic: think of Horace Walpole's *Castle of Otranto* (1764), which is often
viewed as heralding the genre, or Anne Radcliffe's novels that fuelled
the Gothic craze to an unprecedented extent. However, what *Vathek*,
Zofloya and *The Giaour* refuse to offer (unlike Walpole's or Radcliffe's
novels) is a return to domestic bonds after due suspicion or investigation. Here, we encounter three protagonists who conceive personal fulfilment not merely outside, but in vehement defiance of, their inherited
value-system. In particular, the families in *Vathek* and *Zofloya* devour
their own children, as the parents' sins haunt the young. Vathek, in a
rare moment of epiphany while facing eternal damnation, attributes the
greatest share of guilt to his mother: "the principles by which Carathis
perverted my youth, have been the sole cause of my perdition!"
(Richardson 155). Dacre's extra-diegetic narrator and her protagonist
Victoria harp on the mother's bad example at every turn of the plot.
The novel abounds in resounding condemnations of a woman who left
her husband and two children for another man. In her most sympathetic
moments, Dacre describes the murderous Victoria as the "hopeless victim of [the] premature corruption" that resulted from "maternal indis-
cretion" and "destroyed all bonds of respect" (236). The narratives insist
that, despite their propensities to anger or haughtiness, Vathek and
Zofloya's crimes do not spring from unmotivated malignance. Byron's

---

[3] Note that the number before the colon refers to the page in Richardson's edition, the
numbers after the colon to the lines of Byron's poem.

Giaour, although very reticent to share any familial affiliation with the monk who takes his final confession, entrusts the latter with a farewell message and a ring for a childhood friend who had prophesied the Giaour's "doom" already in "many a busy bitter scene" of their "golden youth" (Richardson 217: 1138-1139). This relationship, too, is marked by reluctance to conform: the friend had warned the Giaour in the past, but the latter did not heed the voice of prudence and instead murdered Hassan, thus both fulfilling and succumbing to the prophecy.

As a culmination of this pervading defiance, all three works end with a refusal to integrate their protagonists into their inherited social order. Unlike Anne Radcliffe's prudent and compassionate examples of filial devotion, Vathek abhors his mother's "impious knowledge" (Richardson 156); Victoria witnesses unmoved her mother's death, declaring it to be the just expiation for making the daughter the outcast that she has now become: "on thy head, therefore, will all my sins be numbered" (Dacre 246); and the Giaour, rejecting the absolution of the Monk, remains burdened beyond death by the curse of turning into a vampire that will "ghastly haunt" his country and "suck the blood" of his race (Richardson 205: 757-8).

As intimated by some of the above-mentioned quotes, the absence of a restorative and domestic Radcliffian sentimentality does not entail the absence of a language of affect.[4] These are not works of emotional abstinence. On the contrary, they exhibit an exuberance of emotions triggered by hatred, sexual frustration and raw psychic drives. Beckford depicts violent fantasies in graphic terms, writing that Vathek in the "ebullition of his fury had resolved to open the body of the Alboufaki and to stuff it with those of the negresses and of Carathis [his mother] herself" (Richardson 141); in Dacre's novel, Victoria's "outraged pride swelled her heart to bursting and its insatiable fury called aloud for vengeance, for blood" (Dacre 199), while Byron envisions the cursed Giaour tormented by a heart wrapped in flames. Graphically described emotional uproar and perturbed states of mind transmute into spectacles which in strongly theatrical ways convey the protagonists' narcissist consumption of their own feelings as well as their readers' propensity for voyeurism. Such explicitness of physiological and psychic imagery corroborates David Hume's and Adam Smith's view of sensations and emotional responses being likely to occur upon the spectators' or readers' exposure to lively images. For the eighteenth-century understanding,

---

[4] A famous example, which, in the vein of Radcliffe, endorses misgivings about, but also a final return to, domesticity is Jane Austen's *Northanger Abbey* (1818).

morality is never as pressing as when our senses compel us to ask ourselves: "How do I feel about what is happening before my eyes?"[5] Thus, the question arises: what moral implications could this visual exuberance of emotions that resists integration into an inherited social order have? I would like to offer two possible approaches: the first is informed by the political climate of the 1790s and, the second, by late-eighteenth century aesthetic and cognitive reformulations of sympathy that explore the darkly visceral side of the passions.

II. The Politics of Affect

While for the most part of the eighteenth century, sentimentalism had been (at best) embraced as the glue that held society together or (at worst) satirized for its self-indulging tendencies, the events of the French Revolution saw a thorough politicization of the rhetoric of feeling in fictional as well as political works. Especially after Edmund Burke's *Reflections on the Revolution in France* (1790), both Anti-Jacobins and sympathizers of the Revolution adopted and condemned the display of sentiments. In this political climate, domestic affections, one of the century's most applauded terms within this culture of sentimentalism, suddenly became politically loaded. Domestic affections had been the cornerstone of Frances Hutcheson's theory of passions and were adopted by most Scottish philosophers, who argued that human communities germinated within the family, which they baptized as the "little society," or in Burke's phrase, "the little platoon" (Dwyer 104; Burke 8: 97).[6] In the wake of the Revolution, Burke insisted that domestic affections were proof and warranty for the spread of public affective sensibility and universal benevolence (O'Neill 204). Burke's *Reflections* "polarized the conservative and radical aspects of sensibility," by appealing to domestic or parental affections (Jones 85). Burke conceived the nation as one great British family and the British Constitution as the product of century-long experience and foresight. In this great national family, the aristocracy took over the role of the parent who educated the masses into social discipline. Burke sought to mobilise readers' loyalties to past

---

[5] Terry Eagleton discusses the specular quality of eighteenth-century moral sense in the first two chapters of his *Trouble with Strangers*.

[6] In the introduction to *Jane Austen's Civilized Women*, I elaborate on the ways in which the Scottish Enlightenment valorized human sociability and extracted the duties of the citizen from the basic circumstances of human life, and, in particular, the life of the family.

authority and the principle of heredity, by laying claim to the value of feelings in the name of traditional values and the preservation of an inherited power balance (Jones 85). For him, the French revolutionaries had overthrown the authority of the nobility and the church, and, after doing away with these parent institutions, their democratizing policies were now aimed directly at the family. But what was even more damaging was that the revolutionaries taught the masses to see family ties as not binding, since blood relations are only rarely the result of free choice. This reminds one, of course, of characters like Vathek and Victoria, who lament the fate of having been mothered by unworthy women. It also throws light upon Burke's description of the revolutionaries as "children of their country who are prompt rashly to hack that aged parent in pieces" (Burke 8: 146). This strong image, which for its intensity could have leapt out of the pages of *Vathek*, *Zofloya* or *The Giaour*, visually invokes the savagery caused by such a breakdown of the family (O'Neill 210). Burke calls this breakdown "savagery" because it estranges the masses from "every civil, moral, and social, or even natural and instinctive sentiment," which for him represent the hallmarks of refined manners and civilization (Burke 8: 462).

As Chris Jones demonstrates in a thorough study that traces the polemics around the role of feelings in the aftermath of the French Revolution, many of those who "recanted their radical opinions under the pressure of conservative reaction [. . .] chose to highlight the valuation of domestic or parental affections to mark their return to the fold" (Jones 109). In the face of such reaction, sympathizers of the revolution, such as Mary Wollstonecraft, William Godwin and Charlotte Smith, marked their dissociation from conservatives and penitent radicals by a fierce opposition to parental affections. Extended to other forms of social bonds, opposition to parental affection meant a rejection of any kind of traditional authority. In an attempt to redefine the family, Wollstonecraft attacks parental affections in the same narrative that owes its very existence to maternal love: *Maria, or the Wrongs of Woman* (1798). As a memoir bequeathed upon an infant daughter by her persecuted mother, the novel clearly endorses maternal love; however, it also places its protagonists in harrowingly abusive households, thus deeming domestic ties as toxic and anything but naturally benevolent. The most extreme moment of mistrust in domestic affections is Godwin's famous dilemma, in which he imagines himself having to choose between rescuing Fénélon or his own mother from a burning house. Because Fénélon's writings contribute to the improvement of mankind, Godwin must choose the philosopher.

An even more politicized version of family critique was voiced by Charlotte Smith, who understood the public impact and appeal of Burke's sentimental and conservative domestic politics. She accepted his use of the domestic paradigm to define political matters, but came down on the side of the rebelling children. Thus, in her novel *Desmond* (1792), regarded as the first historical British novel, she interprets the American Revolution as a war between a parent state (Britain) and its child (America). This politicized version of family romance sees the American Revolution as the rightful act of the child who must sever the ties and claim independence from the parent that called her into life.[7] In this context, radical emotional response, or sensibility, materialized in "the capacity of individuals for beneficent action independent of traditional authority" (Jones 111). Universal benevolence that fostered the greatest good of the greatest number rather than usefulness and loyalty in a domestic paternalistic regime drives radical sensibility.

Vathek, *Zofloya* and *The Giaour* absorb the political polarization of sentimentalism, while contemplating the possibility of another dimension of emotional response that differs from both conservative and radical sensibility. Portrayals of the family as either a source of vice (in *Vathek* and *Zofloya*) or as a morbid past (in *The Giaour*) discard the conservative stance that considered sentiments to be founded upon established family values and historical precedent. However, on the other hand, by refusing to subordinate itself to the utilitarian narrative of the greatest good for the greatest number, these stories' propensity to strong feelings disappoints a radical agenda, too: the emotional self-involvement of a Vathek, Victoria or Giaour is a far cry from the universal benevolence that the radicals ascribed to sentiments. The crucial implication here is that such rejection of universal benevolence strips sentiments of their utilitarian value, which explains why these three works have been read as emanations of excessive narcissism. Already earlier in the century, sentimentalism had raised suspicion by its disproportionate distribution of emotions with scant regard for their use-value. The melting tenderness of Sterne's Yorick over a dead ass proved the narcissistic hunger for self-indulging sympathy with one's own ability to sympathize. Consequently, although feeling was able to smooth intersubjective transactions, "it also threatened to derail the whole project in

---

[7] Writing about the American Revolution, Smith states that one does not know "how far the *mother-country* is the worse for this disunion with her colonies, but, I am sure, they are the better," because America has "recovered of those wounds, which its *unnatural parent* hoped were mortal" and is at the time of the French Revolution in "a most flourishing state of political health" (Smith, *Desmond* 106-107, emphasis added).

the name of some less crassly egocentric vision of human society"
(Eagleton 18).

The three works compared here embrace a starkly crass egocentric
vision of society embodied by a young generation, eager to remake itself, among others, by exploring the less sociable side of sentiments.
Vathek's emotionality in particular has been brought into connection
with Beckford's anarchical denial of the need to grow up: Vathek's outbursts, his kicking and treading venerable elders, his biting, pinching,
bellowing and more importantly his unfolding sentiments in face of het-
erosexual love have led critics to think of this tale as a journey through
adolescence, in which the protagonist "is irredeemably damned through
growing up."[8] The tale's iconoclasm is not least mediated through a linguistic extravagance that conveys emotive energy: in the tale's own
words, Vathek is "impelled by an invisible power into extravagance"
(Richardson 93). Without seeking to steer the discussion of affect toward biological determinism, I tentatively use the word exuberance to
describe emotive energy in these three texts, because the term links
emotivity to a surplus of emotional responses implicated in a process of
identity-remaking.[9] In particular, exuberance in neuroscience describes
the development of the teenage brain, that is, an "overproduction" of
tiny branches of brain cells and synapses (Strauch 15). Until little more
than a decade ago, brain growth and wiring was thought to be finished
by age five at the latest. But recent research shows that during puberty
the brain undergoes a thorough re-branching, growth and pruning before it reaches the state of the adult brain in the early twenties. This
exuberance of brain activity reduces inhibition and manifests itself in an
exuberance of impulses, making adolescence the age in which the instinctual energy of the id is less resisted by the policing influence of the
super-ego. Neuroscientific insights, rather than confirming a sort of
bourgeois apprehension of adolescence, should help us interpret the
surplus of emotional responses as an integral part of a process of self-
fashioning.

---

[8] Adam Potkay calls Vathek "the first anti-bildungsroman, ironically poised at the
threshold of the nineteenth-century novel of education" (Potkay, "Beckford's Heaven of
Boys," qtd. in Richardson 301).

[9] I am wary of the possibility that biology can be deployed to substantiate ideology, a
path already taken in the study of emotions and their impact on morality: the eighteenth-
century "cult of sensibility" that explained women's acute emotions (but inferior mental
powers) with their weak nervous system stands as a cautionary tale in the history of
emotions.

Exuberant emotive energy also seems appropriate to characterize Victoria, the protagonist of Dacre's *Zofloya* and Byron's Giaour. Victoria is only fifteen at the beginning of the novel and only twenty at the end. However, unlike Vathek, who vents this exuberance in public, Victoria, once a child of a "wild, ardent and irrepressible spirit," is externally disciplined by conjugal life (40). Nevertheless, during a marriage that reintroduces her into the social order of Venetian society, she yearns for another man, a passion that compels her to poison her husband and kill her rival with a barbarity unequalled by another female protagonist. Victoria's crimes are facilitated by a former slave, Zofloya, the Moor of the title, but she appears no less prone to violence than him. Similarly, Byron's young Giaour entertains no other wish than to avenge the drowning of Leila by killing Hassan. This crime provokes more remorse in him than Victoria or Vathek ever experience, but, at the same time, such brutality makes him indistinguishable from Hassan, whose barbarity he had loathed previously: "And o'er him bends that foe with brow/ As dark as his that bled below" (Richardson 201: 673-4).

Not fortuitously, the rebellious emotive exuberance of these young protagonists is couched in the Oriental tale. Oriental elements found their way into almost all literary genres thanks to the popularity of the *Arabian Nights* in the eighteenth century. However, this does not account for the fascination that the Arabian tales had in the first place. As Saree Makdisi and Felicity Nussbaum argue, the *Arabian Nights* enjoyed a high-culture prominence and influence in the West that was unparalleled in their culture of origin.[10] This fascination, for example, was commented upon by Clara Reeve in *Progress of Romance* (1785), who also located the power of the tales in the force that only a vigorous, youthful culture could produce (Kelly 9). Consequently, while the fanatical aspects of the East under the Gothic dress would be a reminder of the ruthlessness of the French Revolution, it is also interesting to register the fascination of a young generation of writers (Beckford was 21, Charlotte Dacre claimed to have written *Zofloya* at age 24, and Byron was 25) with emotive energies capable of rejuvenating and driving away the *ennui* of the old civilization evoked by Hazlitt. Clothed in the Oriental dress, youthful emotive exuberance seems implicated in a process of refashioning that averts decline by generating new possible ways of being in the world. The vigour of adolescence could resuscitate the very instinc-

---

[10] "The earliest version of the tales had hardly been regarded by Arabs themselves as particularly prominent features of a rich cultural landscape in which, until the late nineteenth century at least, poetry was considered the pre-eminent literary form" (Makdisi and Nussbaum 2).

tual (innate) quality that made emotional responsiveness the watermark of humanity at the beginning of the eighteenth century, or as Godwin put it at the end of the century, "the magnetic virtue, the hidden essence of our life" (Godwin 318). Not only is this exuberance a sign of humanity, but also of an exalted kind of humanity which defends "the doctrine that the enjoyment of high minds is only to be found in the unbounded vehemence and strong tumult of the feelings; and that all gentler emotions are tame and feeble, and unworthy to move the soul that can bear the agency of greater passions" (*Edinburgh Review* 1813: 301).

This is particularly fitting to appreciate the strength of Victoria's character, whose emotional inner world captivates the reader (at times against the novel's moral cautioning) far more than her flat and insipid victims. One is appalled and fascinated by her instinctual energies, which intensify as soon as the beautiful Oriental Zofloya breaks into the *ennui* of her conjugal life. Thus, the emotional excess enabled by the conflation of the Gothic and Oriental can be read in support of Srinivas Aravamudan's proposition to view the Oriental tale as a new template of transcultural utopia that opposed the nationalist "yoke" of domestic realism which ended up having the upper hand in this contest of social visions (Aravamudan 4).

Attempting to understand whether such relish of a visceral emotional exuberance in fiction would mean a departure from that much theorized eighteenth-century moral sentiment that among others Frances Hutcheson, David Hume and Adam Smith called "sympathy," I find Joanna Baillie's revaluation of the term enlightening. Baillie is noteworthy for two reasons: first, she authored 26 plays, tragedies and comedies, all arranged under the title *Plays on the Passions* (1798) – a project that explored the origins and progress of passions; second, in a lengthy introduction, Baillie mapped out the aesthetic concept behind her plays. She named it "sympathetic curiosity." In this concept, Baillie interweaves something old and new: she applies to drama a term whose spectatorial nature originated with Humean and Smithian philosophy and was responsible for many tear-jerking displays of emotions in the eighteenth-century novel. Baillie agrees with Smith that sympathy is a cognitive process through which the self can "see the emotions of their [the spectators'] hearts, in every respect, beat time with his own, in the violent and disagreeable passions" (Smith 27). The theatricality of minutely performed and described emotions (excessive blushing, weeping, fainting) that crowd the pages of the novel evoke the visuality of emotions and the mimetic response they ellicit in the reader.[11] It is this visuality prominent in the novel and its readers' voyeuristic complicity that Baillie renders most visible in her theatre through the concept of "sympathetic curiosity." However, the explicit coupling of visuality with curiosity allowed Baillie to approach an untrodden and even avoided path.

Baillie constructs sympathy as an ambiguous trait that grows out of a primary appetite for spectatorship and particularly of an instinctual lust to view human suffering. Like *Vathek*, *Zofloya* and to a certain extent *The Giaour*, Baillie's drama builds upon crude spectacles of pain, executions, haunting, torture and a tableau of primal emotions and visceral drama. In doing so, these works use violence as a tool essential to the production of sympathy: indeed, others before Baillie argued that the witnessing of sensational scenes could activate the transfer of feelings from character to reader or spectator (Burke made use of public executions to sensitize his readers to the atrocities of revolutions). However, these spectacles are problematic because, first, they could train the reader to view real life as if it were a play or novel, and, second, they could foster pleasure in pain, in particular, the pain of others. Beckford and Dacre acknowledge the second possibility openly: Vathek does not make a secret of the "joy that succeeded to this emotion of terror" (Richardson 83), and Victoria wonders complacently "why, there is certainly a pleasure in the inflication of prolonged torment" (Dacre 205). The reader or viewer of such spectacles could either be prompted to emulate or regard similar scenes in real life as if they were fictions. As David Marshall puts it, "the problem is not what we see *in* the theatre but what we see *as* theatre" (Marshall 23). The most humane people may experience real-life suffering with a theatrical distance which in real life would destroy sympathy or produce false sympathy, that is, the mere stirring of emotions and enjoyment of pain, termed by Freud as masochistic pleasure.

The solution that Baillie offers to such a dilemma is the theatre itself. For her, theatre has an enlightening role to play, by fully representing the passions in their primal unchecked force from their genesis until the bitter end. The death of the passion-driven protagonists serves to discipline the reader or spectator in Baillie's tragedy, and comic social chastisement fulfils a similar goal in her comedies. This theatre consists in

---

[11] David Marshall's *The Surprising Effects of Sympathy* treats the mimetic aspect of sentiments and sympathy as first playing a role in seventeenth-century French classical aesthetics, but crossing transgeneric borders only in the eighteenth century, when it is applied to painting, dramatic arts, poetry and the novel, thus encompassing all aesthetic experience.

unveiling the human mind under the dominion of those strong and fixed
passions, which seemingly unprovoked by outward circumstances, will,
from small beginnings brood within the breast, till all the better dispositions, all the fair gifts of nature are borne down before them, those passions
which conceal themselves from the observation of men; which cannot un-
bosom themselves even to the dearest friend; and can, oftentimes, only give
their fullness vent in the lonely desert, or in the darkness of midnight.
(Baillie 509)

Baillie seems to believe that the more profound disciplining of a community of readers or spectators occurs through a detailed representation
of troubled states of mind and emotional upheavals, as if suggesting that
uncanny emotions are tamed when they are felt, understood and integrated into collective cognition.

Like Baillie's plays, *Vathek*, *Zofloya* and *The Giaour* are similarly un-
apologetic when it comes to depicting the protagonists' undoing. In the
Gothic universe of these tales, too, we encounter protagonists who become slaves to their passions, and, since it is too late to reform, they
meet their due doom: Vathek suffers "eternal unabating anguish" for his
"unrestrained passions and blind curiosity" (158), Victoria is strangled
and hurled into a precipice by Zofloya, her demonic alter ego, and the
Giaour is haunted by his dark past without hope of redemption. However, in narratives like *Vathek* and *Zofloya*, where sublime and exuberat-
ing visceral outbursts have been savoured in their full vigour, the final
punishments of the protagonists pay little more than lip service to morality, whereas the Giaour does not even attempt to relinquish the morbid self-involvement that characterizes him.

It is tempting to interpret the spectacles of pain, torture, murder and
sadistic pleasure in these texts in terms of Baillie's belief that better
knowledge of human passions through verisimilar representations
teaches self-control. However, Dacre and Byron, in particular, seem less
sanguine about the disciplining effect of sympathetic curiosity. Their
works gesture toward the possibility that not only sociable and benign
emotions inspire mimetic doubling in the mind of the spectator, but also
destructive ones, like the body of Victoria darkening as her murderous
alliance with Zofloya thickens, or the hatred of Hassan for the Giaour,
which in a mirroring process blackens the face of the latter: "And o'er
him bends that foe with brow/ As dark as his that bled below"
(Richardson 201: 673-4). In these works, sympathy has indeed become
an ambiguous term (as Baillie rightly observed): its less controllable and
social side that originated with the innate taste of the mind for strong
excitement gains prominence. This ambiguity renders palpable a deep

uncertainty not only about class, race and gender, but the very essence of being social and its resulting pursuit of human values. *Vathek* inaugurates the Western concern with the "outlawed self" as the "projection of an amoral, secret life into the public domain" (Sharafuddin xxxii). Byron picked up on this sensibility when writing *The Giaour*, while Dacre under the guise of moral instruction went to unprecedented extremes by planting the dark, rebellious heart of the outlaw in a woman's body.[12] Hence, while on the surface these texts may reflect what the West thought of the Oriental Other, in their depth, they channel otherness in the West's profound estrangement with its own system of knowledge and ways of life.

Acknowledgement

I am very grateful to Nancy Armstrong for her insightful comments on earlier drafts of this essay and for sharing with me her most recent work on the Gothic and the history of the English novel.

---

[12] It is noteworthy that while the Giaour is only briefly associated with the Albanian rebels in his act of revenge against Hassan, Victoria's life with the *banditti*, whose leader is her brother, takes up the last chapters of the novel.

References

Aravamudan, Srinivas. *Enlightenment Orientalism: Resisting the Rise of the Novel.* Chicago: University of Chicago Press, 2012.

Baillie, Joanna. *"A Series of Plays:* Introductory Discourse." *The Broadview Anthology of the Literature of the Revolutionary Period, 1770-1832.* Ed. D. L. Macdonald and Anne McWhir. Peterborough: Broadview, 2010. 500-514.

Burke, Edmund. *The Writings and Speeches of Edmund Burke.* Ed. Paul Langford. 8 vols to date. Oxford: Clarendon Press, 1981-.

Critical Review. London: A. Hamilton, 1786. Vol. 62. 38-42.

Dacre, Charlotte. *Zofloya; or the Moor.* Ed. Adriana Craciun. Peterborough: Broadview, 2006.

Dixon, Thomas. *From Passions to Emotions: The Creation of a Secular Psychological Category.* Cambridge: Cambridge University Press, 2006.

Dwyer, John. *Virtuous Discourse: Sensibility and Community in Late Eighteenth-Century Scotland.* Edinburgh: John Donald, 1987.

Eagleton, Terry. *Trouble with Strangers: A Study of Ethics.* Chichester: Wiley-Blackwell, 2009.

Edinburgh Review, or Critical Journal. Edinburgh: Archibald Constable and Co., 1813. Vol. 24.48. 321-338.

Godwin, William. *Caleb Williams, or Things as They Are.* Ed. Maurice Hindle. London: Penguin Classics, 1988.

Greenblatt, Stephen. *Shakespearean Negotiations: The Circulation of Social Energy in Renaissance England.* Berkley and Los Angeles: University of California Press, 1988.

Johnson, Samuel. *A Dictionary of the English Language.* 2 vols. London: W. Strahan, 1755.

Jones, Chris. *Radical Sensibility: Literature and Ideas in the 1790s.* London and New York: Routledge, 1993.

Kelly, Gary. "Social Conflict, Nation and Empire: From Gothicism to Romantic Orientalism." *Ariel* 20. 2 (1989): 3-18.

Makdisi, Saree and Felicity Nussbaum. *The Arabian Nights in Historical Context: Between East and West.* Oxford: Oxford University Press, 2008.

Marshall, David. *The Surprising Effects of Sympathy: Marivaux, Diderot, Rousseau, and Mary Shelley.* Chicago: University of Chicago Press, 1988.

Miles, Robert. "The 1790s: The Effulgence of Gothic." *The Cambridge Companion to Gothic Fiction.* Ed. Jerrold E. Hogle. Cambridge: Cambridge University Press, 2002. 41-61.

O'Neill, Daniel I. *The Burke-Wollstonecraft Debate: Savagery, Civilization, and Democracy.* University Park: Pennsylvania State University Press, 2007.

Richardson, Alan, ed. *Three Oriental Tales*. Boston and New York: River-side Editions, 2002.

Sade, Marquis de. "Ideas on the Novel." *The Gothic Novel: A Casebook*. Ed. Victor Sage. London: Longman, 1990. 49-54

Said, Edward. *Orientalism: Western Conceptions of the Orient*. 1975. Har-mondsworth: Penguin Books: 1995.

Sharafuddin, Mohammed. *Islam and Romantic Orientalism: Literary Encounters with the Orient*. London: Tauris, 1994.

Smith, Adam. *Theory of Moral Sentiments*. London: W. Strahan et al., 1774.

Smith, Charlotte. *Desmond*. Ed. Antje Blank and Janet Todd. Peter-borough: Broadview Press, 2001.

Steiner, Enit Karafili. *Jane Austen's Civilized Women: Morality, Gender and the Civilizing Process*. London: Pickering and Chatto, 2012.

Stenner, Paul. "An outline of an autopoietic systems approach to emotion." *Cybernetics and Human Knowing* 12.4 (2006): 8-22.

Strauch, Barbara. *The Primal Teen: What the New Discoveries about the Teenage Brain Tell Us about Our Kids*. New York: Anchor Books, 2003.

Joyce's Transcendental Aesthetics
of Epiphany

Sangam MacDuff

The modern literary epiphany is usually regarded as a subjective, secular experience, but I argue that Daedalus's theory of epiphany in *Stephen Hero* constitutes an aesthetics of transcendence. Epiphanies traditionally present divine apparitions, and Daedalus's definition of epiphany as a "sudden spiritual manifestation" strongly suggests a transcendental event. In contrast to traditional theophanies, though, his theory draws on the poetics of Wordsworth and Shelley, who reimagine the epiphany as a rapturous, but immanent, experience of the sublime. In doing so, they internalise the epiphany, but from an Idealist perspective, the Romantic revelation remains a transcendental moment in which the God-like infinitude of nature and/or the mind is shown forth. Indeed, Wordsworth's epiphanies have all the hallmarks of the Kantian sublime, so that Kant's "Analytic of the Sublime" can be used to understand a Romantic aesthetics of transcendence. If Daedalus's theory is essentially Romantic, it follows that Kant's aesthetics also illuminate *Stephen Hero*, but I argue that they do so in a different way to Wordsworth, by opening up the possibility of a new transcendence, not in the wonder of the starry heavens or the moral law within, but in the sublimity of language itself.

In contrast to the transcendental nature of classical and biblical epiphanies where deities appear directly, the modern literary epiphany is usually regarded as a subjective, secular experience. In *Epiphany in the Modern Novel*, Morris Beja argues that there is a shift "from divine revelations, purely religious experiences, to [modernist] epiphanies, for the most part regarded as secular" (46). Ashton Nichols develops a similar argument in

Emotion, Affect, Sentiment: The Language and Aesthetics of Feeling. SPELL: Swiss Papers in English Language and Literature 30. Ed. Andreas Langlotz and Agnieszka Soltysik Monnet. Tübingen: Narr, 2014. 143-161.

The Poetics of Epiphany, tracing a change of emphasis from the inspired seer of biblical revelations to the Romantic interpreter of oracular epiphanies (13-34). Both Beja and Nichols, like Abrams and Langbaum, see the beginnings of this movement in Wordsworth and its culmination in Joyce; Wordsworth's "spots of time" (1805 *Prelude* 11.258) are frequently compared to Joyce's Epiphanies (Abrams 418-22; Beja 33-34; Nichols 5), while the preface to *Lyrical Ballads,* with its valorisation of "incidents and situations from common life," is typically read as the starting point for Joyce's aesthetics of epiphany – "The Bread of Everyday Life," as Beja puts it (Beja 32, 71-111; cf. Nichols 104-5). Building on his own *Poetry of Experience,* Robert Langbaum formulates the critical concensus concisely: "the epiphanic mode," derived from Wordsworth, "is to a large extent the Romantic and modern mode – a dominant modern convention" whose defining characteristics are "psychological association, momentaneousness, suddenness and fragmentation" (336, 341; see also Tigges 37-84).

Wordsworth's importance in shaping the modern epiphany is indisputable, and Langbaum's criteria are certainly relevant to it, but at the same time, they have little in common with the traditional, *transcendental* manifestations of epiphany, so that their application to Wordsworth overlooks the revelatory aspect of his poetics, just as it ignores the theological significance of the term Joyce devised.[1] Indeed, Daedalus's definition of epiphany as a "sudden spiritual manifestation" (*Stephen Hero* 216 [hereafter *SH*]) strongly suggests a transcendental experience, and in this paper I will argue that his theory of epiphany constitutes an aesthetics of transcendence.

Transcendental aesthetics covers a multitude of things, from heavenly beauty to the grounds of sensory experience, and both senses of both words are relevant to Stephen's theory, since it is framed by a disquisition on beauty which is simultaneously a philosophical enquiry into the "mechanism of aesthetic [empirical] apprehension" (*SH* 217). These terms indicate that Joyce's aesthetics have a strongly Kantian flavour,

---

[1] Epiphany is a recurrent term in the liturgy, referring not only to the feast of the Epiphany on January 6, but to the entire epiphany season which concludes on Joyce's birthday, Candlemas, when Jesus is presented in the temple as a light and revelation. According to the OED the word has two meanings: the first refers to the Catholic festival; the second to divine manifestations in general, but Webster's adds the following senses: "3 *a (1):* a usually sudden manifestation or perception of the essential nature or meaning of something *(2):* an intuitive grasp of reality through something (as an event) usually simple and striking *(3):* an illuminating discovery, realization, or disclosure *b:* a revealing scene or moment." 3a corresponds closely to the definition in *Stephen Hero,* while 3b corresponds to Joyce's literary forms.

but they are also connected, via Wordsworth, to the classico-biblical origins of epiphany as a divine manifestation. As M. H. Abrams has shown, Wordsworth's "Prospectus" to his projected masterpiece, *The Recluse,* is a poetics of revelation (Abrams 21-70), and Joyce's aesthetics owe as much to this aspect of Romanticism as they do to his veneration of the ordinary in unexpected moments of heightened experience. This connection becomes apparent when we see how closely Stephen's theory resembles the poetics of Wordsworth and Shelley, who reimagine the epiphany as a rapturous, but immanent, experience of the sublime, in which the godlike infinitude of nature and/or the mind is shown forth. Thus, from an Idealist perspective, the Romantic revelation remains a transcendental experience insofar as it reveals the pure ideas of unity, the infinite, and God. It follows that if Daedalus's theory is essentially Romantic, then Kant's aesthetics in the *Third Critique* also have a bearing on the aesthetic theory in *Stephen Hero*, which is precisely what I intend to show. Yet I argue that they do so in a different way to Wordsworth, by opening up the possibility of a new transcendence, not in the wonder of the starry heavens or the moral law within, but in the sublimity of language itself.

The Romantic Roots of Daedalus's Definition

In *Stephen Hero*, Stephen defines epiphany as

> a sudden spiritual manifestation, whether in the vulgarity of speech or of gesture or in a memorable phase of the mind itself. He believed that it was for the man of letters to record these epiphanies with extreme care, seeing that they themselves are the most delicate and evanescent of moments.
> (216)

The classico-biblical origins of this "spiritual manifestation" are obvious, but Stephen's emphasis on the delicate, ephemeral nature of these moments, and the fact that they occur in ordinary words and gestures, or in our own minds, rather than divine apparitions, sounds characteristically modern. At first glance, this secular, immanent experience seems far removed from traditional theophanies, confirming the view of Morris Beja and Ashton Nichols, but if we retrace the Romantic roots of Stephen's definition, it becomes apparent that Daedalus's theory in *Stephen Hero* remains a transcendental aesthetic.

Most obviously, there is a striking parallel between this passage and
Shelley's "Defence of Poetry," where in "the best and happiest of moments,"

> We are aware of evanescent visitations of thought and feeling sometimes
> associated with place or person, sometimes regarding our own mind alone,
> and always arising unforeseen and departing unbidden, but elevating and
> delightful beyond all expression. (532)

It is clear from this that Stephen's "most delicate and evanescent of
moments" are remarkably similar to Shelley's "evanescent visitations":
both arise unexpectedly from ordinary places, conversations, or moments of reflection, affecting "those of the most delicate sensibility,"
and leading us back to "the wonder of our being" when poetry touches
"the enchanted chord" (532), "a spiritual state" which "Luigi Galvani,
using a phrase almost as beautiful as Shelley's, called the enchantment of
the heart" (Joyce, *Portrait* 231). Ashton Nichols shows that these parallels run right through Stephen's aesthetics (in both versions), suggesting
that "Joyce imported Shelley's ideas directly into his own theory of
epiphany" (104). Although Nichols ascribes Stephen's theory to Joyce
himself and makes no distinction between the theory in *Stephen Hero* and
the aesthetics in *A Portrait of the Artist as a Young Man* (where the word
"epiphany" does not occur), the parallels are undeniable, showing the
extent to which Joyce drew on Romantic poetics both for his theory of
epiphany in *Stephen Hero* and his conception of the artist in *Portrait*.

This Romantic influence goes beyond "The Defence of Poetry."
Nichols argues that Shelley's and Joyce's theories "derive ultimately
from Wordsworth," specifically the 1802 preface to *Lyrical Ballads*
(Nichols 104-5), where the poet's "lively sensibility" is affected by "absent things as if they were present," throwing over "incidents and situations from common life" a "colouring of imagination, whereby ordinary
things should be presented to the mind in an unusual aspect" (Wordsworth, *Lyrical Ballads* 244). There can be little doubt about the importance of the "Preface" to both Shelley and Joyce, but Nichols's focus is
too narrow. As M. H. Abrams argues, Wordsworth's poetics of epiphany are most powerfully expressed not in the preface to *Lyrical Ballads,*
but in the "Prospectus" which concludes the preface to *The Excursion*, a
poem Joyce cites as an example of Wordsworth's genius. In a letter of
May 1905, Joyce's "history of literature" awards "the highest palms to
Shakespeare, Wordsworth and Shelley" (*Selected Letters* 62); his next letter
judges between them: "I think W[ordsworth] of all English men of let-

ters best deserves your word 'genius'. Read his poem to his lost son in 'Excursion'" (63).[2]

In the 1814 preface to *The Excursion* Wordsworth compares *The Recluse* to the tripartite body of a great gothic church to which *The Prelude* was to be "the ante-chapel" while his lyric poems would form "little cells, oratories, and sepulchral recesses" (Wordsworth, *Poetical Works* 589). In this context, the lines he intended for the end of Book 1 form "a kind of *Prospectus* of the design and scope of the whole poem" (*ibid*) so that its programme can be applied to Wordsworth's poetry as a whole, and if we accept Abrams's assessment of Wordsworth as "the great and exemplary poet of the age" (14), then the revelatory quality of his poetry is characteristic of Romanticism. Abrams traces this revelatory aspect to two key metaphors from Apocalypse – the New Jerusalem as heaven on earth and the marriage of Christ with humanity. Thus, when Wordsworth announces the subject of *The Prelude* as "Creation and Divinity itself . . . for my theme has been /What passed within me" (3.172-74), he is simply internalising the "spiritual sense" of the Bible (Blake to Robinson in Bentley 312) which Winstanley calls "the light and life of Christ within the heart" (*The New Law of Righteousness* 214; qtd in Abrams 53). For Wordsworth, like Blake and Winstanley, God is to be sought in "the Mind of Man" ("Prospectus" 40, in *Poetical Works* 590), whose "discerning intellect,"

> When wedded to this goodly universe
> In love and holy passion, shall find [heaven]
> A simple produce of the common day. (52-55)

Wordsworth's metaphor recalls the nuptial imagery at the end of Revelation where Jerusalem, as the new heaven on earth, is "prepared as a bride for her husband" (21:2), for "the marriage of the Lamb is come" (19:6-7). Christ's words at the crucifixion, *"consummatum est"* in the Vulgate (John 19:30), were traditionally interpreted as signifying that Christ's Passion was the consummation of his marriage with humanity

---

[2] The reference is elusive. Joyce goes on to quote "Where are thou, my beloved son," the first line of "The Affliction of Margaret" (1804). Although book 1 of *The Excursion* consists largely of the tale of "poor Margaret" (I 503), whose provenance is detailed in the Preface (which may account for Joyce's confusion), the lyric itself forms no part of the poem. And the reference is more mysterious still since Joyce appears to read "The Affliction of Margaret" biographically (*"his* lost son"), perhaps confusing the lost son with Wordsworth's abandoned daughter, Caroline (born 1792), or (anachronistically) with his son Thomas (died 1812).

and Wordsworth's image of "love and holy passion" surely recalls
Christ's symbolic union with mankind, as the following lines make clear:

> I, long before the blissful hour arrives,
> Would chaunt, in lonely peace, the spousal verse
> Of this great consummation.   (56-8)

Here "the blissful hour" is again the holy marriage, but in Wordsworth's
version, "the Lamb and New Jerusalem are replaced by man's mind as
the bridegroom and nature as the bride" (Abrams 56), so that the "great
consummation" is transposed from the indefinite future to the present
moment. Wordsworth's "high argument" (*Prelude* 3.182), then, is that
we, through our "discerning intellect," are capable of experiencing paradise through everyday events – "the simple produce of the common
day." The reason this is possible is that Wordsworth conceives of
"Mind" and "World" as "exquisitely . . . fitted" ("Prospectus" 63-8),
and, both, he thinks, have a divine aspect. The question of how exactly
they are related is complex, but it is this notion of the spiritual content
of ordinary experience which gives rise to Wordsworth's epiphanies as
the moments in which the spiritual nature of mind and/or the animating
intelligence of nature is revealed.

Revelation and the Sublime

Thus, while Wordsworth's epiphanies are immanent experiences, the
Apocalyptic (*apokalypsis*: revelation) metaphors behind Wordsworth's
poetics suggest that they are also transcendental revelations, just as their
secular subjects do not preclude spiritual significance. This is a traditional aspect of revelation, but the Wordsworthian epiphany also provides a new form of transcendence, which Joyce takes up and develops
in *Stephen Hero.* Perhaps the clearest example of this is the famous
Snowdon epiphany near the end of the *Prelude,* where Wordsworth fuses
the sublime imagery of full moon, mist and mountains with the deep
chasm and thundering torrents into the sound of "one voice" roaring, a
"universal spectacle" in which "Nature lodged / The Soul, the Imagination of the whole" (60, 64-5).[3] Meditating on this vision, the poet inter-

---

[3] Wordsworth's interest in the sublime can be traced back to the *Descriptive Sketches*
(1793), which include a long note on the sublime (*Prose,* II, 349-60), while his *Guide to the
Lakes* contains many passages contrasting beautiful and sublime vistas (e.g., 21-6, 36, 99,
102).

prets it as "the perfect image of a mighty Mind, / Of one that feeds upon infinity" (69-70). And as *The Prelude* draws to a close, Wordsworth begins to sound again the keynotes of the poem: "an underpresence, /The sense of God" in "Nature. . . most awful and sublime"; or again, those "sublime and lovely forms" which give rise to "the one thought / By which we live, Infinity and God" (72-6, 183-4). In these passages, Wordsworth relates his epiphanic "spots of time" (11.258) explicitly to the sublime and the infinite, celebrating not only the grandeur of nature, or the majesty of its creator, but also the power of the mind. Thus, like Kant's "Analytic of the Sublime," Wordsworth's epiphanic visions reveal both the unity of space and the transcendental nature of the mind, because they awaken our *a priori* concepts of God, unity, and the infinite.[4]

These moments are clearly transcendental in the Kantian sense, but they are also transcendental in the biblical sense, as God's revelation. Both these aspects are evident in book six of *The Prelude,* where Wordsworth describes descending the steep Simplon pass in a series of tumultuous and vertiginous oppositions: an "immeasurable height / Of woods decaying, never to be decayed,[. . .] at every turn /Winds thwarting winds" and "torrents shooting from the clear blue sky." This "giddy prospect" disturbs the poet, becoming a "sick sight" in which the "stationary blasts of waterfalls" from the towering cliffs are personified in "[t]he rocks that muttered close upon our ears, / Black drizzling crags that spake by the way-side / As if a voice were in them." Wordsworth is seemingly unable to reconcile the contradictions in his description; his field of vision is insufficient either to apprehend it in its totality or to describe its full terror and majesty, except by recourse to the overwhelming imagery of the sublime where antitheses are yoked together:

> The unfettered clouds and region of the Heavens,
> Tumult and peace, the darkness and the light –
> Were all like workings of one mind, the features
> Of the same face, blossoms upon one tree;

---

[4] Whether or not Wordsworth actually read Kant is a vexed question, but he was familiar with Kant and German Idealist philosophy, at least in a general sense, through Coleridge. Owen and Smyser note a series of correspondences, both in general ideas and specific phrasing, between Wordsworth's fragmentary essay, "The Sublime and the Beautiful" (1811-1812) and Kant's Third *Critique* (see *Prose* vol. 2 349-60, esp. ll.254-55, 263-66, and *CJ* 245, 250). This may be explained by Coleridge's intensive study of Kant when he stayed with Wordsworth at Allan Bank during 1809-10 (Coleridge 12.3.26) and may not imply that Wordsworth actually read Kant (see Wu 261-62).

Characters of the great Apocalypse,
The types and symbols of Eternity,
Of first, and last, and midst, and without end.
(6.634-49)

In Kant's terms, Wordsworth presents a manifold of intuition too vast
to be assimilated in its totality, so that the mind, being unable to perceive the object in its entirety, must fall back on an *a priori* intuition of
totality, which affords a transcendental glimpse of the infinite (*CJ* §§25-
26); but it is also evident that Wordsworth draws on Revelation for the
imagery of clouds and heavens, darkness and light, the first and last
end.[5] This connection is irrefutable when he calls these contradictory
aspects of nature "Characters of the great Apocalypse, / The types and
symbols of Eternity," explicitly invoking typological and allegorical
hermeneutics to read nature as the revelation of God. But Wordsworth
goes much further than the traditional Enlightenment metaphor of nature as God's book because the revelation he represents is a phenomenological experience, "half create[d]" (*Lyrical Ballads* 116) by the perceiv-
ing subject, and recreated by the poet in his epiphany. This is apparent
at the point at which all the contradictory images Wordsworth uses simultaneously to describe an extraordinary natural phenomenon and the
overwhelming effect it has upon him – its "tumult and peace" – are finally resolved into "the workings of one mind," sustaining an exquisite
ambiguity between the mind of God and the mind of the poet.

This ambiguity is central to Wordsworth's epiphanies, where the
Godlike infinitude of *both* nature *and* the mind are manifest together. As
such, the Wordsworthian epiphany is a Kantian revelation, in which the
pure idea of unity is awoken by an experience of the sublime, thereby
affording a transcendental glimpse of the infinite. Thus, although epiphany becomes a subjective experience for the Romantics, it remains a
transcendental experience in the Kantian sense that it reveals the pure
ideas of God, unity, and the self.

Like Wordsworth, two of the most powerful lenses with which to
focus Joyce's aesthetics of epiphany are the Book of Revelation and
Kant's "Analytic of the Sublime." Joyce copied the entire Book of Reve-

---

[5] Compare Revelation 1: 11: "I am Alpha and Omega, the beginning and the end, the
first and the last." See also Revelation 1: 8, 17-18; 21: 6. Wordsworth may also be recalling Adam and Eve's aubade in book 5 of *Paradise Lost*, where they praise the "Power
Divine" of "him first, him last, him midst, and without end" (153-65). Max Wildi points
out that descriptions of Alpine sublimity were a standard topos in eighteenth-century
travel writing, but the density of Wordsworth's apocalyptic imagery is unusual.

lation by hand from the King James Version between 1903 and 1905 – that is, at the time he was writing his Epiphanies, *Dubliners*, his 1904 essay entitled "A Portrait of the Artist," and the early chapters of *Stephen Hero* (Scholes and Kain 264). Since this manuscript, entitled "The Apocalypse of St John" (Cornell 4609 Bd. Ms.3), also includes three Epiphanies, there seems to be an obvious connection between them, contradicting the standard interpretation of the modernist epiphany as a fundamentally secular form. Indeed, if we take Joyce's title seriously, the Epiphanies "record" a series of revelations, "whether in the vulgarity of speech or of gesture or in a memorable phase of the mind itself" (*SH* 216),[6] just as in the Wordsworthian epiphany heaven is found in the "simple produce of the common day" (Prospectus 55), revealing "the rapture of the Hallelujah sent / From all that breathes and is" (13.262-63). It is evident from this that for both Wordsworth and Joyce, epiphanies show forth the spiritual content of ordinary experience, so that whatever irony there may be in *Stephen Hero,* Daedalus's account of "a sudden spiritual manifestation" in ordinary words and gestures is certainly a transcendental experience.[7]

Joyce's Aesthetics: A Kantian Interpretation

As well as their link to Revelation, Joyce's aesthetics are transcendental in the Kantian sense, but, surprisingly, both connections have been overlooked. Joyce himself cited Aristotle and Aquinas as the sources of his aesthetics, but numerous commentators have shown that the reflections he noted in the Paris and Pola notebooks of 1903-1904 bear little relation to Aristotelian or Thomist doctrine.[8] Although Joyce pro-

---

[6] Stanislaus Joyce's view of the Epiphanies is also revealing: "they were in the beginning ironical observations of slips, and little errors and gestures – mere straws in the wind – by which people betrayed the very things they were most careful to conceal"; later, he says, "[t]he epiphanies became more frequently subjective and included dreams which he considered in some way revelatory" (*My Brother's Keeper* 125-26).

[7] Similarly, the epiphanic nature of Revelation underscores Joyce's conception of *Dubliners* as a series of *epicleti* (referring to the moment of transubstantiation in the Orthodox mass – *Selected Letters* 22); and Stephen's vision of the artist as a "priest of the eternal imagination, transmuting the daily bread of experience into the radiant body of everliving life" (*Portrait* 240).

[8] The best account of Joyce's debt to Aristotle and Aquinas is Fran O'Rourke's essay, "Joyce's Early Aesthetic." O' Rourke demonstrates that Joyce's aesthetics are based on a few isolated quotations from Aristotle's *Nichomachean Ethics* and Aquinas's *Summa Theologiae.*

claimed himself an Aristotelian (Stanislaus Joyce, *Complete Dublin Diary* 53) and characterised Stephen's aesthetic theory as "applied Aquinas" in both *Stephen Hero* (77) and *Portrait* (209), Stephen relies on "only a garner of slender sentences from Aristotle's poetics and psychology" (*Portrait* 176), and the same is probably true of Joyce's early aesthetics.[9] Yet Joyce's "inspired cribbing" (Ellmann xv) brings a hodge-podge of philosophical ideas to bear on these fragments, thereby transforming them into the complex and original aesthetics of *Stephen Hero* and *Portrait*.

This "inspired cribbing" has proved immensely fruitful in propagating a wide range of critical interpretations. For instance, Morris Beja compares Stephen's aesthetics to Schopenhauer's Romantic rereading of Kant, which "does away with the dualism between subject and object" (30), and later to Bergson's "intuition," which affords "absolute" knowledge when one "places oneself within an object in order to coincide with what is unique in it and consequently inexpressible" (Bergson, *Metaphysics* 1, 7, qtd in Beja 55; see Beja 30-32, 54-57). James Caufield explores the connection to Schopenhauer in greater detail, arguing that "Stephen's use of Schopenhauer's aesthetics" can be explained by the fact that "Post-Kantian German Idealism and its Romantic reverberations in *fin de siècle* letters [. . .] were a part of the critical medium in which Joyce's aesthetic sense developed" (714). In the same vein, Robert Scholes and Marlena Corcoran derive Stephen's aesthetics "from the tradition that includes Lessing, August and Friedrich von Schlegel, Kant, Schelling and Hegel" (691). However, Caufield's Schopenhauerian parallels, like Beja's are tenuous, while Scholes and Corcoran provide no evidence for their claim that Stephen's aesthetics are "explicitly indebted" to Hegel, Schelling and the younger von Schlegel, so that these readings are not fully convincing as explanations of Stephen's theory. Nevertheless, they are of interest insofar as they open up new approaches to Joyce's epiphanies, just as an understanding of Bergson's philosophy greatly enhances our understanding of *A la recherche du temps perdu*. And it is with this aim in mind that I propose to reread Stephen Daedalus's aesthetics through Kant's "Analytic of the Sublime"; in doing so, I am not claiming that Joyce's or Stephen's theories are deliberately Kantian, but rather that Kant's approach to aesthetics offers an

---

[9] In *The Aesthetics of James Joyce*, Aubert argues that Joyce was acquainted with Aristotle through Bernard Bosanquet's *A History of Aesthetic*, but it is more likely that Joyce relied on Boedder's *Natural Theology* and Rickaby's *General Metaphysics* – the theology and philosophy textbooks at University College Dublin. See C. P. Curran, "James Joyce Remembered" (36-37, qtd in O'Rourke 118).

illuminating insight into the aesthetics of *Stephen Hero*, and perhaps Joyce's as well.

In fact, Joyce seems to have regarded the aesthetics in the Paris-Pola notebook not as "applied Aquinas" or Aristotle, neither as Idealist or Bergsonian, but as his own, for he signed and dated each entry with a flourish.[10] In *Stephen Hero*, Daedalus tells Cranly that "[n]o esthetic theory [. . .] is of any value which investigates with the aid of the lantern of tradition" (217). His point is that beauty is relative ("Greek beauty laughs at Coptic beauty and the American Indian derides them both" [217]), but it also indicates his desire to formulate a new aesthetic theory with a universal criterion for beauty. This is a recurring theme in the notebook, where Joyce draws on the Greek roots of "aesthetic" (of or relating to sensory perception), in order to equate beauty with apprehension:

> every sensible object that has been apprehended can be said in the first place to have been and to be ~~beautiful~~ in a measure beautiful; and even the most hideous object can be said to have been and to be beautiful insofar as it has been apprehended.   (Scholes and Kain 81; cf. 82-83)

Daedalus makes the same equation between beauty and apprehension in *Stephen Hero* when he says:

> It is almost impossible to reconcile all tradition whereas it is by no means impossible to find the justification of every form of beauty which has been adored on the earth by an examination into the mechanism of esthetic apprehension. . . . The apprehensive faculty must be scrutinised in action.
> (*SH* 217)

Thus Daedalus's aesthetics, like Joyce's, are founded on "the mechanism of esthetic apprehension," by which he means sensory perception. Of course, Kant is widely regarded as having originated this sense of "aesthetic" when, at the outset of his revolutionary "Transcendental Aesthetic," he criticises Baumgartner's "science of taste" on etymological as well as philosophical grounds (*Critique of Pure Reason* [hereafter *CPR*] A 21). Hence, there is a fundamental similarity in what Kant, Joyce and Stephen actually mean by "aesthetics," and although Stephen analyses the "apprehensive faculty" in relation to Aquinas's criteria of beauty –

---

[10] The notebooks are held by the National Library of Ireland (MS 36,639/2/A). See http://catalogue.nli.ie/pdflookup.php?pdfid=vtls000194606_02 (17-19).

"integrity, . . . symmetry and radiance," as Stephen translates them (*SH* 217) – his theory shares a number of similarities with Kantian aesthetics.

First, Stephen asks Cranly to:

> [c]onsider the performance of your own mind when confronted with any object, hypothetically beautiful. [. . .]To apprehend it you must lift it away from everything else: and then you perceive that it is one integral thing, that is a thing. You recognise its integrity. Isn't that so? [. . .]That is the first quality of beauty: it is declared in a simple sudden synthesis of the faculty which apprehends. (217)

This "simple sudden synthesis" is similar to Kant's "synthesis of apprehension" in the *Critique of Pure Reason,* where a manifold of empirical data are "gathered together" in a single "moment" (*CPR* A 99). Of course, for Kant, this intuition of an object, such as a house, is never a conception of "a thing in itself at all but only an appearance, i.e., a representation, the transcendental object of which remains utterly unknown" (A 190). Indeed, the fundamental premise of Kant's first *Critique* is that we can never have access to the transcendental object, the noumenon; what the synthesis of apprehension reveals is the *a priori* idea of unity which structures spatio-temporal experience itself (A 100). For Kant, "[t]he synthesis of apprehension . . . constitutes the transcendental ground of the possibility of all cognition in general. . ."; Stephen's phrase, which seems to echo Kant's, makes the "sudden synthesis of the faculty which apprehends" the necessary precondition for all aesthetic experience.

In the second phase of Stephen's aesthetics, analysis, "[t]he mind considers the object in whole and in part, in relation to itself and to other objects," examining its form and structure in detail (*SH* 217). This second stage of apprehension corresponds quite closely to Kant's "synthesis of reproduction in the imagination," in which the mind comprehends a given object by comparing a series of sensory presentations, relating part to part and part to whole (*CPR* A101-102). The processes are not identical, since Kant emphasises the temporal sequence of apperception and the role of memory in facilitating our imaginative recognition of the unity of the phenomenal representation, while Stephen focuses on the formal "symmetry" of the object, "travers[ing] every cranny of its structure" in order to recognise its integrity (217), but there is nevertheless a marked similarity between the basic analytical procedures they describe.

However, the third phase of Stephen's aesthetics, in which the object is epiphanised, seems at first sight to have nothing in common with Kantian aesthetics. After recognising the object as "*one* integral thing" and then, through analysis, as "an organised composite structure, a *thing in fact*," he says that the mind makes "the only logical possible synthesis," discovering "that it is *that* thing which it is" (218). This is the moment Stephen calls epiphany, when the soul of the object, "its whatness, leaps to us from the vestment of its appearance" and seems "radiant." Ostensibly, Stephen is reinterpreting Aquinas's *claritas* as *quidditas,* but we could easily replace both terms with the noumenon, which shines forth from the vestments of its phenomenal appearance. On this reading, Stephen's third phase amounts to a revelation of the noumenal object, but of course this is unequivocally barred in Kant's doctrine, which may help to explain why Stephen is forced to concede that the Ballast Office clock "has not epiphanised yet."

If Kant's proscription is taken as final, then perhaps there is nothing transcendental about the theory after all, but Stephen's "yet" expresses a certain hope, one that the reader is invited to share, at least to the extent that Stephen's aesthetics are framed as a revelation of truth, and not just any truth, but the truth of their own textual production – that is, the aesthetics of *Stephen Hero.* If we search for a transcendental signifier to unlock the meaning of the novel, then we will be as frustrated as Stephen is by the failure of the clock to epiphanise, but there is another sense in which both Stephen's aesthetics and Joyce's text are transcendental. Again this quality comes from Kant, because the revelation of the immanent truth of our own minds through the categories is central to Kant's transcendental idealism, and this awakening of the pure ideas of reason produces a sublime moment which can be regarded as a subjective epiphany, for Stephen and/or the reader.

Nowhere is this more evident than in Kant's "Analytic of the Sublime," which Derrida convincingly places as the centre of the *Critique of Judgement* (Derrida, *The Truth in Painting* 37-82). As is well known, Kant follows Burke in distinguishing between the beautiful and the sublime. For Kant,

> [t]he beautiful in nature is a question of the form of an object, and this consists in limitation, whereas the sublime is to be found in an object even devoid of form, so far as it immediately involves, or else by its presence provokes, a representation of *limitlessness,* yet with a super-added thought of its totality. (*CJ* 245)

The first thing to note here is that although beauty is a formal quality, consisting in limitation, the sublime is not necessarily formless: a more literal translation of "*das Erhabene ist dagegen auch an einem formlosen Gegenstande zu finden*" is "the sublime can *also* be found in a formless object" (see Pillow 69). Hence, although the sublime is frequently found in objects which appear formless (e.g., a storm, a vast mountain range, the starry heavens), it also refers to objects which are too large to perceive in their totality. When confronted by objects such as these, "our imagination, even in its greatest effort to do what is demanded of it and comprehend a given object in a whole of intuition (and thereby to exhibit the idea of reason), proves its own limits and inadequacy, and yet at the same time proves [. . .] itself adequate to that Idea" (*CJ* 257). In other words, although the imagination is unable to unify vast or complex manifolds of intuition, revealing our finite capacities, this same inadequacy reveals the pure idea of totality supplied by the understanding. This applies most obviously to the "mathematical sublime" (248-50), where the mind submits vast or formless objects to the idea of totality. Since space and past time are infinite, Kant reasons, this totality "does not even exempt the infinite," and our "ability even to think the given infinite without contradiction, is something that requires the presence in the human mind of something supersensible" (254).

Kant argues that nature "is sublime in such of its phenomena as in their intuition convey the idea of their infinity," and these phenomena reveal not only our ideas of totality and the infinite, but also our own freedom, because in the "dynamical sublime" (260-64), when we are confronted by overwhelming forces of nature (hurricanes, volcanic eruptions, tempests, and so on), we first cower in fear and then, provided we are at a safe distance, recognise "the soul's fortitude," a "power to resist [. . .] which gives us the courage to believe that we could be a match for nature's seeming omnipotence" (261). Thus, the dynamical sublime reveals the transcendental concept of freedom (211), just as the mathematical sublime reveals the transcendental concepts of totality, unity and the infinite.

While Kant's examples of the sublime are typical of eighteenth-century aesthetics – cliffs, thunder, lightning, stormy seas, the Milky Way, and so on – suggesting vast, powerful, or formless natural phenomena, there is nothing to prevent smaller objects, even elegant and well-formed objects, including works of art, from being sublime. This is because, in addition to the mind's regress to infinity in the mathematical sublime, Kant argues that "[t]he power of imagination is limited by a maximum of comprehension which it cannot exceed" (Pillow 74). This limitation applies not only to phenomena of great magnitude, but also to our inability to comprehend all the parts of a sufficiently complex object as a whole: "Imagination runs into difficulty in trying to comprehend an object as a unity [. . .] whenever it faces something vast, elaborate, or *complex* enough to overwhelm its powers" (*ibid.*). That this complexity applies not only to physical structures, but also to the ideas of reason is evident from the fact that Kant links judgements of the mathematical sublime to the ideas of God, freedom, immortality, eternity, and even to "aesthetic ideas" which "evoke much thought, yet without the possibility of any definite thought whatever [. . .] and which language, consequently, can never fully capture or render completely intelligible," such as "death, envy and all vices, as also love, fame, and the like" (*CJ* 314). These examples, empirical but "transgressing the limits of experience" (*ibid.*), just as their concepts defy the bounds of language, indicate that sublime reflection, as Kirk Pillow calls it, is also to be found in literary texts.

The Transcendental Language of the Epiphanies

I am not suggesting that there is a direct link between Stephen's aesthetics and Kant's, but the similarities between them are illuminating, both for the light they shed on Stephen's theory, and the implications they have for Joyce's aesthetics. With regard to the former, the close parallels between Stephen's phases of integrity and symmetry and Kant's syntheses of apprehension and reproduction suggest a comparison between Stephen's frustrated longing for a transcendental experience in the mystical unity of subject and object and Kant's proscription against the recognition of the noumenal. In the *Critique of Pure Reason*, Kant argues that these syntheses, which are themselves transcendental faculties, lead us to the "transcendental apperception" of "the original and necessary consciousness of the identity of oneself" (A107-08), and in the same way Stephen's aesthetics can be read as part of his quest to discover his own identity. Of course, Stephen never has his epiphany; *Stephen Hero* is incomplete, and all Dedalus discovers in *Portrait* is that his identity is in flux: "I was someone else then. . . I was not myself as I am now, as I had to become" (261). As the last phrase suggests, though, Stephen's search for identity is a search to understand the destiny he sees written in his own name, which he scrutinises repeatedly (5, 184-86, 276, etc.). Stephen seems to believe that his mythico-biblical name can answer his originary question, "where was he?" (185), providing a transcendental apperception of the self before and beyond experience. But instead, the "perpetual weaving and unweaving" of the self (Pater 236; cf. *Ulysses* 9.376-81) makes Stephen Dedalus the cause of sublime reflection, like one of Kant's "aesthetic ideas" which language can never fully capture. Yet it is not only proper names that occasion this search for original meaning: from the beginning of the novel, Stephen's reflections on language ("belt," "suck," "kiss," etc.) are transcendental, and even as he formulates his aesthetics, Stephen, like Kant, is apt to meditate on the meaning of words like "love," "death" and "spirit."[11]

Thus, Stephen's search for the meaning of aesthetic ideas is none other than the search for the transcendental signifier, a search which is mirrored each time the reader seeks a key to unlock Stephen's aesthetics and complete the analysis of the text. Naturally, the transcendental signifier is no more forthcoming than the noumenal object Stephen seeks; from a deconstructivist perspective, a full analysis of Stephen's theory, like any of Joyce's epiphanies, or indeed any text, is necessarily unattainable. But it is just here that Joyce's aesthetics depart from Kant's, because in Kant's doctrine, even a system of infinite play and deferral offers the promise of unity in its totality, whereas for Derrida,

> totalisation no longer has any meaning, . . . not because the infiniteness of a field cannot be covered by a finite glance or a finite discourse, but because the nature of the field – that is, language and a finite language – excludes totalisation. This field is in effect that of *play*, that is to say, a field of infinite substitutions only because it is finite. . . [I]nstead of being too large, there is something missing from it: a center which arrests and grounds the play of substitutions. (*Writing and Difference* 289)

This would seem to imply that language is not amenable to the mathematical sublime, but Derrida's absent "center which arrests and grounds

---

[11] "–Love, said Stephen, is a name, if you like, for something inexpressible . . . but no, I won't admit that . . ." (*SH* 180; cf. P 261). Isabel's death, based on Epiphany 19, provides the principal occasion for Daedalus to "contemplate the fact of death" (173) in *Stephen Hero*, but compare *Portrait*, where death is a portal "into the unknown and the unseen" (123). On the other hand, in Epiphany 20 and *Exiles* (23), death, not *amor matris*, is the only certainty, and Hugh Kenner, for one, guessed that "death" was the "word known to all men" long before Gabler's corrected edition restored it as "love" (see Kimball). Stephen's reflections on "spirit" are more complex still, and they go to the core of his theory of epiphany as "a sudden spiritual manifestation" in which epiphany occurs when "a spiritual eye" adjusts its vision to "[t]he soul of the commonest object" (216-18). Interestingly, for Kant, spirit "signifies the animating principle in the mind," which is "nothing else than the faculty of presenting *aesethetic ideas*" (*CJ* 313-14).

the play of substitutions" sounds suspiciously like a transcendental idea, one of those regulative ideas of reason Kant postulates as the *a priori* grounds of all experience.[12] And this conjunction of Kant's analytic of the sublime with Derrida's notion of play helps to explain how even texts as complex and indeterminate as *Finnegans Wake* can, at times, inspire a feeling of the sublime. The source of this sublimity is language itself, in its infinite play of *différance*, and Joyce's genius consists in his ability to bring so many of these meanings into play, and so fully, that he gives us a glimpse of their totality, even as his texts open onto the void of infinite deferral.

Does this make Joyce's aesthetics transcendental? Perhaps it does, for his genius is a thoroughly Kantian "genius," filled with that "spirit" or "animating principle in the mind" which for Kant is "nothing else than the faculty of presenting aesthetic ideas" (*CJ* 313-14). An aesthetic idea, we recall, "evokes much thought, yet without the possibility of any definite thought whatever . . . and which language, consequently, can never quite fully capture or render completely intelligible." But Kant concludes that it is "in the poetic art that the faculty of aesthetic ideas can show itself to full advantage" (*CJ* 314), because great poets, like Wordsworth and Shelley, awaken a sense of the sublime through their animating spirit, and it is just this that Joyce gives us in his transcendental aesthetics.

---

12 As Lyotard explains in *Lessons on the Analytic of the Sublime,* "[w]hat is conceived in the transcendent concept exceeds all sensible intuition and escapes all means of proof" (211). The same could be said of Derrida's notions of play, supplementarity, *différance,* etc.

References

Abrams, Meyer Howard. *Natural Supernaturalism: Tradition and Revolution in Romantic Literature*. London: Oxford University Press, 1971.

Aubert, Jacques. *The Aesthetics of James Joyce*. Baltimore: Johns Hopkins University Press, 1992.

Beja, Morris. *Epiphany in the Modern Novel*. Seattle: University of Washington Press, 1971.

Bentley, Gerald Eades. *Blake Records*. 2nd ed. New Haven: Yale University Press, 2004.

Caufield, James Walter. "The Word as Will and Idea: Dedalean Aesthetics and the Influence of Schopenhauer." *James Joyce Quarterly* 35 (1998): 695-714.

Coleridge, Samuel Taylor. *The Collected Works of Samuel Taylor Coleridge*. 12 vols. Vol. 12: *Marginalia*. London: Routledge and Kegan Paul, 1992.

Derrida, Jacques. *The Truth in Painting*. Trans. Geoff Bennington and Ian McLeod. Chicago: University of Chicago Press, 1987.

——. *Writing and Difference*. Trans. A. Bass. Chicago: University of Chicago Press, 1978.

Ellmann, Richard. *James Joyce*. New York: Oxford University Press, 1959.

Joyce, James. *A Portrait of the Artist as a Young Man*. London: Penguin Books, 2000.

——. "Commonplace Notebook." National Library of Ireland MS 36,639/2/A. 18.

——. *Dubliners*. London: Penguin Books, 2000.

——. *Exiles: A Play in Three Acts*. New York: Viking Press, 1951.

——. *Selected Letters of James Joyce*. Ed. Richard Ellmann. New York: Viking Press, 1975.

——. *Stephen Hero: Part of the First Draft of* A Portrait of the Artist as a Young Man. Rev. ed. London: Jonathan Cape, 1975.

——. *Ulysses: The Corrected Text*. New York: Random House, 1986.

Joyce, Stanislaus. *My Brother's Keeper. James Joyce's Early Years*. New York: Viking Press, 1958.

——. *The Complete Dublin Diary of Stanislaus Joyce*. Ithaca: Cornell University Press, 1971.

Kant, Immanuel. *Critique of Pure Reason*. Trans. and ed. Paul Guyer and Allen W. Wood. Cambridge: Cambridge University Press, 1997.

——. *Critique of Judgement*. Trans. James Creed Meredith. Oxford: Oxford University Press, 2007.

Kenner, Hugh. *Joyce's Voices*. London: Faber and Faber, 1978.

Kimball, Jean. "Love and Death in *Ulysses*: 'Word Known to All Men.'" *James Joyce Quarterly* 24.2 (1987): 143-160.

Langbaum, Robert. "The Epiphanic Mode in Wordsworth and Modern Literature." *New Literary History* 14.2 (1983): 335–358.

Lyotard, Jean-François. *Lessons on the Analytic of the Sublime.* Trans. Elizabeth Rottenberg. Stanford: Stanford University Press, 1994.

Nichols, Ashton. *The Poetics of Epiphany: Nineteenth-Century Origins of the Modern Literary Moment.* Tuscaloosa: University of Alabama Press, 1987.

O'Rourke, Fran. "Joyce's Early Aesthetic." *Journal of Modern Literature* 34.2 (2011): 97–120.

Pater, Walter. *The Renaissance: Studies in Art and Poetry.* London: Macmillan, 1917.

Pillow, Kirk. *Sublime Understanding: Aesthetic Reflection in Kant and Hegel.* Cambridge: The MIT Press, 2000.

Scholes, Robert. *The Workshop of Daedalus.* Evanston: Northwestern University Press, 1965.

—— and Marlena G. Corcoran. "The Aesthetic Theory and the Critical Writings." In *A Companion to Joyce Studies.* Ed. Zack Bowen and James F. Carens. Westport: Greenwood, 1984. 689-705.

Shelley, Percy Bysshe. *Shelley's Poetry and Prose: Authoritative Texts, Criticism.* 2nd ed. New York: W.W. Norton, 2002.

Tigges, Wim. *Moments of Moment: Aspects of the Literary Epiphany.* Amsterdam: Rodopi, 1999.

Wildi, Max. "Wordsworth and the Simplon Pass." *English Studies* 40 (1959): 224–32.

Wordsworth, William. *Lyrical Ballads.* London: Methuen, 1986.

——. *Poetical Works.* Ed. Thomas Hutchinson, rev. Ernest de Selincourt. Oxford: Oxford University Press, 1990.

——. *The Prelude* (1805). Ed. Ernest de Selincourt. 2nd ed. Oxford: Oxford University Press, 1959.

——. *The Prose Works of William Wordsworth.* Ed. Warwick Jack Burgoyne Owen and Jane Worthington Smyser. Oxford: Clarendon Press, 1974.

Wu, Duncan. *Wordsworth's Reading 1800-1815.* Cambridge: Cambridge University Press, 1995.

Awe, Terror and Mathematics in Don DeLillo's *Ratner's Star*

Francesca de Lucia

This article explores the role played by emotions, particularly those related to awe and fear, in Don DeLillo's *Ratner's Star* (1976), a novel focusing on scientific research whose protagonist, Billy Twillig, is a teenage mathematical genius. Following Billy's adventures in a research centre peopled by grotesque characters, *Ratner's Star* bears the influence both of Lewis Carroll's Alice books and of E. T. Bell's popular history of mathematics *Men of Mathematics*. My essay deals first of all with how DeLillo represents the process of creative release brought forth by scientific discovery, rendering it in terms of intuition and almost mystical ineffability. Subsequently, both positive and negative emotions associated with mathematics are analyzed using critical tools drawn from the fields of psychology and philosophy. These suggest that awe is an intrinsically ambivalent emotion, something which emerges in DeLillo's descriptions of attitudes towards mathematics. It can also be useful to consider DeLillo's representation of mathematical research within conceptions of the sublime based on Kant and Burke. The article concludes with an analysis of the climactic final scene of the novel, which contrasts apocalyptic views of the "death of science" with a less rigid, and ultimately redemptive perspective which is open to error, correction and change.

Introduction

The aim of this article is to analyze the role played by emotions, in particular those related to awe and fear, in Don DeLillo's *Ratner's Star* (1976), a novel focusing on mathematics. I will draw on psychology and

Emotion, Affect, Sentiment: The Language and Aesthetics of Feeling. SPELL: Swiss Papers in English Language and Literature 30. Ed. Andreas Langlotz and Agnieszka Soltysik Monnet. Tübingen: Narr, 2014. 163-176.

philosophy in order to illustrate these aspects, borrowing in particular from Robert Plutchik's theory of emotions, Mary-Jane Rubenstein's analyses of awe, as well as Kantian notions of the sublime. Two recurring and interrelated motifs of DeLillo's work are a sense of often undefined threat, at times associated with conspiracies and generalized paranoia, as well as a sense of almost religious awe. These elements appear for instance most visibly in *The Names* (1982), where the threatening and primitive backdrop of the novel is strongly connected to DeLillo's interest in forms of archaic religious traditions, be they Christian Orthodox procession or the Islamic pilgrimage to the Mecca. Somewhat similarly, *Underworld* (1997) interweaves a sense of paranoia coming from various sources with an examination of popular immigrant-derived Catholicism in the Bronx, which towards the end of the narrative seems to lead to actual miracles in a context of desperate squalor. More generally, DeLillo's work is informed by a kind of metaphoric mystical mode focused on communal experiences of transcendence. Thus, experiences of collective exaltation which have a redemptive quality, such as the protagonist's visit to the Parthenon in the final part of *The Names*, incarnate a sense of religious "mystery" and contrast with the more threatening mass gatherings of the Unification Church in *Mao II* (1991) or the Nazi parades described in *White Noise* (1984).

These motifs appear in a partially different form in one of DeLillo's little known early works, the 1976 novel *Ratner's Star*. It follows the adventures of Billy Twillig, a Bronx-born fourteen-year old mathematical genius, in a research centre peopled by bizarre and surreal characters, often afflicted by grotesque physical deformities. The plot focuses loosely on the scientists' attempts to decipher a message which is assumed to originate from the "Ratnerians," the alien inhabitants of a planet of the titular Ratner's star. The message turns out to come from the earth's past, though, and much of the tension between characters towards the end of the novel derives from the reasons for deciphering the message. This conflict between scientists with different views becomes a way to represent metaphorically some of the major mathematical debates of the twentieth century.

The novel also functions as a *bildungsroman*, as throughout the narrative, Billy becomes more self-confident and mature. Indeed, Billy is far from the stereotypical image of the "child genius," having been a Bronx street urchin. He also displays several standard teenage attitudes, such as a prurient sexual attitude towards women and a tendency to withdraw and sulk after he is bullied by adults. These aspects of his personality become less evident in the latter part of the novel, suggesting Billy's growth and eventual entrance into adulthood.

The text is divided in two parts, entitled *Adventures* and *Reflections*, something that suggests, along with the presence of a child protagonist endowed with a sensible and straightforward attitude, the influence of Lewis Carroll's Alice books. Carroll's legacy is also important because of the centrality of science in the novel, including to a large extent logical controversies. The second text that plays an important role in *Ratner's Star* is E. T. Bell's *Men of Mathematics*, a popular history of mathematics that was first published in 1937 and which remains widespread. Indeed, "Adventures" follows twelve out of twenty-nine chapters of *Men of Mathematics* from the origins of the discipline in Babylonian times until the beginning of the twentieth century. The structure that DeLillo thus gives to the novel allows him to elaborate, as we shall see, a reflection on different attitudes towards scientific discourse, and in particular, mathematics, which is not, as could be expected, simply limited to the rational sphere but also rife with sometimes violent emotions, both positive and negative ones.

Mathematical intuition: between ineffability and expression

Paul Maltby observes the importance of "visionary moments" in De-Lillo's fiction and points out the "visionary power" of language. This aspect is evident in DeLillo's representations of the process of mathematical discovery, a visionary moment being "a flash of insight or sudden revelation which critically raises the level of spiritual self-awareness of a character" (Maltby 258). On one occasion, Billy is asked to "tell about mathematics," to which he replies laconically, "what's to tell?", thus implying an aspect of ineffability of the discipline (323). Mathematics is seen as belonging to the sphere of the sacred, as an awe-inspiring "language inviolate" (176). At the same time, the culmination of mathematical research means being able to articulate verbally an intuition which is at first almost unutterable:

> The intuition of mathematical order occupied the deeper reaches of cognitive possibility, too old and indistinct for tracing, predating even the individual scrapings of logic and language[. . .]. [Billy] was puzzled by the lack of an adequate vocabulary for mathematical invention, by his inability to understand what made his mathematics happen [. . .]. Thus the simple answer surfaced, deprived at first of linguistic silvering. In the seconds that followed *he knew it in words*. (239, italics added).

This passage suggests the struggle against terrifying forms of "inarticulateness" that haunt the novel, namely with the presence, in Billy's Bronx reminiscences, of a demented woman known as the "scream lady" who shrieks meaningless words. The idea of progress in research as a sort of illumination that gives clarity to previously unformulated mental concepts has indeed been described by mathematicians, as shown in French mathematician Cédric Villani's memoir *Théorème Vivant*:

> L'illumination survint et je *savais* [original emphasis] comment il fallait corriger la démonstration [. . .]. Et ce matin du 9 avril 2009, c'est une nouvelle petite illumination qui a frappé à la porte de mon cerveau pour tout éclairer. Dommage, les lecteurs de l'article ne se rendront sans doute pas compte de cette euphorie, l'illumination sera noyée dans la technique. . . (155)

> [The illumination arrived and I *knew* how to correct the demonstration [. . .]. On this morning of 9April 2009, a new little illumination knocked at the door of my brain to light everything. What a shame that the readers of the article certainly won't be aware of this euphoria, the illumination will be drowned in technics. . .] (my translation)

Like DeLillo in *Ratner's Star*, Villani describes scientific discovery as a form of revelation of the unknown, which can be appropriated and verbalized through a form of enlightenment. In this perspective, mathematics is seen as an incredibly complex language. As pointed out by DeLillo in an interview:

> Aside from everything else, pure mathematics is a kind of secret knowledge. It's carried on almost totally outside the main current of thought. It's a language almost no one speaks [. . .]. This purest of sciences brings out a religious feeling in people.   (qtd. in LeClair 112)

As such, the religious feeling is exemplified in an extreme form by the character of the logician Edna Lown:

> In this hole in the ground Edna knew she lacked nothing, wanted nothing, could easily dismiss all past associations and all prior honours. She lived in the grip of scientific rapture [. . .]. Ambition, love, friendship, the pleasures of giving up and of winning away, the comfort of professional acceptance, the soul's snug glow at the failure of others [. . .] were so much dead air compared with this simple and total absorption, *holism* [original emphasis], a state of unqualified being. (329)

This passage suggests an almost monastic abandonment of the world, the mystical element being reinforced by the use of the term "rapture," alluding to what DeLillo has called the "religious feeling" brought forth by pure science. The notion of rapture is obviously connected to that of awe, which I will now examine using tools derived both from the fields of psychology and philosophy.

Awe, terror and mathematics

In order to define awe as an emotion it useful to borrow from the work of psychologist Robert Plutchik. Plutchik created a scheme known as the wheel of emotions, similar to a colour wheel, to describe how emotions interact with one another.[1] Eight primary emotions constitute the central part of the wheel; they subsequently become attenuated, as shown by the colours becoming lighter: "it is necessary to conceive of the primary emotions as hues which may vary in degree [of] intensity [. . . and are] arrangeable around an emotion-circle similar to a colour-wheel" (109). Amazement and terror are primary emotions which, in their lessened forms, become surprise and fear. When two emotions are combined, they form an emotion compound or dyad: awe is a combination of surprise and fear.

This suggests the intrinsic ambivalence of awe as an emotion. In DeLillo's novel, mathematics is associated not only with the release of creative force in processes of scientific discovery, but also with negative, and sometimes violently paralyzing feelings. In her philosophical exploration of the concepts of wonder and awe, *Strange Wonder*, Mary-Jane Rubenstein develops concepts analogous to Plutchik's representation of awe in the wheel of emotions. She points out that "wonder [. . .] is inherently ambivalent. [It is] the coincidence of marvel and dread, amazement and terror" (29). Rubenstein also alludes to the internalization of notions of awe within Western culture. She refers to the doctrine of "shock and awe" within international policies carried out by the United States, for instance in the context of the second Iraq war. The objective of these policies was to overwhelm the enemy psychologically and create a sense of vulnerability through acts such as extensive damage to infrastructure and a general weakening of society, thus achieving "the military imposition of wonder" (188). "Shock and awe" is meant to

---

[1] Plutchik's wheel of emotions can be viewed here: http://en.wikipedia.org/wiki/-File:Plutchik-wheel.svg

produce an effect similar to that of the bombs over Hiroshima and Nagasaki, without the equivalent physical damage. The association with nuclear weaponry is relevant since, always according to Rubenstein, it elicits feelings almost akin to religious awe, as suggested by the well-known episode of Robert Oppenheimer's quoting of the Hindu holy book Bhagavad Gita while witnessing a test atomic explosion in July 1945: "I have become Death, the destroyer of worlds," thus intermingling the words attributed to a deity (the god Vishnu turning into Shiva) with a sense of terrified awe associated with a scientific discovery whose destructive potential would soon be put into practice. It may be observed that Field Experiment n.1, the mysterious and remote centre to which Billy is flown at the beginning of the novel, resembles Los Alamos, the main location of the notorious Manhattan Project, where the atomic bombs used in the Second World War were produced. Indeed, Stanislaw M. Ulam's memoir *Adventures of a Mathematician* conveys the same sense of alienation and removal from ordinary society in its description of Ulam's arrival to Los Alamos that can be found in the opening of *Ratner's Star*. In both cases, the atmosphere of the place is marked by a surfeit of intellectual resources and fervour, which, however, in DeLillo's case assumes a caricatured dimension. These analogies may suggest that, while *Ratner's Star* eschews the reflections on American history and society that appear in DeLillo's later, more realistic works, it also echoes some of his preoccupation on generalized (possibly nuclear) menaces and overarching conspiratorial networks.

More generally, Rubenstein also points out the connection between the notions of wonder and awe and those of terror and dread, alluding for instance to the concept in Biblical Hebrew of *yrah*, that is "that particular combination of awe, dread and reverence proper to those who have witnessed the signs, wonders and portents of God's work into the world" (9-10). Thus she explains the presence of dread, or even terror, in awe. Terror appears in different ways in relation to mathematics in *Ratner's Star*: in one of the most mundane ways, it is the fear and disgust for mathematics inspired by high school reminiscences, as shown by the following dialogue between Ermintrude and Billy:

"The very word strikes fear in my heart."
"Mathematics?"
"It goes back to early schooling. The muffled terror of those gray mornings, getting out of bed and going to school and opening a mathematics textbook with its strange language and letters for numbers and theorems to memorize. I didn't mind any other subject. But maths struck terror. (239)

Once again, mathematics is perceived as a secret language. The ineffable aspect of this science that we have already seen reappears in a different, much darker key as a deep and fear-inducing loneliness. It is shown thus in Billy's reflections:

> There was no way out once he was in, no genuine rest, no one to talk to who was able to understand the complexity (simplicity) of the problem or the approaches to a tentative solution. There came a time in every prolonged effort when he had a moment of near panic or "terror in a lonely place." (116-17)

The reference to panic in its etymological sense as a condition of deep unease experienced both by animals and humans in the presence of Pan, the Greek god of nature, anticipates genuine forms of terror appearing in relation to rigid views of science which do not allow the process of creative release mentioned above. Rather, scientific inflexibility generates situations of destructive and self-destructive panic. However, in *Ratner's Star*, the sense of apocalyptic threat comes from an apparently harmless event, a solar eclipse which could not be foreseen and thus generates panic, bringing some characters to question the validity of science altogether.

The second part of the novel, "Reflections," which has fewer and more realistic characters, creates an opposition between figures who are completely shattered by the failure of their scientific certainties and those who manage to retain a rational and serene attitude. Examples of the former attitude are foreshadowed early on by the character of Henrik Endor, a brilliant mathematician who has gone to live in a hole in the ground from which he refuses to come out (Endor is a representation of Isaac Newton, who at one point of his life suffered a breakdown). Images of holes, including structures resembling black holes called "moholes," serve as metaphors of states of despairing anguish. Once again, this motif shifts from the mundane, represented by the description of the New York subway early on, to the eerie and terrifying. Billy has a disturbing encounter with Endor, who is described as a great scientist but who presently has been reduced to an animal-like condition, living in a hole (which includes a second hidden hole), constantly digging and eating larvae, behaving in a way that causes Billy to worry that Endor might actually eat him. Endor appears as a negative counterpart of Edna Lown, who also finds herself in a "hole in the ground," where she is, however, uplifted rather than debased. The symmetry is highlighted by the assonance between the names Endor and Edna and, while Edna is one of the few relatively realistic and sympathetic characters of

Ratner's Star, the possible symmetry suggests that, in the economy of the novel, science as complete abstraction from the world is potentially dangerous. Furthermore, these two characters represent symbolically the attitudes of awe and terror inspired by science.

On the other hand, the character of the Chinese American archaeologist Maurice Xavier Wu embodies a more pragmatic view of research and life. He not only displays scientific openness, calm and lack of arrogance but also a form of intellectual self-control even in desperate situations. This is shown in the scene where he manages to control his panic while risking being buried alive in a cave. The passages describing Wu trapped underground in complete darkness refer constantly to a sense of self-imposed calm and how he rationalizes his fear; once again, we can see here the struggle to define in clear language what appears unspeakable, in this case violent and potentially destructive emotions:

> The darkness was total and he was frozen to the stone. He tried to think beyond the level of unchecked hysteria [. . .]. He told himself to remain calm. [. . .] He tried to gauge his panic, to talk to it, to determine its contents. Again he told himself to proceed with utter calm. (390)

It is significant that Wu is also the character who asks Billy to "tell [him] about mathematics" (323). Thus this figure is marked by a constant endeavour to understand and decode what is unknown (as shown by his interest in decoding "secret languages" such as mathematics or Chinese ideograms). This trait extends to the way he behaves in terrifying circumstances. The Italian psychologist Nicola Ghezzani suggests that panic is a reaction to what is perceived as alien and unfamiliar: "il confine fra il noto e l'ignoto, al di qua della porta del panico" ["the border between the known and the unknown, within the threshold of panic"] (*Uscire dal Panico* 18; my translation). Hence Wu is able to deal with fear like he deals with other, less extreme forms of the unknown. Wu is also one of the scientists who is not overcome by mindless terror when the eclipse takes place.

Mathematics and the sublime

Mathematics, with the awe and terror it inspires, might be placed within the concept of the sublime as evoked by Immanuel Kant. It is interesting to observe that, in order to describe this notion in *The Critique of Judgment*, Kant draws a distinction between what he calls the mathematical and dynamic sublime. Instances of the former occur when the individual sees objects of great magnitude that exceed the powers of the senses. It is defined in terms that echo DeLillo's evocations of the ineffability of mathematic discovery:

> For here a feeling comes home to him of the inadequacy of his imagination for presenting the idea of a whole within which that imagination attains its maximum, and, in its fruitless efforts to extend this limit, recoils upon itself, but in so doing succumbs to an emotional delight.
> (*The Critique of Judgment* 60)

In this perspective, it is significant to observe that Endor's speech during his interaction with Billy appears to echo Kant's mathematical sublime, since Endor alludes to the infinite vastness of the universe, which the human senses cannot fully appreciate:

> Planets get torn out of orbit in that kind of density. Too many stars. Too much force and counterforce [. . .]. That's just our galaxy alone. There's no need for everything to be so spread out. Why is the universe so big? And why despite the billions and billions of stars and hundreds of millions of galaxies there is so much space leftover? (84-85)

Rather than experiencing "emotional delight," however, Endor appears overwhelmed by this sense of incommensurability, from which mathematical research offered temporary solace. The enormity of the universe is viewed as a form of fascination (hence the sense of "sublime"), but ultimately acts as a crushing force for Endor. His failure to decode a message assumed to be of extra-terrestrial origin, which he hoped would allow him to measure the universe, triggers Endor's breakdown and eventual dehumanization:

> I turned my panic to empty-field sources and black-body radiation. It was fascinating for a time. You could peer and count and measure and sigh. You could say: "Ahhhh, there it is, look and see." But the size of the universe began to depress me. (85)

Endor finds himself unable to accept and fully comprehend the true dimension of the universe and slides into depression, eventually entering a self-destructive process. Thus, the process of "emotional delight" eludes him. His predicament can be contrasted with that of the character of Dent.

Dent, who lives in a submarine, embodies a more positive view of the mathematical sublime, succeeding in experiencing "emotional delight." Like Endor, Dent used to be a highly acclaimed scientist who at one point found himself overwhelmed by the potentially infinite vastness of scientific research; nevertheless, instead of enduring an eventually devastating "recoiling" of the imagination, Dent has entered a deliberate process of personal and scientific withdrawal, represented by the gradually increasing depth at which his submarine sails. When he refuses to help Softly with the Logicon, he states that, while he still constantly produces ideas, he does so simply for private fulfilment. Hence, in contrast with Endor, Dent has accepted "the inadequacy of his imagination" and the "fruitless efforts to extend this limit." He has become conscious of the limits of the human intellect in the face of the immensity of knowledge in its entirety. This allows him to reach a state of contentment and to continue his work (albeit in a purely private form) rather than to sink into frustration and despair.

The second type of sublime as defined by Kant is the dynamic sublime. It can be encountered when observing natural phenomena that are potentially threatening from a position of security:

> Might is a power which is superior to great hindrances. It is termed dominion if it is also superior to the resistance of that which itself possesses might. Nature, considered in an aesthetic judgment as might that has no dominion over us, is dynamically sublime. If we are to estimate nature as dynamically sublime, it must be represented as a source of fear. (66)

Kant includes amongst examples of the dynamic sublime thunderstorms, erupting volcanoes, hurricanes and maritime storms. He also points out that, in this context, the sublime is not a trait of these natural phenomena, but that it exists within the human mind. *Ratner's Star* concludes with a natural occurrence which carries a sense of threat, even though it is ultimately harmless, that is, an unforeseen solar eclipse. While many characters react with terror, the narrative introduces the figure of a student, in what is presumably a third-world South Asian environment, who is associated with the notion of "mathematics coinciding with the will to live" (431). *Ratner's Star* thus implies that rationality, expressed here by mathematical research, overcomes illusions of the senses (the fear caused by the eclipse is unmotivated) in a fashion analogous to Kant's perception of the sublime.

At the same time, for DeLillo, situations of the sublime similar to Kant's are not deprived of aspects of menace and fear, and from this point of view are thus possibly closer to Edmund Burke's earlier definition of the sublime in *A Philosophical Enquiry*, which highlights more strongly the aspect of terror that is present in the experience of the sublime: "there is something so overruling in whatever inspires with awe, in all things which belong ever so remotely to terror, that nothing else can stand in their presence" (82). He also mentions, in relation to awe, the extreme natural phenomena that in the Bible are associated with divine apparitions, thus echoing the frightening "wonder" inspired by the eclipse. Yet, DeLillo's view of scientific research is not as gloomy and pessimistic as could seem at times, as shown by the final scene of the novel, which I will now turn to.

Conclusion: apocalypse now?

Billy's encounter with Endor is important in relation to the climactic conclusion of the narrative, where Billy's mentor Robert Softly makes a frenzied flight to Endor's hole after the eclipse, while the latter has died and has become a decomposing corpse. Endor's dehumanization is now complete, since he is reduced to "cities of vermiculate life" (437), being presently at one with the larvae he was in the habit of eating. Softly is also entering an increasingly animal-like state, possibly literally turning into a rabbit, as indicated by the "rudimentary and rude" (438) sounds he makes and the repeated references to his "crawling" and "scratching" and "clawing" of the dirt, which create a further analogy with Endor, who "digs and claws" the earth in the hole while discussing with Billy earlier in the novel. Both Endor and Softly adhere symbolically in this way to the perspective of the "death of science." DeLillo fictionalizes in his narrative the debate that took place from the end of the nineteenth century to the mid-1960s between mathematicians with a more pragmatic approach and logicians attempting to create a kind of universal basis for mathematical language which risked becoming completely self-serving. The latter perspective is represented by the Logicon, a project to create a universal language which, however, becomes purposeless.

At the end of the narrative Billy seems at first to be following Softly into the hole:

> On the surface another figure moved, this one on a white tricycle [. . .] madly pedalling, a boy a bit too large for his means of transportation [. . .]. He wore a jacket and a tie. A measured length of darkness passed over him as he neared the hole and found himself pedalling in the white area between the shadow bands that precede total eclipse [. . .]. Laughing as he was [. . .]. Particles bouncing around him, the reproductive dust of existence. (438)

Some critics indicate that in this scene Billy has also been overcome by the unforeseen eclipse: Joseph Dewey writes that Billy's bicycle ride is a "panicked (and absurd) flight [. . .] a gesture of surrender" and that "the boy-genius [is] flummoxed by the great eclipse" (63), while in his book *In the Loop* (1987) Thomas LeClair also assumes that Billy will join Endor and Softly (133). Yet the conclusion of *Ratner's Star* can also be interpreted differently. Indeed, Billy's laugher (which resembles Wu's when he manages to exit the cave) and the image of the "reproductive dust of existence" contrast starkly with the images of decomposition and dehumanization that precede it and imply that the character of Billy will be able provide a form of redemption, hinting at the survival rather than failure of science and adhering to a pragmatist view of science, rather than to the rigid view embodied by Softly and Endor. Furthermore, Billy's jacket and tie and his being too large for the tricycle (which is generally associated with small children) suggest that Billy has reached adulthood.

Thus *Ratner's Star* ultimately rejects a view of science where the unexpected or the possibility of error leads to states of destructive terror. It resembles more the position stated by the group of mathematicians working from the mid-thirties to the early 1980s under the collective pseudonym of N. Bourbaki:

> Nous croyons que la mathématique est destinée à survivre, et que l'on verra jamais les parties essentielles de ce majestueux édifice s'écrouler du fait d'une contradiction soudain manifestée; mais nous ne prétendons pas que cette opinion repose sur autre chose que de l'expérience. C'est peu, diront certains. Mais voilà vingt-cinq siècles que les mathématiciens ont l'habitude de corriger leurs erreurs et d'en voir leur science enrichie, non appauvrie, cela leur donne le droit d'envisager l'avenir avec sérénité.   (9)

> [We believe that mathematics is destined to survive, and that we shall never see the essential parts of this majestic edifice crumble because of the manifestation of a sudden contradiction; but we do not imagine that this opinion is based on anything else than experience. It's not enough, some will say. But it's twenty-five centuries that mathematicians are used to correcting their mistakes and seeing them enrich, rather than impoverish their science; this entitles them to view the future with serenity.] (my translation)

The struggle against inarticulateness takes various different forms in *Ratner's Star*: in the fear induced by the "scream lady" that has been mentioned before but more crucially and centrally, in the rejection of what is embodied by the Logicon, an attempt to create a totalizing "universal logical language" (95).

In the end, *Ratner's Star* suggests a redemptive view of science, highlighting the creative processes of mathematical research and suggesting the control of the possibly destructive negative emotions it sparks; ultimately the novel endorses a perspective where, as noted by the Italian mathematician Ennio de Giorgi: "il matematico ha l'intuizione e il lavoro per rendere l'intuizione comprensibile. Sogno e convivialità" (212) ["the mathematician has the intuition and the work to render an intuition comprehensible and communicable. Dream and conviviality."] (my translation). In this perspective, the mathematician possesses the capacity of making the dreamlike intuition accessible, thus creating a link to others rather than a process of isolation. This indeed is the dimension of "conviviality." In *Ratner's Star* the scientific process personified by the young Billy brings a sense of joyful hope that can overcome even contexts of irrational panic.

References

Bourbaki, N. *Eléments de Mathématiques: Théorie des Ensembles.* Paris: Herman, 1960.

Burke, Edmund. *A Philosophical Enquiry into the Origin of Our Ideas of the Sublime and Beautiful.* 1757. New York: Simon and Brown, 2013.

De Giorgi, Ennio. *Anche la Scienza ha Bisogno di Sognare.* Edited by Franco Bassani, Antonio Marino and Carlo Sbordone. Pisa: Edizioni Plus, 2001.

DeLillo, Don. *The Names.* 1982. New York: Vintage, 1989.

——. *Ratner's Star.* 1976. New York: Vintage, 1989.

——. *Underworld.* 1997. London: Picador, 1999.

——. *White Noise.* New York: Viking, 1984.

de Lucia, Francesca. "'Tell Me About Mathematics': The Representation of Science in Don DeLillo's *Ratner's Star.*" *Atti Accademia Pontaniana* 59 (2010): 159-167.

—— and Paolo de Lucia. "Un Romanzo sulla Matematica: *Ratner's Star* di Don DeLillo." *La Matematica nella Società e nella Cultura* 1 (2011): 433-41.

Dewey, Joseph. "Don DeLillo's Apocalyptic Satires." Ed. John N. Duvall. *The Cambridge Companion to Don DeLillo.* Cambridge: Cambridge University Press, 2008. 53-65.

Ghezzani, Nicola. *Uscire dal Panico: Ansia, Fobie, Attacchi di Panico. Nuove Strategie nella Gestione e la Cura.* Milan: Franco Angeli, 2000 (reprinted 2003).

Kant, Immanuel. *The Critique of Judgement.* Trans. James Creed Meredith. 1790. Radford, Virginia: Wilder, 2008.

LeClair, Thomas. *In the Loop: Don DeLillo and the Systems Novel.* Urbana and Chicago: Illinois University Press, 1987.

Maltby, Paul. "The Romantic Metaphysics of Don DeLillo." *Contemporary Literature* 37.2 (1996): 258-277.

Plutchik, Robert. *The Emotions.* Boston: University of America Press, 1991.

Rubenstein, Mary-Jane. *Strange Awe: The Closure of Metaphysics and the Opening of Awe.* New York: Columbia University Press, 2008.

Ulam, Stanislaw. *Adventures of a Mathematician.* 1966. Berkley: University of California Press, 1991.

Villani, Cédric. *Théorème Vivant.* Paris: Grasset, 2012.

Talk About Flipping Health Food – Swearing and Religious Oaths in Irish and British English

Patricia Ronan

This paper focuses on emotional expressions in Irish English in comparison with British English. More specifically, it examines the use of two categories of high-frequency expressives: religious oaths and expletives related to bodily functions. The data on which the investigation is based stems from the two relevant components of the *International Corpus of English*, ICE Ireland and ICE Great Britain and reveals strong differences in frequency and in the contexts of the use of both religious expressions and particularly of expletives of bodily function. It is argued that in the Irish data expressives like *God, Christ* and *Jesus* play a stronger role than in the British data because the cultural importance of religion is still stronger in Ireland than in England. Expletives based on bodily functions, especially *f*-based swearwords, are highly frequent in Irish English without having an obvious counterpart in British English. The higher frequency in Irish English is also paralleled by a larger pragmatic spread. The reason for the higher frequency in Irish English is explained as a marker of social bonding in Irish culture as compared with British culture.

1. Introduction

The division of speech acts into different subcategories largely goes back to the work of Austin and Searle.[1] Of Searle's five basic categories (Searle "A Classification of Illocutionary Acts"), *assertives, directives, commissives, declaratives* and *expressives*, the first three have received consider-

---

[1] The author would like to thank the anonymous reviewer for the helpful comments.

Emotion, Affect, Sentiment: The Language and Aesthetics of Feeling. SPELL: Swiss Papers in English Language and Literature 30. Ed. Andreas Langlotz and Agnieszka Soltysik Monnet. Tübingen: Narr, 2014. 177-196.

able attention, while the latter two are less well researched. There is a particular dearth of research on expressive speech acts (Guiraud, Longin, Lorini, Pesty and Rivière 1031). So far select categories of expressive speech acts have been investigated; for corpus linguistics these are especially expressions of thanks and of more general politeness (Taavitsainen and Jucker). Even more recently, Guiraud, Longin, Lorini, Pesty and Rivière have used an approach based on emotion theory and formal logic to systemize expressive speech acts. However this, or other formal approaches to expressive speech acts, do not seem to have been applied to corpus data yet.

During the last two decades the research interest in variational pragmatics and studies of the use of Irish English have been growing. The first piece of major work to date has been provided by Schneider and Barron, whose edited volume offers, partly contrastive, descriptions of directness as a feature of politeness. Further, Kallen discusses politeness strategies in general and observes that politeness strategies in Irish English emphasize group identity markers and conventional optimism, and that speakers of the variety tend to avoid assertiveness and directness (see also Farr and O'Keeffe 42). While scientific research is thus particularly interested in the polite and oblique way in which interaction takes place between speakers of Irish English, popular perception often notes that Irish English contains a lot of swearing. The aim of the current study is to investigate the use of two categories of expressives in Irish English: religious oaths and expletives based on bodily functions. More specifically the use of these expressive acts is quantified in comparison with British English to verify to what degree comparable corpora of Irish and British English offer evidence of potential differences in the use of these categories in the two varieties.[2] The findings help us to assess, firstly, to what extent different expressive speech acts are in evidence in the Irish English spoken categories under investigation, and secondly, how prominent swearing is in the corpus data in comparison to British English. The general background of speech acts and expressives is explained in section two. Section three introduces the data and methodology used in the study and section four presents and discusses the results obtained.

---

[2] The ICE Great Britain corpus was used while working as a contract lecturer for the Department of English at the University of Zurich.

2. Expressive Speech Acts, Swearing and Religious Oaths

A discussion of the status and function of expletives as well as of religious expressions would not be appropriate without providing some background on speech acts and research on swearing and religious oaths. Thus, after introducing speech act theory according to Searle, we will discuss existing research on contexts and functions of the use of expletives and religious oaths.

2.1. What are Expressive Speech Acts?

The study of speech acts in general has been highly influenced by Searle's work. He has proposed that while utterances often describe the world around us, they also have other functions (Searle, *Speech Acts*). Searle ("A Classification of Illocutionary Acts") therefore distinguishes five types of speech acts in detail. These are *representatives, directives, commissives, expressives* and *declaratives*. Representative speech acts are utterances in which the speaker's words mirror the world truthfully (Searle "A Classification of Illocutionary Acts" 10), for example:

1. There is a large elm tree in my front garden.

Second, there are directive speech acts, which can be either explicit or implicit, and lead the recipient to carry out a task, for instance:

2. Please shut the door.

Such directive speech acts can also be more implicit, for example uttering the statement *I'm parched* might lead the recipient to offer to put the kettle on for a cup of tea.

In the third category, commissive speech acts, we find a promise by a speaker to carry out a certain action:

3. I promise to give you a lift to the airport on Sunday morning.

The utterance of such a statement does not describe the world, but it makes the world fit the words (Searle, "A Classification of Illocutionary Acts" 11). Further, declarative speech acts are those which, if uttered by the right person under the right circumstances, create situations that fit the words (Searle, "A Classification of Illocutionary Acts" 13), for example:

4. I declare this bazaar open!

Expressive speech acts, in contrast to representatives, do not represent the world. Rather, they express the state of mind, the attitudes, and the feelings of the speaker (Searle, "A Classification of Illocutionary Acts" 12; see also Taavitsainen and Jucker 159) as in the following example:

5. Oh, I absolutely love marshmallows!

Expressive speech acts have been formalized in a model of formal logic by Guiraud, Longin, Lorini, Pesty and Rivière. The authors define expressive speech acts as public expressions of emotional states (1031). They discuss the expression of the emotions of joy and of sadness, of regret, of disappointment and of guilt (1035) and connect the expressive speech acts of delight, sadness, approval, disapproval, sorrow and sympathy (1036), as well as of rejoicing, thanks, regret, deploring, apologies, satisfaction, complimenting, expressing guilt, reproaching, accusations and protests (1037). The two particular types of expressive speech acts with which the present essay is concerned are expressions of deploring and religious oaths. As such, these speech acts are closely linked to the society the speakers live in, and variation can be found within and between different varieties of a language such as English.

Religious expressions, such as *Oh God*, are not mentioned as expressives by Guiraud, Longin, Lorini, Pesty and Rivière but intuitively we would say that of all the speech acts identified by Searle they are more likely to be expressive speech acts than to belong to any other of his categories. Further, there are expressions of deploring, particularly by what has been classified as taboo areas such as swearwords or bad language. Both religious expressions and swearwords – or expletives – are considered taboo language in a classification by Andersson and Trudgill (15). They endorse the categorization of taboo expressions into words concerned with bodily functions like sex and excretion, such as *fuck* and *shit*, into words concerned with religion, such as *God* and *Jesus*, and into animal comparisons, such as *bitch*. The use of these categories is influenced by what is considered a social taboo in a given culture (Andersson and Trudgill 59). The third category of taboo words, animal appellations, differs somewhat from the two former ones in that they are directed towards persons, e.g. *she's such a bitch*, whereas the former ones typically refer to a situation. As it is rather the impersonal use of swearing that interests us in this study, terms of personal abuse will not be considered here.

McEnery points out that different categories of swearwords can also be classified according to how likely they are to cause offence to other speakers of the language. According to this likelihood, McEnery (36) has classified swearwords along the five-item scale ranging from very mild (e.g. *bloody, damn, idiot, pig*), to mild (e.g. *christ* [sic], *cow, shit*), moderate (*arsehole, prick, whore*) strong (*fuck*) and very strong (*cunt*) swearwords. In the following we will particularly consider *fuck* and related items, as well as similar strong swearwords, which could fill the respective envelope of variation in both the British and Irish English corpora.

In considering these items in the two varieties of English under discussion, we will be working on the premise voiced by Wierzbicka that if we can identify common linguistic practices these can point to common ways of thinking: people can be understood best in terms of what they share, such as semantic and conceptual universals (1169-1170). By this token, if linguistic expressions differ, this may point to different attitudes to religious social experiences or different societal taboos.

2.2. Expletives and Religious Oaths

2.2.1. Swearing

Typically swearing is considered to be particularly frequent in youth language, but the use of swearwords has also been observed for older people. Swearwords can also be used where speakers want to portray themselves as youthful and cool (Aitchinson 23) or where the use of such language serves to create feelings of shared community. This use of words that are traditionally called swearwords as in-group markers has been discussed particularly by Wierzbicka, who investigates the use and the semantics of the word *bloody* in Australian English. Wierzbicka notes that the concept of *mate(ship)* is particularly important in Australian society. She also notes that the word *bloody* is ubiquitous in Australian English. In addition to being used as a strong swearword, it can also be used as an intensifier and a mild swearword in a number of different situational contexts (1172-1173). She observes that the adjective has become gentrified by having been used in learned and in political contexts as a symbol of a mix of educated and rough styles in Australia referred to as *larrikin style*. Wierzbicka finds that the use of *bloody* in Australian

English thus functions to show allegiance to the society's cultural values (1175). These would presumably be based on a shared experience of the toughness necessary to colonize and survive in a rough, unwelcoming environment. At the same time, Wierzbicka stresses that the use of *bloody* is by no means accepted by all sections of society (1176). On the contrary, the fact that it is still frowned upon by some increases its attractiveness to others, who we might term the socially rebellious.

In spite of possibly still extant resentments, Wierzbicka (1175, 1177) finds *bloody* to be used significantly more frequently in Australian English than, for example, in American English, and that it plays a more important role in Australian English than in other varieties. It has made its way into genres such as parliamentary debates. As a sign of its positive connotations, it can even be found to collocate with positive expressions such as *bloody good*, leading Wierzbicka to conclude that where *bloody* collocates with nouns it is negatively connoted, but if used with other word classes such as adjectives it functions as an intensifier and can be taken as a sign of truth and sincerity (1181-1182, 1188). As a result, the use of the adjective has become a stereotype of Australian English, and a feature that has developed also in opposition to British culture. Moreover, having been semantically bleached from a swearword, it now expresses high emotionalism and should be considered not only in terms of politeness discourse but also in terms of cultural scripts (1206). Wierzbicka (1179-1180) observes, however, that *bloody* is increasingly being replaced by the still more intense *fuck*. As far as Australian English is concerned, it seems as if the traditional *bloody* is a less relevant cultural taboo for a society in which bodily matters are now widely and publicly discussed. Explicit sexual topics are likely to be still more shunned and thus a better basis for taboo words. As is the case with *bloody* in Australian English, such shared cultural values in other societies should also be observable in distinct linguistic usage patterns of relevant lexical items in discourse.

The expletive *fuck* and its related morphological forms have already been identified as a prominent swearword in Irish English (Murphy 90-91). In Murphy's 90,000 word corpus of male and female speech the only other observed expletives, *shit*, *piss* and the euphemism *feck*, are used to a considerably smaller degree. Murphy finds that the use of *fuck* and its morphological derivatives is significantly more frequent in male than in female data in her Irish English corpus (Murphy 93), which is in line with what has been observed for its use in British English (McEnery and Xiao, 235-268). Of the three age groups investigated, 20s, 40s and 70/80s, the age groups using it most frequently are speakers within the

20s age bracket, followed by speakers in the middle age bracket in their 40s. The most frequently used forms are *fucking*, followed by *fuck*, *fucked* and *fucker*, the collocations *fuck it*, *fuck sake*, *for fuck's sake*, *fuck that*, *fuck off* and *fuck all* also appear (Murphy 93-94). Similar to *bloody* in Australian English, Murphy identifies the use of *fuck* as an "amplifier," which can have negative connotations, but, like *bloody*, can also be used in collocation with positively connoted nouns, though this latter use is more rare (96-98). As Wierzbicka does for *bloody*, Murphy suggests the use of *fucking* to be an in-group marker and a sign of camaraderie, particularly of a younger generation. Particularly for the male language users, semantic bleaching of the expression has taken place to add intensity and dynamism to their discourse and to facilitate bonding by using taboo words which are still disregarded by mainstream culture (Murphy 100), particularly by older speakers who strongly identify with Catholic values (104). Research on both Irish English and Australian English thus suggests that the use of expletives is not necessarily only a phenomenon of uneducated speech, but that it can be used for bonding purposes, and is particularly done so by younger rather than older speakers. These observations concur with McEnery's findings for British English that speakers in the age group up to 25 use more swearing than older groups (McEnery 38), and that educated speakers of the upper middle class are in fact more likely to use strong expletives than are speakers of lower middle classes, who try to use what they consider more polite speech (43).

2.2.2. Religious Oaths

The second category of taboo language considered in this paper is the use of religious expressions. As addressed above, the use of religious expressions has been subsumed amongst linguistic taboo items (Andersson and Trudgill 15), and it has been argued by Stenström that particularly the taboo words used by females often come from this field. In research by Farr and Murphy it has been shown that these items are frequently found in Irish English. In order to determine whether religious expressions are more frequent in written or spoken English, Farr and Murphy (539-540) searched for the key words *Almighty*, *Christ*, *Damn*, *Devil*, *God*, *Hell*, *Holy*, *Jesus*, *Lord* and *Sacred* in one million word extracts from the spoken and the written component of the British National Corpus (BNC). They found that more instances of these are found in the spoken than in the written corpus texts. On the basis of spoken

Irish corpora (Limerick Corpus of Irish English and Limerick Belfast Corpus of Academic Spoken English), a spoken British corpus (Corpus of London Teenage English) and spoken American Corpora (Michigan Corpus of Academic Spoken English and Corpus of Spoken Professional American English) it was also determined that these items are considerably better represented in informal than in formal contexts (Farr and Murphy 541-543) and only about 10 percent of the overall tokens in fact refer to religious contexts. The types *God* and *Jesus* were found to be the best-represented with 785 and 462 tokens per one million words respectively in the Limerick Corpus of Irish English data. *God* collocates, amongst others, with appropriate religious expressions such as *oh my God, honest to God, thank God* or *God almighty* creating notions of honesty, help, hope and gratitude, and particularly in female speech it is used in contexts of surprise, annoyance, pity, emphasis and excitement (Farr and Murphy 543, 552), but its use is also observed to cause laughter and nervousness. Particularly high instances of *Oh my God* have been observed in female speech from the 20s age bracket, which the authors related to the popularity of this expression in the wake of the American TV series *Friends*.

Jesus and *Jesus Christ* are thought to be stronger expressions than *God* (Farr and Murphy 555) and found in contexts of excitement and may be used to intensify accounts (545), for younger female speakers it particularly expresses surprise (554). Overall, the use of religious expressions was observed to be higher for males than for females. For the female speakers it was highest for adult speakers of the oldest age group, 70/80 years of age, the 40s age group providing a middle ground and the 20s age group providing the lowest use (Farr and Murphy 547-551). Overall, younger speakers use religious expressions with higher frequencies in what might have been considered offensive uses by older speakers or in the past (558). Based on these findings we will assume that the level of religious references will correlate with the level of importance of religion in society, and that the comparison of religious expressions in the ICE corpora for Ireland and Great Britain will allow us to judge the relative importance of religious references in this data.

3. Data and Methodology

The current study is corpus-based and the data on which this study is based stems from ICE Great Britain and from ICE Ireland. The ICE-family of corpora spans a growing number of first and second language varieties of English throughout the world. All corpora contain approximately one million words from clearly specified domains in 500 files of about 2,000 words each. Throughout the corpora, 300 files are from spoken categories, the remaining 200 files are from written categories (Greenbaum). The language that is aimed for in the collection of the corpora is a standardized version of the local variety of English, expressly vernacular or basilectal varieties are not included. This, as well as the fact that similar categories from both formal and informal registers are present in each of the corpora, ensures maximum comparability of the different varieties of English, even though certain idiosyncrasies in each corpus can of course not be avoided. These similarities were used as a basis for the present research project. Common expletives and religious expressions found in the literature (Farr and Murphy, Murphy, McEnery) have been searched for in ICE GB and ICE IRE by using the online interface provided by corpus web-interface Corpus Navigator.[3]

4. Expletives and Religious Oaths in ICE Ireland and ICE Great Britain

As indicated in section three above, the two expressive categories investigated here are from the taboo expression areas of expletives and of religious expressions. It has been shown for varieties of English, both British (McEnery) and Australian (Wierzbicka) as well as indeed for Irish English (Murphy), that far from being used only to express anger, expressions belonging to the expletives category may also be used as in-group markers to increase bonding. Further, as Ireland is well known for being a religious country, religious expressives may also be considered to convey shared cultural values and should thus be found with some degree of frequency particularly in Irish English. In the following we will therefore compare the use of overtly religious expressions that have been found to be most frequent in the Limerick Corpus of Irish English, *Jesus, Christ* and *God* (Farr and Murphy 541) on the one hand, and the frequent expletives *bloody* and *fuck* on the other hand.

4.1. Religious Expressions in the ICE Corpora

In the following we will compare the uses of *God, Christ* and *Jesus* in the two corpora under investigation. A fourth possible appellative for God, *Lord*, has been left out of scrutiny as only a small number of its occur-

---

[3] http://es-corpnav.uzh.ch/

rences were used in this sense. The vast majority of attestations of *Lord* in both corpora stem from political and legal contexts and only very few examples with a religious context were observed in both corpora.

For the first item under investigation, *God,* a comparison of the roughly one million-word ICE Ireland and ICE Great Britain reveals strong similarities in use, but there are considerably higher numbers in ICE Ireland than in ICE Great Britain. In ICE Ireland, we find a total of 454 attestations of *God.* Most of the instances of *God,* 396, come from the spoken component, only 58 derive from written genres. There are four examples referring to Celtic deities, one example refers to other gods, the "Elephant God" (W1B-011:1:1), 59 examples stem from religious discourse. The majority of examples can thus be seen as invocations of God, either just as *God,* or *my God* or *oh my God,* but we also find clear utterances with religious senses, such as *God rest him* (S1A-004:1:48:A), *God love him* (S1A-051:1:72:E) or *God bless us* (S1A-023:1:83:B).

Searches in ICE Great Britain reveal 300 examples of references to *God* or *god(s).* Of these, 41 are in the context of religious discourse. In 33 examples, other deities are referred to, such as *Goddess* or *Sun God.* The remaining 168 instances can be seen as types of invocation, such as *Goodnight and God bless* (s2b-030:1:75:A), or the frequent *God, oh God* or *my God.* References to *God* are more frequent in spoken discourse (219 examples) than in written discourse (48 examples). Thus, the cultural importance of the reference to God is very similar in both British and Irish English, but invocative use of *God,* or *oh God* and *my God* is highly significantly higher in the Irish English corpus.[4]

Searches for the stem *Christ* reveal 38 true positives in ICE Ireland, the majority of which are religious references, such as:

6. <W2B-005:2:3> The four Sundays of Advent are days of preparation for the celebration of Christmas and Christ's coming into the world.

The remaining 9 instances are expressives. In the ICE Ireland corpus we find *Christ* being used both in agitation or exasperation, as in 7, and like an invocation as in 8 and 9:

7. <S1A-042$A> Shut up <S1A-042$B> *Jesus Christ* it's only a Kit Kat <S1A-042$C> It's not a giant Snicker, which you'll probably get in Angela's anyway.

---

[4] The p-value according to chi-square is <.0001.

8. < S1A-065$A> We'd never done this before. <S1A-065$C> Oh God. *Christ.* He crawled out of where <#> Out of that.

9. <S1A-065$B> (. . .) We thought the thing was going to go right off the edge <S1A-065$C> (. . .) Yeah, *Christ* (. . .) <S1A-065$B> <#> It's going so fast. And then you come down and you just go into a twist (. . .).

ICE Great Britain has 28 examples of *Christ.* Of those 28, 23 stem from religious discourse, 5 are expressive examples; the context suggests that all of these are examples of exasperation or agitation. The arguably most interesting example is the following:

10. <w1b-010:2:92> I'd have to exclude all the theological people because if I wasn't allowed *Christ* I'd certainly have a few questions for St. Peter and the Virgin Mary.

Here religious discourse is mixed with what seems an expressive indicting agitation rather than invocation of divine help. Farr and Murphy (556) classify *Christ* as a strong form, indicating shock, surprise and incredulity, and these semantics are visible here as well. *Christ* is further used in exasperation, but also an invocation and perhaps a plea for divine support.

Finally, ICE Ireland contains 89 examples of *Jesus,* 20 of which stem from religious discourse, and only 4 from written sources. The majority of the other examples can be considered expressives such as:

11. <S1A-066:1:184:C> *Jesus* don't eat me.
12. <S1A-067:1:51:C> *Jesus* I've no messages at all now so I haven't.

However, overtly religious contexts have not been found with this form, there is one example of *Sweet Jesus,* but the context *Sweet Jesus they weren't calling Lou good-looking* (S1A-003:1:220:C) is not at all religious.

Jesus is considered a stronger evocative than *God* by Farr and Murphy, expressing surprise and disbelief, and it may still be a taboo word for the oldest age group (Farr and Murphy 554-555). Interestingly, it is the only religious expressive which is explicitly used in the context of swearing in the corpus:

13. <S1A-011:1:63:B> We were like oh for fuck sake like *Jesus*
14. <S1A-051:1:178:A> She went to put her hand through it and he goes *Jesus* fuck's sake don't touch my hair
15. <W2F-004:1:164> I might have expected it, you worthless creeping *Jesus.*

If indeed *Jesus* is the strongest of the group of religious terms and still a taboo word for some parts of society, this may mean that it is explicitly selected in the context of swearing to increase the impact of the utterance.

In ICE Great Britain, we only find 28 instances of *Jesus*, from which two references to *Jesus College* should be deducted. 20 of the examples stem from religious discourse, leaving us with only 6 examples of expressives, five of which are from spoken language. All of these are either just single-word appellations or use *Oh Jesus*. On the basis of these few examples, no special pragmatic value can be described for the use of *Jesus* in ICE Great Britain.

An overview of the use of *God, Christ* and *Jesus* in ICE Ireland and ICE Great Britain is given in Table 1.

Table 1: Uses of *God, Christ* and *Jesus* in ICE Ireland and ICE Great Britain in raw values (and normalized per one million words in brackets).

Corpus	God	Christ	Jesus	Total
ICE Ireland	454/(430)[5]	36/(24)	89/(85)	582/(554)
ICE IRE excluding religious discourse	395/(374)	16/(15)	69/(66)	480/(457)
ICE GB	267/(249)[6]	30/(28)	26/(24)	323/(302)
ICE GB excluding religious discourse	226/(211)	10/(9)	6/(6)	242/(226)

These religious exclamations are used significantly more frequently in the spoken than in the written genres: of the 89 examples of *Jesus* only 4 (4.5 percent) stem from written corpus data, of the 454 examples of *God*, 58 (13 percent) are from the written components in ICE Ireland. In ICE GB, *God* appears more often in the less spontaneous written discourse, 48 out of the 267 attestations (18 percent), while *Jesus* is mostly a spoken appellation also in ICE GB, with only 4 of the 26 examples (15 percent) stemming from written data. Thus, as already noted for a different set of corpora by Farr and Murphy, in the ICE corpora the use of religious expressions is clearly mainly a feature of spoken language, except where religious discourse is concerned. Appellations to *God, Christ* and *Jesus* in non-religious contexts are considerably more frequent in

---

[5] Additionally there are four references to Celtic deities (Lug, Goibhniu, Cailleach Bhéara). Place names and references to godparents are not considered.

[6] Additionally there are 33 references to various deities from international pantheons or to godparents.

Irish than in British English. While this might indicate that there is a greater taboo associated with using the name of God in Britain than in Ireland, the already good attestation of the appellation in everyday contexts makes this unlikely. On the other hand it may also indicate that religion is a more central component of life in Ireland than in Britain and that therefore more invocations are based on expressives from the religious field. Further information on this issue could be gleaned from investigations of more varied corpora, and from investigating a larger set of religious expressions in the two corpora.

4.2. Expletives in ICE Ireland and ICE Great Britain

As noted in section 2.2.1 above, authors working on expletives in varieties of English have repeatedly stressed that such expressions can fulfil various functions. In the current study we want to examine two strong expletives that have been observed in a number of varieties of English, *bloody* and *fuck(ing)*. There seem to be few swearwords that have the same breadth of syntactic and pragmatic variation. Therefore we are restricting our approach to these two, plus the variants of *bloody*, *bleeding* and that of *fuck*, *feck*.

In ICE GB, the arguably most prominent swearword, *fuck* and its derivations, appear 14 times in total, 5 times in a rather linguistic style discussion:

16. <s1a 092:1:134:B> Can you say bo-*fucking* ring?

This discussion accounts for 5 of the 14 examples. In the other examples, the corresponding gerund is used like an adverb of quality three times: *I'm fucking weak* (s1a-052:2:110:a), *do some real fucking journalism then* (s1a-052:2:127:A) and *It's fucking yellow* (s1a-085:1:149:A). The negative entity is used as an intensifier in these cases. This use of a negatively perceived entity as an intensifier is a well-documented pattern cross-linguistically, and can also be observed in the use of the English adverb *terribly* (Jing-Schmidt).

Additionally, in the same conversation *fuck* is used twice in a semantically intransitive context with the particle *around*, in the sense of pottering about:

17. <s1a-074:5:336:A> I'm still *fucking around* sorting things out
18. <s1a-074:5:337:B> Well don't be *fucking around* sorting things out

Here we observe an interesting semantic shift from a taboo word denoting a specified action towards the unspecific description of a (perceivedly) unproductive action. Finally, *fuck off* is attested twice (s1a-052:2:94:B and s1a-052:2:129:A). And in the only attestation of the item in the written corpus, it is used in its literal sense (w2f-003:1:127). The use of this item is thus found with a frequency of 0.2 attestations per 10,000 spoken words and 0.14 attestations per 10,000 words in the written and spoken material from ICE Great Britain.

The situation is different in the ICE Ireland data. There, the *f*-word is used 130 times. The majority of the attestations, 96 are in spoken discourse, 34 in written discourse. Of the spoken discourse, 79 are in face-to-face and 18 in telephone conversations. This yields a ratio of 1.56 examples per 10,000 words in the total spoken component of ICE Ireland as compared to the 0.2 per 10,000 from ICE GB. This difference is statistically highly significant at $p < 0.0001$ according to chi-square, as are the differences in the combined written and spoken frequencies of 1.24 in ICE IRE and 0.14. The higher frequency of *fuck* and its derivatives in the Irish data is also confirmed by a comparison with data from the British National Corpus, where its frequency is somewhat higher than in ICE GB, namely 0.56 per 1 million words, but the difference is still statistically significantly lower than in ICE Ireland.

The *f*-word also shows a considerably broader semantic spread, expressing, in addition to the items named for ICE GB above, also general swearing (example 19), semantically transitive expressions of flinging (example 20) or intransitive moving (example 21):

19. <S1A-017:1:186:B> Och for *fuck*'s sake
20. <S1A-015:1:166:A> He's had a few too many to drink and the cops *fucked him back* into the house again
21. <S1A-014:1:71:D> One of them drinks a pint of Bass and then *fucks up* to bed again.

Its use as a personal characteristic includes indicating something like an idiot (*awkward fucker* S1A-024:1:52:D), a rascal (*cheeky fucker* S1A-044:1:13:A), and expressing that someone is in trouble (*you'll be fucked* S1A-024:1:119:D).

In contrast to British English, there is also a larger selection of corruptions, such as *frigg* (4 examples), with similar semantics of general swearing (see example 22), but also of troubledness (example 23):

22. <S1A-041:1:151:D> See the whole film it's brilliant up until you find out that he's a *frigging* half bat creature thing.
23. <S1A-036:1:103:B> He smoked all his life and his breathing's absolutely *frigged.*

Further we find *feck* (9 examples), which is used similarly to *fuck*, as an expression of despise (<S1A-049:1:117:A> *I said ah feck it I'll go down*), as a negative adjective (<W1B-004:2:95> *Maybe she's got the right feckin' idea eh what!),* and as a verb of movement (<S1A-050:1:7:C> *Give me the shitty mattress and you feck off*). *Feck* and its derivatives seem to be taken by most speakers as corruption of *fuck*, even though, as also indicated by Murphy (91-92), it can in fact be derived from Old English *feccan* "fetch, bring, draw" (Bosworth s.v. *feccan*) and may have been connected to *fuck* due to its phonetic similarity.

There further are three examples of *flipping,* for which only examples with a more restricted semantic spread are attested, namely a modifying adjective, probably suggesting a stupid entity or an entity of low value such as in:

24. <S1A-031:1:80:A> I mean talk about *flipping* health food!
25. <S1A-017:1:197:A> And he got on the *flipping* minibus with his kilt on him.

None of these corruptions are found in ICE GB, but they are frequent and have a high semantic spread in ICE IRE. This indicates that even though *fuck* is better established, both in terms of numbers and semantic spread, in Irish colloquial speech, it retains a taboo value for a number of speakers who try to avoid the stronger expletive by using a softer corruption.

The use of this semantic cluster of swearwords does not seem to replace other well-known examples of English swearwords, such as *bloody* or *bleeding. Bloody* appears 48 times in ICE GB and 44 times in ICE IRE. In both varieties, its use is restricted to adjectival, typically pre-nominal contexts:

26. <w1b-003:1:92> *bloody* cheek!
27. <ICE GB w1b-002:3152:3> I already get excited thinking about it. <W1b-002:3:153> it's going to be *bloody* excellent!
28. <ICE IRE S1A-033:1:106:B> Probably goes back to the *bloody* ark

Negatively connoted uses of *bloody* by far dominate in the two ICE corpora under investigation, with 27 above forming the only exception where it is used in a positive context. In all these contexts it seems to serve predominantly as an intensifier. In contrast to *fuck* and its corruptions, *bloody* is more similarly distributed amongst written and in spoken data both in ICE Great Britain (32 spoken out of a total 48) and in ICE Ireland (23 spoken out of 44), and is particularly used in fictional writing. Thus the use of *bloody* is quite similar in ICE Great Britain and ICE Ireland. It is mainly in evidence as a noun-modifying, intensifying adjective. The related adjective *bleedin(g)*, used as an expletive, only features once each in the corpora, e.g. *Another bleeding cowboy stupidity* (ICE GB w2f-001:1:84) and *The bleeding nuns'll do the same* (ICE IRE S1A-037:1:93:C).

A survey of these items in both ICE Great Britain and ICE Ireland is given in Table 2.

Table 2: The use of *f*-based and *b*-based expletives in ICE GB and ICE IRE in raw frequencies (relative frequencies per one million words given in brackets.)

Corpus	*Bloody*	*Bleedin(g)*	*Fuck-*	*Feck-*	*Frig-*	*Flip-*	Total
ICE GB	48/(45)	1/(1)	14/(13)	0	0	0	63/(59)
ICE IRE	44/(42)	1/(1)	130/(124)	9/(8)	4/(4)	3/(3)	191/(182)
Total	92	2	144	9	4	3	254

Especially the use of *f*-based swearwords is significantly larger in the Irish English than in the British English data. Their semantic spread shows that they are used not only as swearwords, but that their usage has also been bleached to include use as intensifiers and expressions of general movement. This semantic bleaching, together with the increased applicability, is likely to make the original swearword more broadly applicable in colloquial speech. However, the higher use of the expletive *fuck* in Irish English as compared to British English does not seem to have led to a lower use of *bloody* in Irish English, but the relatively high use of *f*-forms in Irish English seems to be in addition to the forms of *bloody*. It may thus have a slightly different pragmatic value; it clearly has a more varied semantic content and subjectively seems to still have a higher taboo value than *bloody* as shown by the continued absence from more monitored genres of spoken language, such as broadcasting and classroom language. The data examined here gives further support to the idea that *f*-based swearwords, particularly *fuck* and its derivatives, may be used to increase group bonding within a certain cultural identity.

An interesting question is of course how items with this semantic content come to be used as intensifiers in the first place. Traugott (34-35; 48-51) traces the typical pathways of change, which expressions undergo when developing subjective pragmatic or discursive functions. During linguistic development items will increasingly come to be used as discourse markers, as hedges, interjections, in swearing or politeness markers and textual and conversational routine expressions; this process is known as *pragmaticalisation* (Claridge and Arnovick 165-167). Along these lines, Traugott (49) argues that the items in question newly transmit information on speaker attitude in the communicative situation. Throughout linguistic history, she argues, such shifts are often metaphorical.

From the vantage point of the evolutionary development of humans, Jing-Schmidt explains that negative, potentially threatening events are more salient to human perception than positive events because they have the potential of endangering our lives. Such negative experiences lead us to being over-cautious and lower the threshold of fear (Jing-Schmidt 418-422). Therefore, expressions of fear, disgust and anger are more salient than positive expressions, which makes them more accessible for becoming grammaticalized as intensifiers in various languages. Most often they stem from the domains of fear, from contexts of both emotional and threat-related fields such as religious domains (*damned*), threats to life (*terribly*) or moral threats (*sinfully*) (Jing-Schmidt 426-429). Jing-Schmidt affirms that the literal senses of these symptoms are usually bleached and the intensifiers primarily come to signal high emotive intensity (429). Items from the other typical negative domains, disgust and anger, are typically based on human and animal characteristics (*stinking*) or body products or on abstractions of the threat caused towards their environment by a person's anger. She shows that emotive intensifiers therefore boost dramatic effect; they elicit attention and establish inter-speaker rapport (Jing-Schmidt 425). The emotional intensity of the situation is first distilled through processes abstraction and metonymic relations. This meaning-component of high emotional intensity is then metaphorically mapped to semantic intensity. This schema is also applicable to our case, in which *fuck* and its derivatives can be seen initially as moral taboos (with high emotional intensity), which would be sufficient ground for electing them as a negatively biased intensifier. A similar process has been described for Australian English and its use of *bloody* (Wierzbicka).

5. Conclusion

This essay has investigated the use religious expressions and of swearwords in Irish English compared to British English. Returning to
Wierzbicka's study of *bloody*, we wanted to answer the question what the
differences observed in the use of swearing and religious oaths might
tell us about the differences in Irish and English culture. The use of religious expressions is rare in the semi-formal registers, as is the use of
swearwords in both varieties. A comparison of the general use of religious expressions and swearwords in ICE Ireland and ICE Great Britain
shows that these categories are considerably more frequent in the Irish
data than in the English data, and that the spread of their usage is also
wider than in the English data. The higher use of religious expressions
in Irish English confirms that religion plays a larger role in the mind of
Irish people than it does in the minds of English people and the taboo
to use religious expressions is more frequently broken in Irish English
where the stronger cultural impact of religion results in higher evocative
power of religious expressions.

As far as swearwords are concerned, in Irish English they particularly
derive from the field of sexual taboo language. Their considerably
broader semantic spread and their higher frequency in Irish English indicate that their lexical contents have, at least for some speakers,
bleached to express more general senses. These general senses do not
only include the cross-linguistically common extension of negative-bias
expressions towards intensifiers but also more general verbal senses like
movement verbs.

References

Aitchinson, Jean. "Whassup? Slang and swearing among schoolchildren." *Education Review* 19.2 (2006): 18-24.

Andersson, Lars and Peter Trudgill. *Bad Language*. London: Blackwell, 1991.

Austin, John L. *How to Do Things With Words*. Oxford: Oxford University Press, 1962.

Barron, Anne and Klaus P. Schneider. "Irish English: a Focus on Language in Action." *The Pragmatics of Irish English*. Ed. Klaus P. Schneider and Anne Barron. Berlin: Mouton de Gruyer, 2005. 2-15.

Bosworth, Joseph. *An Anglo-Saxon Dictionary Online*. Ed. Thomas Northcote Toller and Others. Comp. Sean Christ and Ondřej Tichý. Faculty of Arts, Charles University in Prague, 2010. http://bosworth.ff.cuni.cz/044609 (last accessed 30 July 2013).

Claridge, Claudia and Leslie Arnovick. "Pragmaticalisation and Discursisation." *Handbook of Pragmatics: Historical Pragmatics*. Ed. Andreas H. Jucker and Irma Taavitsainen. Berlin: de Gruyter, 2010. 165-192.

Farr, Fiona and Anne O'Keeffe. *"Would* as Hedging Device in an Irish Context: An Intra-Varietal Comparison of Institutionalised Spoken Interaction." *Using Corpora to Explore Linguistic Variation*. Ed. Randi Reppen, Susann M. Fitzmaurice and Douglas Biber. Amsterdam and Philadelphia: John Benjamins, 2002. 25-48.

—— and Bróna Murphy. "Religious References in Contemporary Irish-English: 'For the Love of God Almighty. . . . I'm a Holy Terror for Turf'." *Intercultural Pragmatics* 6.4 (2009): 535-560.

Greenbaum, Sidney. *Comparing English Worldwide: The International Corpus of English*. Oxford: Oxford University Press, 1996.

Guiraud, Nadine, Dominique Longin, Emiliano Lorini, Sylvie Pesty and Jérémy Rivière. "The Face of Emotions: A Logical Formalization of Expressive Speech Acts." *10th International Conference on Autonomous Agents and Multiagent Systems (AAMAS 2011)*. Ed. Kegan Tumer, Pinar Yolum, Liz Sonenberg and Peter Stone. Taipei, Taiwan: IFAAMAS, 2011. 1031-1038.

Jing-Schmidt, Zhuo. "Negativity Bias in Language: A Cognitive Affective Model of Emotive Intensifiers." *Cognitive Linguistics* 18.3 (2007): 417-443.

Kallen, Jeffrey L. "Politeness in Ireland: '. . . In Ireland, It's Done Without Being Said'." *Politeness in Europe*. Ed. Leo Hickey and Miranda Stewart. Clevedon: Multilingual Matters, 2005. 130-144.

—— and John M. Kirk. *SPICE-Ireland: A User's Guide.* Belfast: Cló Oll-scoil na Banríona, 2012.

McEnery, Anthony. *Swearing in English: Bad language, Purity and Power from 1586 to the Present.* London: Routledge, 2006.

—— and Xiao, Zhonghua. "Swearing in Modern British English." *Language and Literature* 13 (2004): 235-268.

Murphy, Bróna. "'She's a *Fucking* Ticket': The Pragmatics of FUCK in Irish English – An Age and Gender Perspective." *Corpora* 4.1 (2009): 85-106.

Schneider, Klaus P. and Anne Barron. *The Pragmatics of Irish English.* Berlin: Mouton de Gruyter, 2005.

Searle, John. *Speech Acts.* Cambridge: Cambridge University Press, 1969.

——. "A Classification of Illocutionary Acts." *Language in Society* 5 (1976): 1-23.

Stenström, Anna-Brita. "Expletives in the London-Lund Corpus." *English Corpus Linguistics: Studies in Honour of Jan Svartvik.* Ed. Karin Aijmer and Bengt Altenberg. London and New York: Longman, 1991. 239-253.

Taavitsainen, Irma and Andreas Jucker. "Expressive Speech Acts and Politeness in Eighteenth Century English." *Eighteenth Century English: Ideology and Change.* Ed. Raymond Hickey. Cambridge: Cambridge University Press, 2010. 159-181.

Traugott, Elizabeth Closs. "On the Rise of Epistemic Meanings in English: An Example of Subjectification in Semantic Change." *Language* 65.1 (1989): 31-55.

Wierzbicka, Anna. "Australian Cultural Scripts – *Bloody* Revisited." *Journal of Pragmatics* 34 (2002): 1167-1209.

Attitudes of Students in Switzerland Towards Varieties of English

Sarah Chevalier

This paper explores attitudes of students in Switzerland towards different varieties of English. These students, just like native speakers of English, are increasingly exposed to different national and regional varieties through the media and travel. It is therefore postulated that they will also be affected by the phenomenon that Mugglestone has observed among native speakers, namely the "rise of the regional" (273). Accordingly, one hypothesis investigated is that Swiss students will not overwhelmingly consider British English as the most desirable variety to speak despite the fact that it is traditionally the national variety of English taught in schools. Instead, they will have different preferences, influenced by where they have spent time abroad and thus by emotional attachments formed towards a particular national variety. Further, it is hypothesised that when students only consider the English spoken in Britain they will no longer generally favour non-regional Received Pronunciation, the traditional prestige accent in Swiss schools. Rather, for some students the class associations of this variety will create negative affective dispositions. Results support these hypotheses and reveal two further tendencies. The first is that American English and British English are equally popular while the second is that among British varieties students favour a regional variety which traditionally has not been associated with overt prestige, namely the English spoken in London.

1. Introduction

For some people, hearing a particular language variety can evoke a strong emotional reaction. Such reactions include embarrassed discomfort ("makes me cringe"), claims of physical suffering ("painful to listen

Emotion, Affect, Sentiment: The Language and Aesthetics of Feeling. SPELL: Swiss Papers in English Language and Literature 30. Ed. Andreas Langlotz and Agnieszka Soltysik Monnet. Tübingen: Narr, 2014. 197-213.

to"), admiration ("I'm always impressed by the way they speak") or even envy ("I wish I spoke like that").[1] Emotional responses to a language variety such as those described above are one type of manifestation of an *attitude* towards that variety. Oppenheim (39, quoted in Garrett 19), states that attitudes are expressed via (among other things) "verbal statements or reactions," "selective recall, anger or satisfaction or some other emotion." Since attitudes themselves cannot be directly observed, it is only via manifestations such as emotional responses that the investigator can attempt an analysis of language attitudes.

But why should a particular language variety trigger such an emotional response in the first place? And, of particular interest here, what attitudes towards varieties of English can be observed today? This paper explores these questions within the theoretical and methodological framework of language attitudes research. The following section provides some answers to the first question, while the main part of the paper is devoted to investigating the second. Section three outlines key research undertaken by various researchers on current attitudes, while sections four to six report on previously unpublished research carried out in Switzerland on attitudes of non-native speakers towards native varieties of English.

2. The "Inherent Value" of a Variety versus "Imposed Norms"

Some non-specialists (as well as scholars in the past) believe that certain varieties of language are inherently better (or worse) than others. These varieties are felt to be per se more beautiful, logical or correct. This has been termed the *inherent value hypothesis*. Thus, a variety which is believed to be intrinsically superior may cause feelings of admiration or even envy in the listener while a variety believed to be inferior may evoke feelings of discomfort, disgust or even, if it is the speaker's own variety, "linguistic self-hatred" (Giles and Niedzielski 87). While acknowledging the reality of such emotional responses to certain language varieties, the inherent value hypothesis has long been undermined by linguistic research. Giles, Bourhis, Trudgill and Lewis, for example, in a study published four decades ago, examined subjects' reactions to two varieties of Greek, namely Athenian and Cretan. The former holds higher prestige within the Greek language community and is perceived as pleasanter

---

[1] These statements were made directly to the author both by informants in the context of data collection as well as by acquaintances.

than the latter (407). If the Athenian dialect were inherently pleasanter, then hearers who could not understand the varieties should also judge it to be so. This was tested among forty-six British undergraduates who had no knowledge of Greek. A *matched guise experiment* (Lambert, Hodgson, Gardner and Fillenbaum) was conducted with the same bidialectal speaker reading two identical texts, once in the Athenian variety and once in the Cretan variety. In addition, speakers of four further languages (Spanish, Italian, German and Persian) were recorded and played as distracters, so that the subjects would not realise that the speaker of Athenian Greek and Cretan Greek was the same person. The subjects were asked to identify each language and to rate the voices on scales of pleasantness and prestige (among other tasks). The results revealed that none of the subjects recognised either variety as Greek and that no significant differences were found in the ratings of the two varieties (Giles, Bourhis, Trudgill and Lewis 408). Thus, the authors see the *imposed norm hypothesis* – the idea that judgements concerning language varieties simply reflect the status that variety has in society – as validated.

3. Current Research on Attitudes towards Varieties of English

The imposed norms of language varieties today, however, are not always clear-cut; the social connotations of language varieties appear to be becoming more diverse. According to Coupland, "linguistic varieties referred to as 'standards' and 'dialects' are coming to hold different, generally less determinate and more complex values in a late-modern social order" ("Dialects, Standards and Social Change" 43). In Britain today, for example, it is no longer the case that non-regional Received Pronunciation is a prerequisite for entering certain professions (Trudgill 176). Mugglestone speaks of the increasing presence of regional accents in prestigious spheres as the "rise of the regional" (273). A large-scale survey conducted by the BBC in 2005 provides quantitative evidence of this phenomenon. While in 1970, Giles found that among his British informants the accent considered socially most attractive was Received Pronunciation, the BBC online survey in 2005 found that the accent rated as the socially most attractive was the accent identical to the respondent's own. It should be noted that concerning the results for the *prestige* of the variety rather than the *social attractiveness*, English spoken without a regional accent was rated highest in both the older and the more recent study (see Garrett 172-177 for a comparison of the two studies). Outside the British Isles, Bradley and Bradley found a similar phenomenon.

In Australia, in the period from 1984-1998, the accent known as "General Australian," and spoken by the majority of the population (Mitchell and Delbridge 37), received increasingly positive ratings. The opposite happened in the case of the accent labelled by Mitchell and Delbridge "Cultivated Australian." The latter is the accent in Australia which is most similar to Received Pronunciation (see Wells 594-595) and therefore the least regionally marked as Australian. While Cultivated Australian English was still considered prestigious by the informants at the end of Bradley and Bradley's investigation, it did see a clear devaluation in the time period investigated.[2]

The BBC's study on attitudes towards varieties within Britain and Bradley and Bradley's Australian research provide clear evidence of the "rise of the regional" within nations. In the following, I would like to discuss the extent to which the same phenomenon can be observed in the global context. Do, for example, speakers hold more positive attitudes towards their own national variety compared to other national varieties? Bayard, Gallois, Weatherall and Pittam explored this issue in their investigation of attitudes towards four national varieties of English among subjects of three of the four nationalities. The four national varieties were Australian English, New Zealand English, North American English and Southern English English. The three groups consisted of students from Australia (N=99), New Zealand (N=257), and the United States (N=53). The method was a *verbal guise experiment*, similar to the matched guise technique above. Both of these techniques are designed to elicit attitudes indirectly, that is, without the subjects realising that they are judging language. The difference is that with the matched guise the same speaker is used for the different varieties, whereas in the verbal guise each variety is represented by a different speaker. The advantage of the matched guise technique is that with the same speaker variables such as voice quality remain constant. The disadvantage, however – especially when more than two varieties are involved – is the difficulty of finding a speaker who is truly multidialectal. In Bayard, Gallois, Weatherall and Pittam's study, the task of finding two speakers (female and male) who could sound authentic in four national varieties would

---

[2] It should be pointed out within this overview of language attitudes research that attitudes are of course not monolithic, and people may hold different attitudes towards a language variety depending on the particular context in which they find themselves, and the role they are assuming at a particular moment in time. However it is not essential for the research questions in this paper to discuss the influence of context in any detail (see, e.g., Coupland "Accommodation at Work" for an exploration of this aspect).

have been extremely difficult. In their study, eight different speakers were used. The subjects listened to recordings of a female and male pair who spoke one of the four national varieties. The listeners had to rate the voices according to 22 traits on Likert scales. The traits fell into four basic types: status (e.g. "speaker's level of education"), power (e.g. "authoritativeness"), solidarity (e.g. "friendliness") and competence (e.g. "intelligence"). They summarise their results as follows:

> [T]he American female voice was rated most favourably on at least some traits by students of all three nationalities, followed by the American male. For most traits, Australians generally ranked their own accents in third or fourth place, but New Zealanders put the female NZE voice in the mid-low range of all but solidarity-associated traits. All three groups disliked the NZ male. The RP voices did not receive the higher rankings in power/status variables we expected.
>
> (Bayard, Gallois, Weatherall and Pittam 22)

While we could observe the "rise of the regional" in studies comparing varieties within a country, the same cannot be said when national varieties are compared. If this were the case, we would expect each group to give their own variety the highest overall rating, which in this study is not the case. Thus, rather than witnessing a rise of the regional, we may be observing, according to Bayard, Gallois, Weatherall and Pittam, the rise of American English as a prestige model. This is especially striking since the prestige model in Australia and New Zealand has traditionally been Received Pronunciation.

Garrett, Williams and Evans also consider "attitudinal data from New Zealand, Australia, the USA and UK about each other's Englishes" (211). They make reference to the findings of Bayard, Gallois, Weatherall and Pittam, published four years previously in 2001, and state that they wish to re-examine such attitudes after political change in the United States and with a different methodology. In their study, Garrett, Williams and Evans employ a "folklinguistic methodology," namely by eliciting associations subjects hold about different varieties. Altogether 517 undergraduates were asked to name countries in which English was spoken as a native language (apart from the respondents' own country) and to answer the following: "tell us how the English spoken there strikes you when you hear it spoken" (217). Answers were categorised according to six categories (218-219): linguistic features (e.g. "clipped"), affective (e.g. "snobbish"), status and social norms (e.g. "incorrect"), cultural associations (e.g. "McDonald's"), diversity (e.g. "many regional accents") and comparison (e.g. "similar to New Zealand"). Concerning

American English, Garrett, Williams and Evans summarise their results as follows: "US English was viewed strikingly negatively in terms of its affective associations, and there were references to 'excess' from all respondent groups (e.g. overassertive, overenthusiastic)" (211). Three main themes emerged from the negative affect comments: arrogance and power (e.g. "they think they are better than everyone else"), exaggeration (e.g. "over the top") and insincerity (e.g. "phoney") (228). Thus, while Bayard, Gallois, Weatherall and Pittam's 2001 study suggests that American English is increasingly regarded as a high status variety, with different methodology (and in a different political climate), Garrett, Williams and Evans' 2005 study reveals that it also evokes strong negative feelings.

Bayard, Gallois, Weatherall and Pittam (43) state that one way their findings could be further tested would be by examining which variety L2 speakers[3] of English in non-English speaking countries prefer. They report on research carried out in the Netherlands (by van der Haagen) and Sweden (by Bayard and Sullivan). In the former study, it could be seen that despite the fact that Received Pronunciation was the traditional prestige accent in the Netherlands, American English was rated "equally high in status and much higher in dynamism" (as described by Bayard, Gallois, Weatherall and Pittam 43). In the latter study, while Received Pronunciation still retained first place in power and competence traits, the North American male voice was rated higher in the other traits. A study conducted in Denmark by Ladegaard also examined reactions to varieties of English among L2 speakers. Ladegaard examined responses to five varieties of English in Denmark: American English, Australian English, Cockney, Received Pronunciation and Scottish English. While Received Pronunciation rated highest on traits of status and linguistic competence, the other accents scored higher than Received Pronunciation on traits of personal integrity and social attractiveness. The picture emerging from these studies of responses of L2 speakers is therefore that of the continued importance of British English as a prestige model. But it also reveals American English (and indeed other varieties) to be attractive as models for L2 speakers.

In the studies outlined in this section, we see evidence of greater linguistic tolerance with regard to regional accents among native speakers of English within their own countries. When national varieties are compared, we can observe the importance of American English, whether as

---

[3] In this paper the term *L2 speakers* is used to denote speakers of English for whom English is not their first language.

a possible new prestige model (Bayard, Gallois, Weatherall and Pittam), in strong affective reactions (Garrett, Williams and Evans) or as a contender as a speech model for L2 speakers (e.g. van der Haagen). The goal of the present study is to further investigate – and provide evidence for or against – the picture described above.

4. Aim and Scope of the Swiss Study

This study explores the attitudes of university students in Switzerland towards varieties of English. Non-native speakers of English, just like native speakers, are increasingly exposed to different national and regional varieties through the media and via travel. Thus, it is hypothesised that students in Switzerland will not overwhelmingly consider British English as the most desirable variety to speak despite the fact that it has traditionally been the national variety of English taught in schools. Instead, students will have different preferences, partially influenced by where they have spent time abroad. Further, based on the research outlined in the previous section, it is postulated that American English will be an important contender as the new prestige model. It is also hypothesised that when students only consider varieties of English spoken in Britain they will no longer generally favour the non-regional accent of Received Pronunciation, in spite of it being the traditional model in Swiss schools.

5. Method

The research questions outlined above were investigated via two different types of surveys carried out among university students of English linguistics at the University of Berne. In the first survey, students were asked by the author within a lecture and a seminar to fill in a very short questionnaire. Approximately half of the participants were graduate students and all of the students were familiar with linguistic labels for varieties of English. Answers of native speakers of English were not considered. The final number of valid questionnaires was seventy-seven. The students were asked to write down their answers to the following five questions:

1. Age:
2. Native language(s):
3. English speaking countries you have lived in for more than three months:
4. What national variety of English would you prefer to speak?
5. If you had to choose a British variety only, which would you choose?

Question three was asked to see whether there was a correlation between Anglophone countries students had lived in and their preferences, while questions four and five concerned the preferences themselves. With regard to question four (national varieties), the aim was to discover to what extent there was a diversity of preferences, as well as the extent to which American English may be "catching up" or may have even overtaken British English as a prestige model. Question five was posed in order to focus more precisely on the issue of whether the "rise of the regional" is affecting L2 speakers.

The questionnaire could be criticised on ideological grounds since it was assumed that (the majority of) students would want to be able to speak English like a native speaker. An L2 speaker may, in fact, prefer to be recognised as a speaker of their L1 (native language) for reasons of identity. Further, L2 speakers who achieve near-native proficiency and who are sometimes mistaken for native speakers sometimes report on misunderstandings in conversation since their L1 interlocutor assumes pragmatic competence or cultural knowledge that the L2 speaker does not possess. However, for the purpose of this survey it was not considered necessary to take these issues into account; respondents were of course free to write that they did not have a preference, and in fact several did.

In contrast to this closed-question survey, the other survey was based on open questions and followed the folklinguistic method used by Garrett, Williams and Evans (described above). In this case, only national varieties were considered since it was assumed that a group of L2 speakers as a whole would not have enough familiarity with a given set of more localised regional varieties. In this survey, one undergraduate class (twenty-one students) was asked for their spontaneous responses to the English spoken in three countries: England, the USA and Australia. They were asked exactly the same question as the one used by Garrett, Williams and Evans (217), namely, "tell [me] how the English spoken there strikes you when you hear it spoken." It can be argued that these participants do not correspond to the "naïve" respondents who should be used in folklinguistic studies on attitudes. However, the exercise took place in a seminar which had nothing to do with either language attitudes or varieties of English; it was sprung upon the students with no warning and they were asked to respond spontaneously and personally and not as students of linguistics. Although some of these students also happened to fill in the questionnaire on preferences described above, the folklinguistic data collection had been carried out in the previous semester, so it was impossible for the questionnaire to have had any influence on the association responses.

6. Results and Analysis

In the first survey, the demographics were as follows: the average age of the students was twenty-four, and the native language of the majority was Swiss German (68 percent). Their answers to the question concerning choice of national variety can be seen in Table 1. It should be noted that when answers to this question gave more information than that of "national variety," this extra information was ignored. For example, the answer "Southern United States," which is also a regional designation within the country, and the answer "sophisticated American English," which is also a social designation, were both simply categorised as "American English." Further, national varieties were defined by state borders, so that the one answer of "Scottish English" was categorised as British English. This is an oversimplification, obviously (see, e.g., Ferguson on "nation" and "state" with respect to language issues). However,

Table 1: Preferred national variety of English among 77 students in Switzerland

Preferred national variety	Number of students
American English	27
Australian English	4
British English	28
Canadian English	7
Irish English	2
New Zealand English	5
South African English	2
No preference	2
Total	77

in order to gain a broad overview of tendencies it made sense to have no overlapping categories. Further, for question five, the opposite method was used, so that fine detail is captured there. These results reveal a diversity of preferences in that all the "inner circle" varieties of English (Kachru) are found. The other main result is the high and more or less equal preference for American and British English.

The following table shows the results for correlations between national variety preferred and the place of an extended period of stay in an English-speaking country.

Table 2: Correlation between preferred national variety and country in which students have stayed for an extended period of time

Correlation	Students
Yes	32
No	9
Not in English-speaking country for more than 3 months	36
Total	77

In Table 2, a clear correlation can be observed between students' preferred national variety and the country in which they had stayed for an extended period of time. Of the 41 students who had lived in an English-speaking country for more than three months, 32 stated that the variety of that country was also their preferred national variety. Further evidence is also found when examining some of the answers to question five: for example, those respondents who chose Welsh English or Belfast English as their preferred British variety stated that they had lived in Wales or Belfast respectively (many, however, did not specify which region within the country they had stayed). Since this survey contains only quantitative data, it is not possible to know whether respondents came to prefer the variety of the place in which they stayed abroad after being immersed in the speech community or whether they chose the place because they preferred the variety of that region in the first place. Given, however, that students do not usually have extensive financial means and sometimes stay abroad wherever they can manage to obtain an affordable university place or a job, it is certainly likely that in some cases the former scenario applies, namely that students come to identify with and prefer the variety of the region in which they happen to live.

Table 3 displays the results for question five of the survey, which asked about students' preferred variety within Britain. Unlike with question four, the responses have not been placed into any overarching categories; the answers have been left as they are, and the labels in the table correspond to what the students actually wrote. This was done in order to capture the mixture of regional and social categorisation, considered particularly important with respect to the exploration of the "rise of the regional."

Table 3: Preferred British variety of English among 77 students in Switzerland

Preferred British variety	Number of students
Belfast	1
Cockney	2
East Anglia	1
Glaswegian	1
Liverpool	1
London (1: "sophisticated London")	29
Mancunian / Manchester	3
Oxford English	2
Received Pronunciation / RP	14
Scottish (1: "mild Scottish")	12
South Wales	1
Southern English	2
Standard British English	1
Welsh	1
No preference	6
Total	77

These results are very interesting for two reasons. The first is that four-teen different varieties of English are mentioned, eleven of which are regional. Concerning the answers that indicate a non-regional variety, Received Pronunciation, unsurprisingly, makes an appearance, as does Standard British English (which of course can be spoken in a regional accent – it is in fact difficult to know precisely what the respondent had in mind here), and Oxford English, which is clearly a social rather than a regional designation. The second finding of interest is that the variety which was the most popular by far was a regional variety, namely London English. Twenty-nine respondents stated that this was the variety of British English that they would most like to speak, not to mention two further students who wrote Cockney. This number (31) is higher than the number of people who stated Received Pronunciation (14) and higher than all of the answers naming a non-regional variety together (17). The finding matches that of the BBC survey, which showed the increased popularity of London speech compared to other varieties within Britain. Garrett (174) suggests that it is a combination of stereo-

types of working class speech, the dynamism of the capital and its overall prosperity, which serve to create favourable associations with London speech today.

I turn now to the results of the open-question survey, where students were asked to spontaneously write down their associations with
the varieties of English spoken in England, the USA and Australia. The
total number of items participants gave was 105. There were 40 items
for England, 37 for the USA, and 22 plus 6 responses of "I don't know"
for Australia. Since the responses for Australia were considerably fewer
than for the other two countries, they will not be discussed here. For
England and the USA, responses ranged across all of the categories described by Garrett, Williams and Evans. For American English, the largest category was negative affect (11/37 items). Students felt that the
English spoken in America was, for example, "superficial," "self-
centred," and consisted of a "big use of exaggerating and dramatic
words." Overall, the responses in this category were very similar to
those described by Garrett, Williams and Evans for native speakers of
English. With regard to the English spoken in England, two main categories emerged. The largest comprised comments referring to the variety's perceived high status (15/40 items), e.g. "high-brow," "noble,"
"elegance," "sophisticated" and "high status." The other category was
that of negative affect with 9/40 items; mentioned once each were "arrogant" and "stiff," while the other 7 items were the words "snobby" or
"snobbish."

The responses show that these twenty-one Swiss undergraduates still
consider English English as the main prestige variety. This matches the
findings of both Bayard and Sullivan and Ladegaard. At the same time,
quite a few responded in an emotionally negative way towards the perceived "snobbishness" of the variety. American English also evokes
negative emotional responses, if rather different ones. The number of
responses in the category of negative affect for both varieties seems – at
least for L2 speakers who have chosen to study English at university –
surprisingly high. Yet the diversity of the remaining comments reveals
that these attitudes are not uniform. The English spoken in England is
also seen as "funny," "witty," "polite," and "chummy." American English is seen as "classy" by one person; another respondent finds it
"cool," and several find it "straightforward" or "direct." It also evokes
positive emotional reactions due to personal connections, such as "it
makes me feel at home because I spent an exchange year there" or "it
reminds me of my friend [. . .] I love the American English accent."

One noticeable difference between the two varieties concerned how easy the participants considered each of them to be. The English spoken in England was considered more difficult by a number of people; one student, for example, wrote that it was "either uber posh, or you simply can't understand them at all." This was never mentioned for American English, which was, on the other hand, sometimes found to be easier, or the variety that was the "most natural."

This method of asking for spontaneous associations with language varieties has, by its nature, resulted in more complex data than the closed-question survey. However, we have been able to observe a number of patterns: American English evokes negative emotional responses due to its perceived excessiveness and superficiality, while the English spoken in England is felt by roughly a quarter of the respondents to be arrogant or snobbish. In addition, the latter retains its place in the minds of these students as a variety associated with high prestige, while American English, for a number of them, is the "most natural" variety, or the most straightforward. If we return to the hypothesis that participants will have a diversity of preferences, this is supported by these findings in the sense that neither variety is a clear "favourite." With regard to the question of American English becoming the new prestige model, these findings do not offer any particular indication of this. However, its importance can be seen in the fact that the participants made an approximately equal number of comments for both American and English English, unlike the considerably lower number that they were able to make for Australian English.

7. Summary and Conclusion

One of the issues examined in this paper has been that of why language varieties can trigger strong emotional responses. In addressing this question, I discussed the *inherent value* versus the *imposed norm hypothesis* and described the work of Giles, Bourhis, Trudgill and Lewis. Their research (and other studies, e.g. Giles, Bourhis and Davies) validates the imposed norm hypothesis: people react to and form judgements about language not due to any inherent quality in the language variety in question, but due to its status in society. However, it was also pointed out that the status of a variety may be multifaceted, and that the social connotations of language varieties today are increasingly heterogeneous (Coupland "Dialects, Standards and Social Change"). While English spoken without a regional accent remains the most prestigious variety in Britain according to the recent, large-scale survey conducted by the BBC, it is no longer considered to be socially the most attractive. Regional accents are rated more positively than in the past and are increasingly heard in prestigious spheres (Mugglestone; Trudgill). Likewise in Australia, the more obviously geographically marked accent, termed by Mitchell and Delbridge as General Australian, is increasingly appreciated at the expense of the less regionally marked variety, namely Cultivated Australian (Bradley and Bradley). Where comparisons of national varieties are concerned, the picture is a little different. Here, evidence shows that American English is admired by Australians and New Zealanders, both compared to British English, and also compared to their own varieties. Thus, it has been suggested that American English may be becoming the new global prestige model (Bayard, Gallois, Weatherall and Pittam). This idea has been explored by a number of researchers in L2 contexts and findings point to a possible tendency in this direction (Bayard and Sullivan; van der Haagen; Ladegaard).

The present paper has also examined attitudes towards English in an L2 context, reporting on research undertaken among university students in Switzerland. The hypotheses of the study were confirmed. Swiss students show a diversity of preferences with regard to native varieties of English. When seventy-seven students were asked which national variety they would prefer to speak, the varieties of every inner circle country were mentioned. Further, when the question concerned varieties within Britain only, fourteen different varieties were named, eleven of which were regional. It was assumed that students' increased exposure to different varieties of English through the media and travel would result in precisely such a diversity of answers. While no question concerning media was actually asked, there was a clear correlation between preferred variety and the place in which students had spent time abroad.

Despite the diversity outlined above, clear tendencies concerning popularity could be observed. American English and British English were highly and equally popular as the national variety students would most like to speak. This is interesting in light of the fact that high school students generally still use British textbooks and Received Pronunciation has traditionally been the speech model. Thus, despite socialisation in British English, American English is equally popular. Within Britain, London English was preferred far and above non-regional Received Pronunciation. This preference is in accordance with the findings of the BBC survey, which revealed that London speech has greatly increased in social attractiveness within Britain (BBC).

The associations of a (mainly) different set of twenty-one university students with American English and English English revealed considerable diversity and a surprising number of comments showing negative affect. Negative affect was the largest category for American English and the second largest for the English spoken in England. The largest category for English English was that of high status, which shows that its traditional place as a prestige variety is still well-anchored in this L2 environment. American English on the other hand was felt to be natural, direct and straightforward. Neither variety was clearly preferred, lending further support to the hypothesis that students in Switzerland today have a diversity of preferences.

How L2 speakers feel towards native varieties of English can be explained, I suggest, both by their traditional school socialisation and particularly by their easy access to different varieties of native speech both via the media and via personal travel. While only the correlation with travel and preferred variety could be confirmed with actual data in this study, it is a fact that university students of this generation spend a considerable amount of time immersed in English language media and communicating online in English. Students have instant and constant access to English language films, music clips, *youtube* tutorials, interactive computer games which they play with people around the world, and so on. With regard to American English, the participants' familiarity with (associations survey), and equal preference for (questionnaire), surely reflects the dominance of American English in the English language media that they are exposed to, something which Bayard, Gallois, Weatherall and Pittam (44) label an "unceasing global media onslaught." This dominance may also possibly be reflected in some of the negative comments referring to excessiveness.

For some people, hearing a particular language variety can evoke a strong emotional reaction. Linguistics students are no exception. Yet, the main picture this study has drawn is that of a diversity of preferences, and thus – as is being observed increasingly among native speakers – a greater appreciation for, or at least tolerance of, linguistic diversity itself.

References

Bayard, Donn and Kirk Sullivan. "Perception of Country of Origin and Social Status of English Speakers by Swedish and New Zealand Listeners." *Proceedings of Fonetik 2000*. Ed. Antonis Botinis and Niklas Torstensson. Skövde: Högskolan Skövde, 2000. 33-36.

——, Cynthia Gallois, Ann Weatherall and Jeffery Pittam. "Pax Americana? Accent Attitudinal Evaluations in New Zealand, Australia and America." *Journal of Sociolinguistics* 5.1 (2001): 22-49.

BBC Voices. 2005. Available online at: http://www.bbc.co.uk/voices/ (last accessed on 1 June 2012).

Bradley, David and Maya Bradley. "Changing Attitudes to Australian English." *English in Australia*. Ed. David Blair and Peter Collins. Amsterdam: John Benjamins, 2001. 271-285.

Coupland, Nikolas. "Accommodation at Work: Some Phonological Data and their Implications." *International Journal of the Sociology of Language* 46 (1984): 49-70.

——. "Dialects, Standards and Social Change." *Language Attitudes, Standardisation and Language Change*. Ed. Marie Maegaard, Frans Gregersen, Pia Quist and J. Normann Jørgensen. Oslo: Novus, 2009. 27-49.

Ferguson, Gibson. *Language Planning and Education*. Edinburgh: Edinburgh University Press, 2006.

Garrett, Peter, Angie Williams and Betsy Evans. "Attitudinal Data from New Zealand, Australia, the USA and UK about Each Other's Englishes: Recent Changes or Consequences of Methodologies?" *Multilingua* 24 (2005): 211-235.

——. *Attitudes to Language*. Cambridge: Cambridge University Press, 2010.

Giles, Howard and Nancy Niedzielski. "Italian is Beautiful, German is Ugly." *Language Myths*. Ed. Laurie Bauer and Peter Trudgill. London: Penguin, 1998. 85-93.

——, Richard Bourhis and Ann Davies. "Prestige Speech Styles: The Imposed Norm and Inherent Value Hypothesis." *Language in Anthropology IV: Language in Many Ways*. Ed. William McCormack and Stephen Wurm. The Hague: Mouton, 1975. 589-596.

——, Richard Bourhis, Peter Trudgill and Alan Lewis. "The Imposed Norm Hypothesis: A Validation." *Quarterly Journal of Speech* 60 (4) (1974): 405-410.

——. "Evaluative Reactions to Accents." *Educational Review* 22 (3) (1970): 211-227.

Kachru, Braj, ed. *The Other Tongue: English Across Cultures.* Urbana, Illinois: University of Illinois Press, 1982.

Ladegaard, Hans J. "National Stereotypes and Language Attitudes: The Perception of British, American and Australian Language and Culture in Denmark." *Language and Communication* 18 (1998): 251-274.

Lambert, Wallace E., Richard C. Hodgson, Robert C. Gardner and Samuel Fillenbaum. "Evaluational Reactions to Spoken Languages." *Journal of Abnormal and Social Psychology* 60 (1960): 44-51.

Mitchell, Alexander G. and Arthur Delbridge. *The Speech of Australian Adolescents: A Survey.* Sydney: Angus and Robertson, 1965.

Mugglestone, Lynda. *Talking Proper: The Rise of Accent as Social Symbol.* Oxford: Oxford University Press, 2003.

Oppenheim, Bram. "An Exercise in Attitude Measurement." *Social Psychology: A Practical Manual.* Ed. Glynis Breakwell, Hugh Foot and Robin Gilmour. Basingstoke: Macmillan, 1982. 38-56.

Trudgill, Peter. *Sociolinguistic Variation and Change.* Washington DC: Georgetown University Press, 2002.

van der Haagen, Monique. *Caught Between the Norms: The English Pronunciation of Dutch Learners.* The Hague: Holland Academic Graphics, 1998.

Wells, John C. *Accents of English 3: Beyond the British Isles.* Cambridge: Cambridge University Press, 1982.

"All I could do was hand her another tissue" – Handling Emotions as a Challenge in Reflective Texts by Medical Students

Miriam A. Locher and Regula Koenig

In some medical teaching institutions, students have to partake in compulsory training in communication skills. They are required to demonstrate good listening skills, to repeat, mirror and summarize information, structure an interview and use open and closed questions. They are also informed that they will be confronted with their own and their patients' emotions during a consultation and they are asked to develop methods of signaling empathy. This essay reports on data collected from medical students at a British university who wrote a reflective text in which they explore their communicative behavior in connection with a memorable encounter with a patient. While they are prompted to think about how they felt during their encounter and hence the mention of emotions is frequent in the texts, our thematic content analysis reveals that some of the students choose the topic of handling emotions during a patient encounter as particularly noteworthy. We observe that students are affected by the positive and negative emotional stance of the patients and draw on an impressive scope of emotion words. When creating an emotional stance in their text, students draw on verbal cues and they use language to describe vocal, body, physiological and facial cues. They also enact emotions in constructed dialogue.

1. Introduction

This essay presents results on how the topic of emotion emerges in a corpus of English texts written by medical students of the University of Nottingham, UK. These texts were written as part of a compulsory clini-

Emotion, Affect, Sentiment: The Language and Aesthetics of Feeling. SPELL: Swiss Papers in English Language and Literature 30. Ed. Andreas Langlotz and Agnieszka Soltysik Monnet. Tübingen: Narr, 2014. 215-236.

cal communication skills module and belong to the genre of reflective writing. The students were asked to recall a memorable encounter with a patient and to discuss the communication skills that they employed, how they felt about the interaction, and what conclusions for future behavior they draw from the experience. Reflective writing – texts written to critically examine one's own practice, conduct or position – has been recognized as a valuable tool in teaching in the discipline of medicine for some time, but is still not widely used according to Branch and Paranjape (1185). Its purpose can be defined as follows: "In medical and health science courses you are required to produce reflective writing in order to learn from educational and practical experiences, and to develop the habit of critical reflection as a future health professional" (Monash University). Doctors are encouraged to engage in this kind of writing throughout their careers.

From a linguistic perspective, the texts offer ample research possibilities such as the discussion of linguistic identity construction or character positioning (cf. Gygax, Koenig and Locher), genre analysis or the study of metaphors. From an applied perspective, our analysis can feed back into the development of clinical communication skills teaching. In this essay, we discuss if and how the students talk about emotions. We first turn to positioning our study in its context and to describing the data in more detail (section 2). In section 3 we turn to the analysis of the texts by applying a mixed method. More specifically, this involves (i) a quantitative analysis of the vocabulary used in the corpus, (ii) a quantitative thematic content analysis of a sub-corpus and (iii) a close reading of how emotions surface in one particular text. Section 4 draws conclusions and offers an outlook for the research.

2. The Context of the Study and the Data

This essay draws on data that was collected in connection with the interdisciplinary project "Life (Beyond) Writing: Illness Narratives," funded by the Swiss National Science Foundation. The project brings together research interests in narrative in health contexts from different disciplines. Franziska Gygax ("On Being Ill"; "Theoretically Ill") explores autobiographies that deal with illness in the field of literary and cultural studies, while the linguistics team studies reflective writing texts that were written by medical students at the University of Basel and the University of Nottingham, as well as reflective texts by doctors published in medical journals. It is one of the aims of the project that the results of these research efforts inform the further development of clinical communication skills teaching at the University of Nottingham (Victoria Tischler) and Basel (Alexander Kiss) (e.g. Gygax, Koenig and Locher).

The data for this study consists of 189 reflective writing texts that medical students from the University of Nottingham composed in connection with their communication skills course taught by Dr Victoria Tischler. The average length of the texts is about 1,500 words. When the students submitted their texts (a task that was optional), they were in their second year of medical training (of a five year degree; three years *Bachelor of Medical Sciences* BMedSci plus two years *Bachelor of Medicine, Bachelor of Surgery* BM BS). They have had clinical interaction through attachment to a general practitioner and during regular hospital visits. They have also completed a Clinical Communication Skills module in the first year of the course, in which the following topics are introduced: how to structure a clinical interview; use of different question types; signaling empathy and other verbal strategies; rapport building; non-verbal communication; and roles of doctor and patient. The texts were collected in 2010 and 2011. The task completed by the students can be summarized as follows:

– The students write about a *memorable encounter with a patient* during their internship at a GP surgery or a clinical surgery.
– They are invited to *introduce / describe* the situation and the characters of their narrative and to use constructed dialogue for key passages.
– They are asked to *reflect* on their communication skills, on their emotional reactions and *to draw conclusions* about future behavior.

The instructions thus follow the classical set-up for a reflective writing task: description – reflection – conclusion (Hampton; for a more refined description see Watton, Collings and Moon). The actual information that the students received about the task was much more detailed and the image in Figure 1 shows that the information was structured with relevant questions given for the students to respond to. For our purposes here it is especially noteworthy that the students were explicitly invited to reflect on their emotions (*Describe what you felt after the encounter*, and *How did I feel during the conversation and afterwards?*) and that they were asked to use constructed dialogue.

Reflections on communication with a patient

Instructions:

Think about which conversation/encounter with a patient impressed you most. The questions listed below will help you to structure your thoughts about this encounter from memory. Those questions marked with an * **must** be addressed. The other questions can be chosen if relevant to the specific context of the described situation.

Before you start writing up your text, write down everything that you remember about the encounter. Then you can proceed according to the points listed below.

Situation:

DESCRIPTION

* Describe the patient (age, relevant diagnosis, first impression – appearance, posture, language, anything else noticeable, etc.).
* Describe in which context the encounter took place (what was the reason for the encounter?).
* Describe what you talked about by using verbatim speech (the exact words) as much as possible. If you cannot remember the exact wording, reconstruct the dialogue for the crucial moments as well as possible.
* Describe how you felt after the encounter.

Reflection:

REFLECTION

The following questions should help you to structure your reflections.

* 1. The uniqueness of the encounter
a) Why do I remember this particular encounter so well?
b) What was so special about the patient or my behaviour that I remember it so well?

* 2. Communicative aspects
a) Did I communicate with the patient as I intended to?
b) Did the conversation proceed as planned?
c) If yes, why and in what ways have I achieved this?
d) If no, what went wrong and what could I have done differently?

CONCLUSION

Aims:

* What have I learnt from this encounter?
* What would have helped me to manage/shape the encounter in a better way?
* What aspects of my behaviour and language will I change in order to improve my next encounter with a patient with a similar problem?

Hints for writing the text

Please anonymize the names of all parties involved.

For crucial moments in the conversation, indicate reported speech in the following way:

Mrs. XY: *"and none of the doctors told me anything about a mistake; they wanted to simply not talk about it and I now have to suffer for it. That's outrageous, isn't it?"*

Student: *"You are very angry, aren't you?"*

Mrs. XY: *"Yes, of course I am! If they had properly told me and bad apologized, it would have been only half as bad."*

Mrs. XY: *"... and then the surgeon said it will be all my fault if the operation won't succeed; as I didn't have the best conditions, and being so overweight, the situation is always difficult."*

Student: *"Yes, a doctor shouldn't say anything like this."*

How did I feel during the conversation and afterwards?

For example: *I was absolutely crestfallen afterwards. During the conversation, I never knew what was okay to say. Am I allowed to criticize a surgeon? Did he really say what the patient reported, or is this only the patient's version? Was it wise to encourage the patient to speak more about her experience or should I have stopped it? I didn't dare put an end to it because I didn't want to appear like yet another 'bad doctor'.*

What would I change for the next interaction?

...

[Administrative pointers]

Figure 1: The instructions to the students (the designations *description*, *reflection* and *conclusion* have been added)

A questionnaire on the students' linguistic background handed in together with the consent form indicates that the Nottingham contributors are female in 63 per cent of all cases and 92 per cent are aged between 19 and 21 years. Eighty-eight per cent of the students indicate English as one of their first languages. The other first languages mentioned are of European origin, but, importantly, include also many languages spoken in Asia and some in Africa.

In what follows, the content analysis is based on a thematic reading of 50 texts, the analysis of emotional stance is illustrated on one text and the vocabulary analysis draws on the entire corpus of 249,708 words.

3. The Surfacing of Emotions in the Corpus

To study how emotions surface in the corpus, we have chosen a mixed methodology. In a first step, we use a quantitative vocabulary analysis that allows us to get a crude overview of the semantic fields that the students draw vocabulary from. In a second step, we establish what the students write about in their texts and whether they table emotions as a topic in its own right by conducting a quantitative thematic analysis of a sub-corpus. This quantitative overview is followed by a qualitative close reading of how a particular student writes about emotions. After presenting these analyses, their main results will then be briefly discussed against previous studies on emotion management in medicine/medical training.

3.1. The Vocabulary of the Corpus

In order to gain a first impression of the use of emotion words in the corpus, a quantitative vocabulary analysis is conducted. The aim is to detect the semantic fields that characterize the texts and to gain a rough understanding of the overall composition so as to better understand the role of emotions within the corpus. The analysis is based on the corpus of all 189 texts, which amounts to a total of 249,708 words, or 108,017 words when stop words (such as articles, conjunctions and prepositions) are excluded.

Figure 2 displays a frequency cloud of the first 100 most frequent words in the corpus (excluding stop words). The words are shown in alphabetical order and their respective size indicates their frequency. The chart nicely illustrates the semantic fields of the patient encounter (e.g. *patient, GP, student, [patient] history, consultation, hospital*), the focus on communication skills (e.g. *communication, interview, question, rapport*), and the reflective part of the task (e.g. *feel, felt, think*).

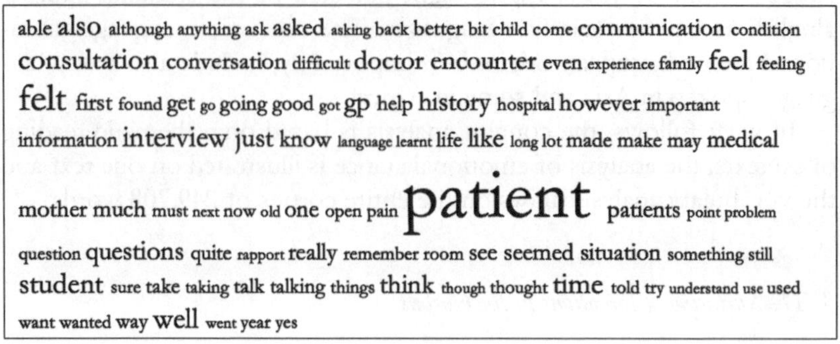

able also although anything ask asked asking back better bit child come communication condition consultation conversation difficult doctor encounter even experience family feel feeling felt first found get go going good got gp help history hospital however important information interview just know language learnt life like long lot made make may medical mother much must next now old one open pain **patient** patients point problem question questions quite rapport really remember room see seemed situation something still student sure take taking talk talking things think though thought time told try understand use used want wanted way well went year yes

Figure 2: Frequency cloud Nottingham I and II (first 100 words, excluding stop words, ordered alphabetically)

The same topics emerge when we conduct a keyword analysis (Stubbs 129; Scott). Using AntConc (a free program for corpus linguistics), all words of the corpus (not lemmatized and including stop words) are compared to the reference corpus of the BNC (British National Corpus) in order to establish the set of words that are particularly characteristic of the reflective writing corpus. The following list shows the first twenty most typical words (ordered according to their log-likelihood values):

I, 10245; *patient*, 3829; *felt*, 960; *student*, 736; *interview*, 656; *consultation*, 651; *feel*, 642; *gp*, 593; *doctor*, 580; *encounter*, 564; *history*, 543; *questions*, 541; *me*, 2159; *mrs*, 453; *seemed*, 432; *medical*, 388; *patients*, 387; *conversation*, 383; *communication*, 379; *asked*, 371

The importance of the pronoun *I*, which is in first position, can be explained with the focus on first person reflection in the corpus. The role of emotions is not visible within the 100 most frequent words (see the cloud) or the 20 most typical keywords (see the list above). While the verb *feel* is frequent and the noun *feeling* occurs as well, we cannot know from the list alone whether the words refer to semantic fields of reflection or to the field of emotion. While looking at word lists out of context constitutes an obvious disadvantage, we argue that exploring the lists further will nevertheless result in giving us a crude understanding of the overall vocabulary composition of the texts. Our search for emotion words thus led us to look at the frequency list of the entire corpus (with the stop words excluded; N=108,017). The percentages reported below present an approximation due to the limitations of the word list analysis just mentioned.[1]

Our perusing of the lists confirmed the semantic fields of patient encounter, the focus on communication skills, and the reflective part of the task. In addition, we found that names of body parts, technical medical vocabulary and emotion words define the corpus. About 12.3 per cent of the words (N=13,755) pertain to either body parts (e.g. *ankle*, 7; *anus*, 4; *arm*, 24; *armpit*, 3; *arms*, 27; *bones*, 3; *brain*, 10) or medical jargon (referring to medication and conditions; e.g. *abdominal*, 20; *abdominous*, 1; *abortion*, 10; *ache*, 8; *aching*, 2; *adhd*, 2; *aeds*, 1; *aetiology*, 1; *aftercare*, 3; *agammaglobulinaemia*, 1; *aids*, 21). The low frequency of the words with many single occurrences is particularly noteworthy.

Turning to lexemes that indicate either emotions or reflection, the overall frequency of about 5 per cent (N=5,846) is lower than for medical jargon, but many of them occur quite frequently. The following list is ordered according to overall frequency:

felt, 960; feel, 642; think, 577; feeling, 248; empathy, 142; happy, 139; comfortable, 135; upset, 128; feelings, 119; believe, 112; worried, 98; sorry, 94; emotions, 81; emotional, 78; confidence, 60; confident, 59; thinking, 55; calm, 54; confused, 54; nervous, 54; concerned, 53; involved, 50; worry, 50; anxious, 48; embarrassed, 47; sympathy, 43; angry, 41; frustrated, 40; sad, 40; pleased, 38; sensitive, 37; feels, 36; empathetic, 35; fear, 32; emotionally, 31; mood, 28; satisfied, 25; empathise, 24; glad, 24; shy, 24; worrying, 24; annoyed, 23; frustrating, 23; love, 23; believed, 22; comfort, 22; emotion, 21; frustration, 21; guilty, 21; judge, 21; brave, 19; grateful, 19; afraid, 18; loved, 18; sympathetic, 18; stress, 17; empathize, 15; anger, 14; disappointed, 14; happier, 14; satisfaction, 14; comforting, 13; polite, 13; upsetting, 13; worries, 13; apprehensive, 12; unhappy, 12; upbeat, 12; ashamed, 11; distressing, 11; fears, 11; lonely, 11; pleasure, 11; sympathise, 11; annoying, 10; desperately, 10; judgmental, 10; pleasant, 10; saddened, 10; stressed, 10

---

[1] The word lists were gone through manually by two raters, who might have missed some lexemes. As mentioned before, word lists do not allow the rater to make decisions as to whether, for example, *back* is used as a noun or a preposition. These comments are valid for all subsequent presentations of frequencies in this sub-section. In other words, the reported percentages are to be taken as a rough indication of the overall corpus composition and not as precise numbers.

Emotion and reflection vocabulary is here presented together as – on the basis of the word list alone – there can be made no meaningful decision whether words such as *felt/feel/think/feeling*, etc. refer to emotions or the process of reflection. Nevertheless, we can glean from the list a surprising scope of emotion words, ranging from those with negative connotations (22 per cent, N=1,278) and positive connotations (23 per cent, N=1,312) to those that have either neutral or unclear connotations out of context (56 per cent, N=3,238).

In the list of emotion words with negative connotations, we can make out clusters of word fields that are notable because of their comparative high frequencies: WORRY (N=185), BEING UPSET (N=143), FRUS-TRATION (N=87), NERVOUSNESS (N=67), SADNESS (N=62), EMBARRASS-MENT (N=60), ANXIOUSNESS (N=55), CONFUSION (N=54), FEAR (N=52), ANGER (N=41) and STRESS (N=40). While the list itself does not yield any insights as to whether these emotions are assigned to the patient or the student, the mere scope of them is noteworthy.

The emotion words with positive connotations are equally varied in scope. The most frequent clusters are around EMPATHY (N=240), COM-FORT (N=181), HAPPINESS (N=165), CONFIDENCE (N=120), SYMPATHY (N=83), CALMNESS (N=69), PLEASANTNESS (N=64), and SATISFACTION (N=43). The frequent mention of *empathy* can be explained with the fact that this concept does not only refer to genuinely felt emotions but also to a strategy taught in the communication skills module and recommended for the purpose of enhancing rapport with patients (see, for example, l. 40-42 in the Appendix).

To illustrate the use of positive emotion words in context we present extracts from a text written by a 20 year old, female medical student, who indicates English and Thai as her first languages (N-088). The memorable encounter is about a patient who impressed the student with her positive attitude. The patient is a dancer with diabetes whose legs were amputated. The student starts the text by setting a dark scene (the extracts are quoted without any corrections; italics added):

> 1 It was a dark, rainy morning when my colleague and I visited the patient
> 2 during our first hospital visit of the year.

> [371 words: Description of the history taking, the feeling of shock and being at a loss at learning that the patient had been a dancer whose legs had been amputated ("I felt shocked"; "I was lost as to how to react")]

36 I was really *sad* to hear that, a dancer who no longer had legs! That
37 must've felt *awful*. My colleague and I *failed to find appropriate*
38 *consoling words* for the patient. *We stayed silent. I was at lost.* [sic.]
39
40 But we did try to [b]e *empathetic*, offering kind words of support
41 and understanding as the interview went on. I *nodded and mirrored the*
42 *patient's slight gestures and frowns, hoping to convey my empathies.*

The student explicitly states that the tragic fate of the dancer was *not why [she] remembered the encounter so vividly* (l. 16). Instead, the student is affected by the positive and optimistic outlook of the patient. An extract that is positioned after several passages with constructed dialogue illustrates this nicely (note the repeated use of metaphors):

57 I felt a *revitalizing energy* from the patient. She was *strong*. I saw her
58 as *powerful and hopeful*. She would never let something like this
59 *"drag [her] down."* I was *taken aback, surprised, and proud of the*
60 *optimism* all at the same time.
61 She was *marvelous*.
62 The patient herself must've felt *proud* as well. She was *smiling*
63 *brightly, laughing*, and her speech and language was *uplifting*. She
64 must've felt that she could not give up, even with this condition, and so

65 she *refused to feel down.*
(N-088)

In this extract we witness how the emotions of the patient directly affect the student. In addition, and from a stylistic point of view, the description of the student's emotions as a reaction to the patient's fate are the leitmotif for the composition of the text. The patient's worldview is so uplifting that the student's emotions also change as a consequence.

Finally, there is a set of words that have to do with reflection and emotion, which have neutral or ambiguous connotations out of context (as mentioned above, an analysis of word frequency out of context defies easy assigning of these lexical items to either emotions or reflections only). Particularly striking are the clusters around FEEL/ FEELINGS (N=2,005), THINK (N=641), and BELIEVE (N=146). *Think* and *feel* also belong to the 100 most frequent words in the corpus overall (excluding stop words).

3.2. Thematic Analysis of 50 Reflective Writing Texts

After having established that the students draw on the semantic fields of emotions as an important aspect of their vocabulary use, we now turn to a quantitative analysis of the topics the students choose to write about in a sub-corpus of 50 texts. The first 25 texts from the two cohorts were analyzed with respect to the main themes that students raised in their texts (N=50; 27 per cent of the entire corpus).[2] A team of three raters achieved consensus by discussing the question *What is this text about?*[3] The results are presented in Table 1. Up to three categories could be chosen in order to understand why the students had chosen the particular memorable encounter they wrote about. Table 1 shows that the students make the explicit discussion of communication skills a central aspect in 37 of the 50 texts (74 per cent). This means that the students do not only reflect on communication skills in the reflective part, but they also choose a memorable encounter in which (successful or unsuccessful) communication skills present a central point. This thematic preference is then followed by singling out special medical conditions (28 per cent; e.g. depression) and talking about (lack of) professional experience on the part of the medical student (20 per cent).

Importantly, two topic categories have to do with either the patient's emotions (18 per cent) or the student's emotions (16 per cent). In one text both emotion topics are raised, so that there are 16 texts in total, in which emotions play an important thematic role (32 per cent). This finding shows that rather than just mentioning emotions in the reflective parts of the texts (the instructions require reflections on emotional reactions), the students raise the topic of emotions and how to cope with them in its own right. This high percentage of emotion topics confirms that it is challenging for medical students to deal with emotional patients as well as to deal with their own emotional reactions to patients. This problem will be discussed more thoroughly against previous research below.

---

[2] Since there is no underlying ordered principle (other than the name of the student before anonymization) for the sequence of texts in the corpus, this choice amounts to a random selection.

[3] The core researcher Regula Koenig developed a catalogue of bottom-up thematic categories, and then trained two raters in recognizing them. Since a text could raise many issues in passing and the question was about the "main themes" raised, the team decided to reach a consensus about one to three important themes per text by discussion rather than independent coding (see MacQueen, Mclellan-Lemal, Bartholow and Milstein; Namey, Guest, Thairu and Johnson).

Table 1: Thematic analysis (only categories of more than 10 per cent are displayed)

	No. of texts	% of N=50
Communication skills explicitly present	37	74
Special conditions	14	28
(Lack of) Experience	10	20
Emotions patient	*9*	*18*
Impact of illness on patient's life	9	18
Emotions student	*8*	*16*
Setting (several participants/people)	6	12
Successful encounter	5	10

Furthermore, taking a closer look at the 37 texts in which communication skills are explicitly focused on as a topic, it transpires that the use of *empathy* is mentioned in a third of all texts (N=16, 32 per cent), preceded only by mention of the use of *questions* (N=21, 42 per cent) and *structuring an interview* (N=18, 36 per cent), and followed by the mention of *rapport* (N=15, 30 per cent). Once again we therefore see the importance of dealing with emotions for the medical students as a critical part of their professional training.

Medical educators including our collaborator Victoria Tischler have recognized the need for giving guidance to medical students by introducing lectures on communication with patients who are distressed. This issue is a legitimate concern for young people on their way to becoming doctors since they are on the one hand encouraged to find ways of expressing empathy with patients (see, e.g., Maguire and Pitceathly) and on the other they are warned against *compassion fatigue* in order to prevent burn-out (see, e.g., Pfifferling and Gilley). It is striking that these young students, who are reporting on their first experiences in the field, already single out this topic as problematic and thus put their finger on an important aspect of their profession, which has been termed *emotional labor* (Hochschild *The Managed Heart*, "Emotion Work"; Erickson and Grove), a term to which we will return at the end of the next section.

3.3. Illustration: Dealing with a Distressed Patient

Having established in the previous sections that students highlight emotions as an important topic and that they use a wide range of emotion words, we now turn to illustrating how an emotional stance (cf. Matoesian) is created in the text of a particular student, which combines writing about the patient's emotions and the student's emotions in the same text.

The theoretical framework for our analysis is inspired by Planalp's work on emotional cues in face-to-face interaction. Table 2 shows that these cues are multimodal, ranging from vocal, verbal, body, and physiological to facial cues. When taken together, they constitute a *composite signal* which is created *online* and designed for the identification by the recipient (Clark 178-179; for overviews on emotional cues, cf. Ochs and Schieffelin; Langlotz and Locher). In our data, we have to rely entirely on the linguistic power of evoking emotional stance. In other words, the writers use language for the emotional *verbal cues* listed in Table 2, but they can also choose to use language to report on and describe the other cues (vocal, body, physiological, facial) in retrospect.

Table 2: Planalp's overview of emotional cues (see also Langlotz and Locher)

Class of cues	Forms of realization
Vocal	voice quality: low, loud, slow, fast, trembling, high-pitched, monotonous, animate voice
Verbal cues	language-specific emotion vocabularies metaphors speech acts emotional discourse practices, e.g. therapeutic discourse
Body cues	animated, energetic movement physical actions: throwing things, making threatening movements, kissing, caressing gait: walking heavily, lightly, arm swing, length/speed of stride body posture: stiff/rigid, droopy, upright hands/arms gestures: hand emblems, clenching hands or fists
Physiological cues	blushing, pupil dilation, heart rate, breathing, skin temperature
Facial cues	facial expressions of emotions through forehead and eyebrows, eyes and eyelids, and the lower face (mouth, lips, labionasal folds)

The chosen text (N-85, see Appendix for the entire text) was written by a 20 year old female student with English as a first language. The main issue described in the chosen encounter is the role and impact of the patient's and the student's emotions on how the encounter develops. In addition, the student also focuses in particular on empathy as a communication skill in the reflective parts of the text. The chosen encounter is about a patient who becomes very distressed during the consultation due to her condition (a persistent viral infection and pregnancy) and starts crying. The student recounts that she does not know how to handle this outburst. The patient becomes even more upset when a blood test is required because of her severe phobias about needles and blood. At this point the patient starts to scream and hyperventilate. After the encounter the student feels emotionally drained and is not satisfied with how she dealt with the situation.

Since the topic of this text is how an encounter with a distressed patient did not go smoothly, the text is brimming with emotion cues. Lexical emotion cues are indicated in italics in the extracts below and in the appendix. The student is assigning emotional mental states to the patient and to herself during the encounter by employing verbal cues of language-specific emotion vocabularies. A selection of examples is given here in italics:

- She smiled but it struck me that she looked *unhappy*. (l. 8-9)
- I was left alone with the patient who was becoming more and more *upset* (l. 18-19)
- *I felt awful* that I couldn't do anything to help her. [. . .] (l. 29)
- I tried to adopt a *soothing tone of voice* when speaking and *felt desperate* to say something to *make her feel better*. (l. 54-56)
- This made the patient even more *upset*, I felt utterly *helpless*. (l. 59-60)
- The *fear in her eyes* made me *feel even worse* – I knew how *scared and upset* she was but I couldn't make it better. (l. 62-64)

The student uses emotion adjectives and collocations as verbal cues of emotional stance (*unhappy, upset, scared, feeling awful/ desperate/helpless*), describes a vocal cue (*soothing tone of voice*) and a facial/physiological cue (*fear in her eyes*).

The student does not only assign mental states by means of emotion vocabulary to herself and the patient, but also stresses how the patient's distress affects her own emotional state. As a consequence of the patient's distress, she herself feels *awful, desperate* and *helpless*. This is primarily the case because the student feels that she cannot adequately help the patient. Indirectly the student thus highlights her expectations that a doctor should be able to improve the patient's situation (*I couldn't do anything to help her*, l. 29; *make her feel better*, l. 56; *couldn't make it better*, l. 64). The fact that doctors often in fact cannot help patients (medically or emotionally) is rarely talked about as doctors are usually trained to intervene. In contrast, Johansen, Holtedahl, Davidsen and Rudebeck, in a study on GPs treating terminally ill cancer patients in Norway, point out that acknowledging a shared humanness can enable a doctor to simply "be" with a terminally ill patient where medical intervention is no longer effective. This requires understanding of both physiological and existential suffering, which is often absent in biomedical training.

The student also uses the description of actions to signal the patient's and her own emotions (italics added):

- She *smiled* but it struck me that she looked unhappy. (l. 8-9)
- The patient began to *cry*. (l. 24)
- I reached into my bag and *leaned towards* the patient *asking if she needed a tissue*. (l. 28-29)
- Later, Dr Name began to prepare the patient for blood to be taken, when she realised what was happening *she screamed and began to hyperventilate*. (l. 60-62)
- Between *her sobs* she explained that she had severe phobias of both needles and blood. *All I could do was hand her another tissue*. (l. 64-66)

The emotion cues in these examples once again represent lexical items that have emotional connotations (*smile, cry, scream, hyperventilate, sobs*). However, there are also a number of actions that are indexical of showing concern and empathy in the context of such an encounter (*lean towards the patient, offer a tissue*). The student recalls these actions (body cues and speech acts) that indexed emotional stance at the time and reports them by means of language.

In other instances, the student describes a situation in words that only become emotionally charged when interpreted in context:

- I found it *difficult* to know what to say: I had *no idea of how someone in this situation would feel and I didn't want to sound insincere or make matters even worse*. (l. 24-26; see also l. 34-35)

The sentences in lines 24 to 26 describe an emotional situation in which the student could be described as feeling helpless and worried about doing the right thing, but the words in themselves are not strongly emotionally indexical.

In addition, the student employs a more indirect means of evoking the emotional state of the patient in that she uses *constructed dialogue* (cf. Tannen).[4] By presenting the patient as using her own words to signal emotional distress, the emotions are *enacted* rather than assigned (italics added):

- Patient: *"I'm sorry about all this."* (l. 20)
- Patient: "It's just . . . this has been going on for so long and *I can't cope anymore."* (l. 22)

The literature on oral narratives of personal experience reports that constructed dialogue can be used to create involvement in the listeners, create immediacy and can move the narrative plot forward (Tannen). Rather than summarizing or paraphrasing a dialogue, the listeners are invited to draw their own conclusions. However, the student who creates the story world of her memorable encounter does not use the passage with constructed dialogue to advance the story much. Instead, she uses it as an illustration to give her own assessment of the patient's unhappiness more credibility since it is the patient herself who implies that she is desperate (*I can't cope anymore*, l. 22).

In the reflective passages, the student explicitly highlights that she was surprised about the force of the emotional contagion (also note the use of the container metaphor in the first example):

- I know that this encounter was *emotionally draining for me* and *I can only imagine that it was ten times worse for the patient.* (l. 38-40)
- I wasn't aware of how much of an effect the patient's upset would have on me; (l. 80-81).

She explicitly refers to the use of *empathy* as a strategy that she tried to employ in order to counteract the distressing situation:

- *I hope that by at least offering her a tissue and showing some empathy towards her this made her feel slightly better.* (l. 40-42)

Students are introduced to the use of empathy in the communication skills course as a strategy that can be signaled verbally and non-verbally. Empathy is encouraged in clinical communication as a powerful tool for

---

[4] The students are explicitly invited to use constructed dialogue in the instructions for the reflective writing task. The presence of constructed dialogue is thus not surprising but how it is used is of interest for our study.

enhancing rapport and therefore relationship building with patients. Empathy is a type of emotional resonance that students and clinicians are advised to develop as it has therapeutic benefits such as encouraging disclosure and reducing anxiety (Halpern). Students are advised to try to imagine the patient's experience by emotionally attuning to verbal and non-verbal cues that they can express for example in their tone of voice or use of emotive language.

In addition, the student proposes that showing (more) empathy and being *more confident, less anxious* and *embarrassed* could be a solution for handling future situations in a more satisfying way:

- As I gain more experience talking to patients and relatives who are distressed *I will become more confident and less anxious.* I realise that *my anxiety wasn't helpful* in this situation and could have *made the patient feel worse. In the future I think I will be better equipped for this type of situation where hopefully I will be able to reassure the patient by saying something like "I understand that you are upset".* (l. 43-48)
- On reflection I think that *I should have felt less embarrassed about saying the wrong thing. I should have just used more empathic statements and provided more of an opportunity for the patient to discuss how she felt. I think that as long as I was sincere the patient would not have been offended by my discussing her distress. Al though afterwards I have consoled myself with the fact that at least the patient felt comfortable enough in the consultation to remain there, continue talking to us and show her emotions.* (l. 71-78)
- Hopefully I will be *less anxious and more confident* in talking to patients about why they are upset [. . .] (l. 91-92)

In developing these future scenarios, the student discusses the potential emotional consequences that a change in her communicative behavior might have. Finally, the student also points out that showing too much empathy might be negative:

- I wasn't aware of how much of an effect the patient's upset would have on me; in the future I will try to remain empathic *but I must also be aware of maintaining a professional amount of distance.* (l. 80-83)

Finding the balance between empathizing and not being drawn into an emotional situation at the expense of the medical practitioner's own health is indeed a difficult task. The student uses the phrase *maintaining a professional amount of distance* to refer to this challenge. However, students also often use this or similar phrases not only to express concern for their own health, but also because they are worried that they cannot remain professional if they get too drawn into the emotional world of the patient.

So how can these insights be related to the more general topic of reflective writing in medical training and corresponding challenges of emotion management? Erickson and Grove convincingly argue that all interaction between people involves the need to manage emotions (707). Drawing on Hochschild's work (*The Managed Heart*), they propose to make a distinction within emotion management between "emotion work" "to refer to the management of emotion in personal interactions (e.g., with family and friends)" and "emotion labor," which "should be used only in occupational contexts where one is managing emotions because it is part of what the job requires" (Erickson and Grove 707). In healthcare and therapy contexts, the need to address the patient's emotions is particularly prominent as the latter are given help in coping and managing their emotions (Erickson and Grove 707). Learning how to manage the professional's emotions, however, is also part of learning about the practice. In their review of work about nursing, Erickson and Grove show that there are conflicting norms at play. On the one hand, "we generally expect that our doctors and nurses approach our health care with a certain level of empathic concern," and on the other hand, "emotional detachment, neutrality, and/or emotional control" are taught as "fundamental to providing quality care and to preserving their own health and well-being" (712). It is exactly this dilemma that is described by the student in her description of neutrality and empathy above, which points to the importance of making emotional labor a topic in medical teaching.

The quantitative thematic analysis of the fifty texts and the qualitative discussion of a sample text have illustrated that very early on in their training students are aware of the emotional challenges of their profession. The role of emotions transpires as an important issue in the descriptive/narrative part of the texts as well as in the reflective parts. As illustrated with an exemplary analysis of one text, when creating an emotional stance in their text, students can draw on verbal cues and they use language to describe vocal (*soothing tone of voice*), body (*lean towards somebody, offer a tissue*), and physiological/facial cues (*fear in her eyes*).

4. Conclusions and Outlook

Our thematic content analysis of reflective writing texts of medical students shows that handling emotions in doctor-patient interaction transpires as a challenge early in the training of medical students. The students report that they are affected by the patients' positive or negative emotions and that their own reaction is especially difficult to handle in the case of distressed patients. It is therefore important to offer tailored input on dealing with distressed patients and also dealing with one's own emotions and psychological welfare.[5]

The students use language to create emotional cues. The most straightforward ones are verbal cues, such as the use of language-specific emotion vocabularies, metaphors or speech acts. The students also use language to describe vocal, body, physiological and facial cues. Finally, they use constructed dialogue to give the patient a voice in expressing emotions themselves. The lexicon analysis shows that a wide variety of emotions are discussed and that positive and negative connotations are equally present.

Future research on these texts can explore a number of linguistic and applied issues in connection with emotions. It would be worthwhile to pursue the question of metaphors more, to understand better what exactly students mean when they write about "empathy," to see whether they propose solutions of their own to deal with their own or their patients' emotions. Finally, the use of such texts as a vehicle for catharsis could be examined as a potential way of combating stress and burnout.

*

Acknowledgements

We would like to thank all the Nottingham medical students and Victoria Tischler who have allowed us to use their texts for this study and the Swiss National Science Foundation (126959, 144541) for funding our research. We also thank Victoria Tischler for her constructive feedback on this essay. In addition, we express our sincere thanks to the interns who helped us with data analysis at various stages of the project: Ellen Brugger, Olga Brühlmann, Florence Bühler, Evelyne Iyer-Grüniger, Dino Kuckovic, Nathalie Meyer, Ruth Partl, and Andrea Wüst. Finally, we thank the anonymous reviewers for their constructive criticism.

---

[5] Other challenging situations for doctor-patient communication are dealing with patients who are impaired in their capacities as communicators (physically or mentally, children), and situations in which the patient is accompanied by a caretaker or interpreter. In Nottingham specific lectures deal with these issues in addition to how to deal with distressed patients.

Appendix

Lexical patient emotion cues (<EP . . .>) and student emotion cues (<ES . . .>) are indicated in diamond brackets and italics:

1 As the patient stood up and walked towards the consultation room I
2 guessed that she was around 35 years old. Her face was slightly flushed
3 and she was holding a tissue⁶ – I assumed that she was coming to the
4 surgery about a cold or flu. She entered the room and sat down; under the
5 bright lights of the consultation room I noticed how much the patient
6 reminded me of my neighbour. As "Dr Name" looked for her notes I saw
7 that the patient was sat towards the front of her chair with her legs crossed
8 looking towards the floor. *<EP She smiled>* but it struck me that *<EP she looked*
9 *unhappy>*.

10-17 [Summary of information on the patient's condition provided by Dr Name]

18 Dr Name left the room to get a syringe for some blood tests. I was left
19 alone with the patient who was becoming *<EP more and more upset>*:

20 Patient: *<EP "I'm sorry about all this.">*
21 Student: "It's OK"
22 Patient: "It's just . . . this has been going on for so long and *<EP I can't cope anymore.>*
And things I would normally take, you know like Echinacea, I can't with being pregnant."
23 Student: "It must be really difficult."

24 *<EP The patient began to cry.>* *<ES I found it difficult to know what to*
25 *say: I had no idea of how someone in this situation would feel and I*
26 *didn't want to sound insincere or make matters even worse.>* I wanted to
27 break the silence but couldn't think of anything to say to make her feel
28 better. I reached into my bag and leaned towards the patient *<EP asking*
29 *if she needed a tissue.>* She smiled as I handed her a tissue. *<ES I felt*
30 *awful>* that I couldn't do anything to help her. After the patient had left
31 Dr Name asked me if I was OK. *<ES I explained that I found it difficult*
32 *knowing what to say when the patient started to cry.>* It was easier in
33 hindsight to think I should have said "I understand why you are upset"
34 but I wasn't sure that I did understand. At the time I was concerned with
35 *<ES sounding insincere or even patronising>*; but in reflection, the
36 patient probably wouldn't have been that critical of the exact phrasing I
37 used and *<EP might have been comforted and felt more able to discuss*
38 *her feelings with me>*. I know that this encounter was *<ES emotionally*
39 *draining for me>* and *<ES I can only imagine that it was ten times worse*
40 *for the patient>* I hope that by at least offering her a tissue and
41 *<ES showing some empathy towards her>* *<EP this made her feel*
42 *slightly better.>*

43 As I gain more experience talking to patients and relatives who are
44 distressed *<EP I will become more confident & less anxious. I realise*
45 *that my anxiety wasn't helpful in this situation and could have made the*

---

⁶ The mention of the tissue is a foreshadowing that the patient is in distress, but the student is careful to point out that she first interpreted this sign as indexing a cold rather than distress.

46 *patient feel worse. In the future I think I will be better equipped for this*
47 *type of situation where hopefully I will be able to reassure the patient by*
48 *saying something like "I understand that you are upset".>* After
49 speaking to Dr Name and consulting relevant literature I have also
50 learned the value of a brief silence. This can give the patient an
51 opportunity to discuss their feelings or simply for everyone concerned to
52 reflect.

53 I feel that this encounter was memorable because it was the first time that
54 was alone with <EP *a patient who was so obviously upset>*. I tried to
55 adopt a <ES *soothing tone of voice* when speaking and *felt desperate to*
56 *say something to make her feel better.>* As the consultation progressed
57 The patient revealed that she was <EP *fearful of losing her job>* as she
58 had had to take time off due to her illness and would then be going on
59 maternity leave. <EP *This made the patient even more upset,>* <ES *I felt*
60 *utterly helpless.>* Later, Dr Name began to prepare the patient for blood
61 to be taken, when she realised what was happening <EP *she screamed*
62 *and began to hyperventilate. The fear in her eyes>* <ES *made me feel*
63 *even worse>* – I knew how <EP *scared and upset she was>* but I
64 couldn't make it better. Between <EP *her sobs>* she explained that she
65 had severe phobias of both needles and blood. <EP *All I could do was*
66 *hand her another tissue.>*

67 I didn't communicate with the patient as I had intended. I didn't
67 anticipate how difficult it would be for me to remain calm and say
68 something comforting to the patient. As the conversation between the
69 patient, Dr Name and myself continued the <EP *patient became*
70 *increasingly upset;>* I had been hoping that it would have been the
71 opposite to this. On reflection I think that <ES *I should have felt less*
72 *embarrassed about saying the wrong thing. I should have just used more*
73 *empathic statements and provided more of an opportunity for the patient*
74 *to discuss how she felt. I think that as long as I was sincere the patient*
75 *would not have been offended by my discussing her distress. Although*
76 *afterwards I have consoled myself with the fact that at least the patient*
77 *felt comfortable enough in the consultation to remain there, continue*
78 *talking to us and show her emotions.>*

79 <EP *I have learnt how difficult and how emotionally demanding some*
80 *consultations can be. I wasn't aware of how much of an effect the*
81 *patient's upset would have on me; in the future I will try to remain*
82 *empathic but I must also be aware of maintaining a professional amount*
83 *of distance.>* As I have mentioned previously, this encounter has also
84 taught me that sometimes a silence can be helpful in getting the patient to
85 discuss their emotions and concerns with you. I don't think I could have
86 been any more prepared for this encounter. Learning about the theory
87 behind communication in these situations was useful but seemed to go
88 completely out of the window when I was actually presented with a <EP
89 *patient who was so distressed.>* I think now that I have been in this
90 situation I will be more capable of shaping such an encounter in the
91 future. Hopefully I will be <ES *less anxious and more confident>* in
92 talking to patients about why they are upset although I appreciate that not
93 all patients will react in the same way in these types of encounters
94 therefore I must be flexible in my approach to them.
(Corpus: Nottingham, Text 85)

References

Branch, William T. and Anuradha Paranjape. "Feedback and Reflection: Teaching Methods for Clinical Settings." *Academic Medicine* 77 (2002): 1185-1188.

Clark, Herbert H. *Using Language.* Cambridge: Cambridge University Press, 1996.

Erickson, Rebecca J. and Wendy J. C. Grove. "Emotional labor and health care." *Sociology Compass* 2 (2008): 704-733.

Gygax, Franziska. "On Being Ill (in Britain and the US)." *European Journal of Life Writing* 2 (2013): 1-17.

——. "Theoretically Ill: Autobiographer, Patient, Theorist." *The Writing Cure: Literature and Medicine in Context.* Ed. Alexandra Lembert-Heidenreich and Jarmila Mildorf. Münster: LIT, 2013. 173-190.

——, Regula Koenig and Miriam A. Locher. "Moving across Disciplines and Genres: Reading Identity in Illness Narratives and Reflective Writing Texts." *Medical Communication in Clinical Contexts.* Ed. Rukhsana Ahmed and Benjamin Bates. Dubuque: Kendall Hunt, 2012. 17-35.

Halpern, Jodi. "What is Clinical Empathy?" *Journal of General Internal Medicine* 18.8 (2003): 670-674.

Hampton, Martin. *Reflective Writing: a Basic Introduction.* 2010. Available at: www.port.ac.uk/media/contacts-and-departments/student-support-services/ask/downloads/Reflective-writing-a-basic-introduction .pdf (last accessed on 4 February 2014)

Hochschild, Arlie R. "Emotion Work, Feeling Rules, and Social Structure." *American Journal of Sociology* 85 (1979): 551-575.

——. *The Managed Heart: Commercialization of Human Feeling.* Berkeley: University of California Press, 1983.

Johansen, May-Lill, Knut Arne Holtedahl, Annette Sofie Davidsen and Carl Edvard Rudebeck. "'I Deal with the Small Things:' The Doctor-Patient Relationship and Professional Identity in GPs' Stories of Cancer Care." *Health* 16.6 (2012): 569-584.

Langlotz, Andreas and Miriam A. Locher. "The Role of Emotions in a Discursive Approach to Relational Work." *Journal of Pragmatics* 58 (2013): 87-107.

MacQueen, Kathleen M., Eleanor Mclellan-Lemal, Kelly Bartholow and Bobby Milstein. "Team-Based Codebook Development: Structure, Process, and Agreement." *Handbook for Team-Based Qualitative Research.* Eds. G. Guest and K. M. MacQueen. Lanham: Altamira, 2008. 119-136.

Maguire, Peter and Carolyn Pitceathly. "Key Communication Skills and How to Acquire Them." *British Medical Journal* 325 (2002): 697-700.

Matoesian, Greg. "Struck by Speech Revisited: Embodied Stance in Jurisdictional Discourse." Journal of Sociolinguistics 9.2 (2005): 167-193.

Monash University. *What is Reflective Writing?* 2012. Available at: http://-www.monash.edu.au/lls/llonline/writing/medicine/reflective/1.xml (last accessed on 13 March 2013).

Namey, Emily, Greg Guest, Lucy Thairu and Laura Johnson. "Data Reduction Techniques for Large Qualitative Data Sets." *Handbook for Team-Based Qualitative Research*. Eds. Greg Guest and Kathleen M. MacQueen. Lanham: Altamira, 2008. 137-162.

Ochs, Elinor and Bambi Schieffelin. "Language Has a Heart." *Text* 9.1 (1989): 7-25.

Pfifferling, John Henry and Kay Gilley. "Overcoming Compassion Fatigue." *Family Practice Management* 7.4 (2000): 39-44.

Planalp, Sally. "Communicating Emotion in Everyday Life: Cues, Channels, and Processes." *Handbook of Communication and Emotion: Research, Theory, Applications, and Contexts*. Ed. Peter A. Andersen and Laura K. Guerrero. San Diego: Academic Press, 1998. 29-48.

Scott, Mike. "PC Analysis of Keywords – and Key Key Words." *System* 25.2 (1997): 233-45.

Stubbs, Michael. *Words and Phrases: Corpus Studies of Lexical Semantics*. Malden: Blackwell, 2001.

Tannen, Deborah. *Talking Voices: Repetition, Dialogue, and Imagery in Conversational Discourse*. Cambridge: Cambridge University Press, 1989.

Watton, Pete, Jane Collings and Jenny Moon. *Reflective Writing: Guidance Notes for Students*. 2001. Available at: www.exeter.ac.uk/fch/work-experience/reflective-writing-guidance.pdf (last accessed on 13 March 2013).

Political Emotions: Civil Religion and Melodrama in Spielberg's *Lincoln*

Agnieszka Soltysik Monnet

This essay focuses on how Spielberg's film engages with and contributes to the myth of Lincoln as a super-natural figure, a saint more than a hero or great statesman, while anchoring his moral authority in the sentimental rhetoric of the domestic sphere. It is this use of the melodramatic mode, linking the familial space with the national through the trope of the victim-hero, that is the essay's main concern. With Tony Kushner, author of *Angels in America*, as scriptwriter, it is perhaps not surprising that melodrama is the operative mode in the film. One of the issues that emerges from this analysis is how the film updates melodrama for a contemporary audience in order to minimize what could be perceived as manipulative sentimental devices, observing for most of the film an aesthetic of relative sobriety and realism. In the last hour, and especially the final minutes of the film, melodramatic conventions are deployed in full force and infused with hagiographic iconography to produce a series of emotionally charged moments that create a perfect union of American Civil Religion and classical melodrama. The cornerstone of both cultural paradigms, as deployed in this film, is death: Lincoln's at the hands of an assassin, and the Civil War soldiers', poignantly depicted at key moments of the film. Finally, the essay shows how film melodrama as a genre weaves together the private and the public, the domestic with the national, the familial with the military, and links pathos to politics in a carefully choreographed narrative of sentimentalized mythopoesis.

Emotion, Affect, Sentiment: The Language and Aesthetics of Feeling. SPELL: Swiss Papers in English Language and Literature 30. Ed. Andreas Langlotz and Agnieszka Soltysik Monnet. Tübingen: Narr, 2014. 237-256.

Few national figures inspire the emotions that Abraham Lincoln does. Even during his life Lincoln was both passionately revered and hated. His violent death on Good Friday at the hands of a Confederate patriot and Lincoln-hater, merely a month after his second inauguration, transformed the end-of-war gratitude of a nation into the high-pitched worship that only martyrdom can confer. Steven Spielberg's recent film, *Lincoln* (2012), is about the last three months of Abraham Lincoln's life, and more specifically about the complex political effort to pass the controversial Thirteenth Amendment, abolishing slavery. The film's focus on Lincoln's skill as Washington operator and manager of people, both friends and enemies, comes from the book that inspired Tony Kushner's screenplay: Doris Goodman's *Team of Rivals* (2005), which is concerned with, as Goodman's subtitle tells us, "The Political Genius of Abraham Lincoln." The film departs in several important aspects from the book, however. One is the more narrow focus on Lincoln himself, while the book examines the other men in Lincoln's cabinet, the "team" of the title. Secondly, Kushner introduces an attention to Lincoln's domestic life as well as his intimate moments with his male secretaries, telegraph workers, and other young men such as soldiers in camp or at the hospital. A third element that Spielberg and Kushner bring to the story is a narrative mode structuring the emotional choreography of the film that is best understood as a form of melodrama. And finally, the film emphasizes an aesthetic and performative aspect of Lincoln that we can read through the concept of American Civil Religion.

My main argument about the film is that it weaves these last two dimensions, melodrama and Civil Religion, together to perform cinematographically a task that national heroes have traditionally accomplished, namely, inspire increased devotion to the cause of national coherence at a time of conflict or patriotic lassitude. I take the word "devotion" from Lincoln's own Gettysburg Address, where he uses the word interchangeably for patriotism and the willingness to die for one's country. The one other time that Lincoln was conjured so insistently through the movies to unite and inspire a weary nation was on the eve of World War II, where two Lincoln films in a row, both focusing on his humble origins, were deployed to heal the wounds of a decade of the Depression.[1] At present, at least five films have been released since 2010.[2] Two are

---

[1] *Young Mr. Lincoln* (1939, dir. John Ford) and *Abe Lincoln in Illinois* (1940, dir. John Cromwell).

[2] *The Conspirator* (2010, dir. Robert Redford), *Abraham Lincoln vs. Zombies* (2012, dir. Richard Schenkman), *Abraham Lincoln: Vampire Hunter* (2012, dir. Timor Bekmanbetov), *Lincoln* (2012, dir. Steven Speilberg), *Saving Lincoln* (2013, dir. Salvador Litvak).

explicitly Gothic, one portraying Lincoln as a vampire hunter, just as the title promises, and another portraying him as a zombie killer. A third focuses on the trial of Booth's co-conspirators, especially Mary Surratt, the first woman hung by a federal court. All are reverential towards Lincoln and portray him as a great humanitarian and super-human hero (in two of these films, literally). All focus on his last years or months of life, and assassination, unlike the earlier films, which were concerned with Lincoln's poor, rural and working class background, an aspect of Lincoln that spoke to a Depression-wracked nation.

Why the current interest in resurrecting the late Lincoln on screen? One possible answer is the link between the struggle for abolition and the election of a black President to the White House. In this perspective, Obama's election is the culmination of a process of political enfranchisement that begins with the Emancipation Proclamation. Another answer might lie in the "house divided" trope, a phrase from one of Lincoln's most famous speeches, where he argues that a "house divided against itself cannot stand." The prospect that the American political divide between liberals and conservatives, or simply left and right, is more extreme now than ever before, could therefore account for an appeal to Lincoln since he has traditionally served as a unifying figure. A Southerner by family background and birth, a Northerner by education and adult experience, an easy-going tall-tale telling Westerner in manners, and an Eastern political operator by necessity, Lincoln has often been viewed as the first truly national President. His fervent belief in the Union, and his willingness to accept a Civil War in order to preserve it, also contribute to this aspect of his iconic definition. Lincoln serves as a symbol of unity in yet another way, as a somewhat androgynous figure, a man of feeling, who sympathizes with the grieving mothers of soldiers and who offers pardons at every opportunity. A Southern literary tradition, immortalized in the film *Birth of a Nation*, calls Lincoln the "Great Heart."

A third reason of course is that Lincoln was a war president, and America has been a country at war since 2003, and arguably since 12 September 2001, when Bush announced that the terrorist attacks on New York were "acts of war" and would be retaliated in kind. This is a darker and more complex dimension of Lincoln, one linking him to the 600,000 Civil War deaths, and generating cultural work of memorialization, national definition, and ideological containment that is best approached through the sociological paradigm of Civil Religion.

We can see all three elements acknowledged in the film: the slow but progressive advancement of the African American into the body politic is evoked by the first scenes of the film, where Lincoln chats with black Union soldiers. The divided nature of American politics and a president's need to procure support from a rival party by any means necessary constitutes the main drama as well as comic relief in the film. And finally, the burden of the Commander in Chief of the Armed Forces, as American Presidents are defined, to authorize death and wage war establishes the moral and emotional gravity of the film as it opens and closes with battlefield scenes reminiscent of the unforgettable first thirty minutes of *Saving Private Ryan*, created by the same cinematographer, Janusz Kaminski.

In short, the film engages with various key aspects of the Lincoln myth, as they speak to the current national moment, and weaves them together into a generically hybrid text that invites viewers to renew their faith in the American national project. What I mean by "hybrid" is that the film borrows from several different genre traditions, including the historical biopic, the war film, a congressional variation on the courtroom drama, and of course melodrama, which will be the main focus of this essay. Since the screenplay is written by a playwright, a man in love with words and their complex power, the film is unusually verbose for a Spielberg film. In the first half of the film especially, it feels like we move from one room of talking men to another, with occasionally Molly or Tad to break the monotony. Not that the conversations are themselves monotonous, if you follow their import, but the tone of the film remains fairly subdued in the first two-thirds of its running time before it begins a series of dramaturgical spikes and plateaus that lead to the climax. In fact, I will argue that emotion is central to a thorough understanding of the film and its project, both in terms of the melodramatic portrayal of Lincoln as virtuous victim, and in terms of the way the film is structured emotionally. Melodrama is used to leaven the political hagiography with glimpses of Lincoln's domestic life, while comedy is used to lighten the melodrama with a comic subplot of the three political fixers procuring votes through a variety of schemes and bribes.

In addition, the film adapts melodrama to a contemporary context where the conventional emotional excess of the form yields to a surprising emotional restraint. In fact, some of the most important scenes of the film involve characters *hiding* their emotions, disciplining themselves, and putting on a public mask of moderation or even hypocrisy. One is a flashback of Molly hiding her grief for Willy while hosting a reception at the White house, and another is Thaddeus Stevens refusing to be provoked into a politically inexpedient admission of his radical views. In short, as a modern adaptation of the melodrama genre, the film shies away from emotional excess and advocates a middle road of pragmatism and moderation. Yet emotion remains at the center of the film, both in its portrait of Lincoln as sufferer, and in its melodrama-heavy second half, where the speechifying of the first half pays off in a series of emotionally intense moments beginning with a violent quarrel between Lincoln and his son Robert and culminating with his assassination.

Melodrama

First of all, it is important to clarify and demystify the term "melodrama," a term that is used loosely in common parlance for any kind of emotionally exaggerated narrative or situation. The stigma that Modernism attached to emotional response continues to exert its toxic influence on literary study even if scholars of American culture have been challenging its assumptions since at least the 1980s. Works like Jane Tompkins' *Sensational Designs* (1986) revolutionized scholarship on the nineteenth century by taking seriously the role and effects of genres like melodrama and the sentimental novel. Tompkins' expression "cultural work" has in the meantime become the defining term of the field of Cultural Studies insofar as the project of this discipline is to examine cultural texts of all kinds for their inscription of power relationships and ideology. Tompkins specifically looked at the political power imbricated with the sentimental effects of texts such as *Uncle Tom's Cabin* (1852). In the meantime, the field of melodrama studies in film and drama was developing since the 1970s, where works like David Grimstead's *Melodrama Unveiled* (1976) and Thomas Elsaesser's "Tales of Sound and Fury" (1972) set the groundwork for a rich investigation of social melodrama in popular culture.

The study that probably had the most influence of all on both literary and popular culture melodrama studies was Peter Brooks' *The Melodramatic Imagination* (1976), which argued that melodrama emerged from a post-religious European society as a way of coping with lost moral blueprints and frames of reference. This argument, which gave serious cultural significance to precisely those elements that were most despised in melodrama, namely, its moral simplicity, its emotional overdetermination, and its domestic situations, and identified these characteristics in canonical writers such as Henry James, launched a generation of scholars to investigate how melodrama operates in a variety of cultural texts and contexts.

Besides Tompkins', the most influential and important work to focus specifically on American culture is Linda Williams' *Playing the Race Card* (2001), in which she argues that melodrama is "the fundamental mode by which American mass culture has 'talked to itself' about the enduring moral dilemma of race" (xiv). I would take this insight a step further, and argue that American mass culture talks to itself in a melodramatic mode about American history and identity in general. Like Brooks, Williams sees melodrama as more than a mode seeking emotionalism for its own sake but rather a genre with larger stakes, such as the quest for a "hidden moral legibility" in what Brooks calls a "post-sacred world" (Williams 18; Brooks 15). Brooks' term "the moral occult" is also important and describes the tendency of the genre to assume that there is a domain of "operative spiritual values which is both indicated within and masked by the surface of reality" (Brooks 5).

The fact that the moral occult of melodrama is both secular and yet gestures towards a hidden spiritual dimension or significance aligns it in an unexpected way with the cultural work of Civil Religion, which too is a secular discourse but which presupposes a dimension beyond the physical and empirical informing the agency and meaning of the nation as living entity. Historically, in fact, melodrama and modern Civil Religion are both linked to the emergence of the nation-state and its promise of transcending class, ethnic and religious differences in the dissolving magic of national unity. Like the nation, melodrama seeks to unite and forge links between people, affective links based on a common sensibility. It is no accident that many of the great nationalist novels of the nineteenth century are also very much influenced by melodramatic conventions. These include what Williams calls a "dialectic of pathos and action" (wherein pathos often leads to action), an idealization of a "space of innocence" (often a home or a natural space, in either case a locus of play), the use of character types embodying "primary psychic roles" such as nurturing mother, stern father, good son, or selfish opportunist. Williams also argues, contrary to popular misconceptions about the genre, that melodrama uses the latest devices associated with representational realism in the service of its desire to create identification between characters and readers or spectators. This would explain, for example, why contemporary melodrama is more sober and restrained than nineteenth century melodrama. A final crucial convention, the central one in fact, for Williams, is the focus on a victim-hero and on recognizing his or her virtue. This is the main work of melodrama, and is organized around the depiction of suffering, either mental or physical. Recognizing the virtue of the victim-hero is also the key to the moral legibility orchestrated by the text (Williams 29).

To these conventions, I have added another one (Soltysik 2008) which I view as a crucial extension of the function of the victim-hero, and that is the death of a virtuous character, usually (but not always) the protagonist. In keeping with the semi-magical logic of the moral occult, the death of a virtuous victim possesses an extraordinary agency, and can convert others to the values espoused by the victim, or can serve as catalyst for action that advances those values. A good example is the death of Uncle Tom in Stowe's *Uncle Tom's Cabin,* which converts two up to then sadistic and clownish black slaves on Legree's plantation to Christianity. It also serves as a catalyst for young William Shelby to free all the slaves on the Shelby plantation. In a larger cultural frame, it could be argued that the pathos generated by Uncle Tom's death served as a catalyst for the Civil War. In any case, that is how Abraham Lincoln is said to have described the novel in an anecdote of how he welcomed Harriet Beecher Stowe to the White House with the words "so you're the little woman who wrote the book that made this great war!" (cited in Weinstein" 1).[3]

Although Lincoln's words are probably apocryphal, there is perhaps a core of emotional truth in Lincoln's desire to share the blame for the Civil War, or even to slough it off entirely on Stowe, as this quote suggests. And here we come to a possible answer to a question that is begged by the preceding description of the cultural work of melodrama, namely, if the cultural work of melodrama is to produce recognition of the virtue of a victim-hero, why would Lincoln need such recognition? Wouldn't it be redundant, since he's already a national hero? We can see why the black slave in 1852 could need such recognition, or the fallen woman in 1792, when Susanna Rowson wrote the first great sentimental novel of American literature, *Charlotte Temple,* or even the lawyer with AIDS, as Tom Hanks plays him in the melodramatic film *Philadelphia* in 1993. These are all characters that can be said to exist on the margins of social acceptability and the cultural work of melodrama is to render them sympathetic and includable in the body politic of American society. But Lincoln? Isn't he already at the center of the body politic? I would argue that, precisely because Lincoln was President during the

---

[3] Although Lincoln probably never said these words, the anecdote has been reproduced by countless critics and clearly strikes a chord among readers and scholars (see Vollaro). The real impact of Stowe's novel on antebellum attitudes towards African Americans can never be measured but nineteenth-century abolitionists certainly believed it helped their cause (Vollaro 28-29).

Civil War, he needs redemption and recognition in order to be included in the nation as conceived by popular culture. His potential exclusion stems partly from the precarious position occupied by any sovereign, paradoxically both the leader and the potential scapegoat of the national collectivity.[4] However, an even more obvious reason for Lincoln's need for redemption is suggested by the comment to Stowe that has been so persistently attributed to him. After all, Lincoln is the president with the largest number of deaths of Americans on his hands, 600,000, which is more than World War One, World War Two and the Vietnam War combined. The work of recognizing his virtue is a cultural task that can never be accomplished once and for all but must be re-performed by every generation that wishes to claim him as a unifying figure.

On a third and more mundane level, as this film focuses on the micro-political aspects of Lincoln's leadership, his manipulation of people and votes, and especially his frequent equivocations, this also produces a less than saintly Lincoln who needs to have his higher purpose and deeper virtue recognized by the film audience, since many people in the world of the film fail to perceive it. For example, some senators call him a tyrant, others see him as full of "tricks," and even the film audience sees him playing with words in a distinctly Clinton-esque manner to achieve his purpose.[5] This was part of Spielberg's plan to invite Lincoln off the "alabaster pedestal," as he puts it in an interview, referring to the way the film tries to shows Lincoln's personal and domestic side (Fleming). However, the irony of Spielberg's strategy is that he takes Lincoln off his pedestal only to better hoist him onto an altar, inscribing the film within a long tradition of national hagiography in which Lincoln occupies pride of place as national martyr and quasi-divinity (one need only to think of the temple-like appearance of the Lincoln Memorial).

---

[4] According to Marvin and Ingle, the sovereign and the military together belong to what they call the "totem class," defined by both the power to kill and the ritualistic offering of themselves as sacrifices for the collectivity (6, 248-253).

[5] The most striking example is when Lincoln sends a note to the House floor asserting that "So far as [he] know[s], there are no peace commissioners in the city nor are there likely to be." This was technically true only because Lincoln has instructed the Richmond commissioners to be denied access to the city.

Civil Religion

Here the concept of Civil Religion needs to be explained. Originally coined by Rousseau, there are two principle ways in which it can be understood. One is the way that Rousseau originally meant it, which was an artificially invented but politically expedient religion of the state (see Cristi 17-27, and Gentile 18-20). The other way, which has been more influential in an American context, has been as a kind of natural emanation of a national culture and statecraft. This is the sense in which Robert Bellah understood the concept when he wrote the essay that launched a decades-long debate among American historians: "Civil Religion in America" (1967). Although scholarly interest in the concept waned after a decade of intense debate, it remains a compelling framework through which to understand the emotional and quasi-mystical dimensions of American politics and has even enjoyed something of a revival in recent years.[6] I use Civil Religion to refer to the way in which national institutions, rituals and ideologies function like religion, in the Durkheimian sense. For instance, national civil religion divides the world into sacred and profane spheres (e.g. punctuating the yearly calendar with national holy days: Fourth of July, Memorial Day, Flag Day, etc.), provides members with a sense of supra-individual transcendence and collective continuity (the nation for which the flag stands, as the Pledge of Allegiance terms it), and tries to offer an emotionally satisfying framework for coping with death in military service (i.e. dying *for* one's country).[7] If national civil religion resembles traditional religions in these three aspects, the modern nation has wrested from religion two other aspects that it now monopolizes completely: the power to kill non-members for the sake of its self-preservation and the right to ask members to die in its name. Currently, only the nation legitimately holds this power, which is why the nation can be said to have replaced religion in the social organization of death (Marvin and Ingle 25).[8]

---

[6] See for example, Marvin and Ingle, Cristi, Gentile, Pahl, and Haberski.

[7] See Billig for a discussion of the importance of nationalism in Amercans' lives even if it seems unnoticed (8).

[8] I follow Aviel Roshwald in not making a distinction between patriotism and nationalism, which are commonly differentiated into a healthy versus a fanatical devotion to an existing or aspiring state (4). Similarly, making a distinction between civic nationalism and religious nationalism provides no significant critical traction with respect to the United States, which has been defined in terms of the latter as often as the former despite the officially secular status of its foundational documents.

Lincoln: *The Project*

Keeping in mind the cultural work of both melodrama and Civil Religion, we can turn now to Spielberg's film and begin to understand how it
draws on both frameworks in its depiction of Lincoln as melodramatic
victim-hero and national martyr and how these two are made to overlap.
I will examine several scenes from the film, paying particular attention
to the musical score, as it plays a key role in the emotional choreography
of the film. The very first scene is a direct inter-textual reference to
Spielberg's other major patriotic war film, *Saving Private Ryan,* which is
best remembered for its gory depiction of the landing on Normandy
which set a new and possibly unsurpassed bar for gruesome realism in
battlefield scenes. *Lincoln* also opens with a combat scene from the Civil
War. Much shorter, but even more dense and intimate, the scene depicts
hundreds of men engaged in fierce hand to hand combat, stabbing each
other with knives and bayonets in a muddy, rainy field that recalls medieval depictions of hell. Since death by bayonet was relatively rare during the Civil War, we must understand the scene rhetorically as part of
the film's desire to make history intimate by thrusting the spectator in
the midst of a very personalized form of combat. Thus, against the
backdrop of a deafening human roar, we see the faces of men murder-
ing each other personally and up close, stepping on each other and
drowning each other in the mud. Quickly, however, a voice-off narrator
pulls us out of the scene and we discover that the battle is a memory
being recounted by an African American Union soldier to Lincoln as he
chats with the men in a military camp. With no remorse, the soldier reports not taking any prisoners among the Southerners that day, in re-
taliation for the execution of black soldiers by Confederates in an earlier
battle. We are thrust immediately into the ugliness of the Civil War as it
was driven by emotions of vengefulness and racial hatred, where white
racism is paid back in kind by black Union men.

Listening calmly and sympathetically to this gory account we discover Abraham Lincoln, as first we hover with the camera just over his
shoulder. A black soldier reproachfully reminds Lincoln that black soldiers were initially paid far less than their white counterparts, and that
there are still no black officers in the Army. This complaint offers an
occasion for the film to show its first example of Lincoln's "political
genius," namely, his skill at diffusing awkward or tense situations with
diversion and humor. First he asks the soldier what he will do after the
war (the diversion) and then answers the soldier's allusion to the limited

job prospects open to black men with a joke about how no barber can cut his wayward hair (the strategic humor).

We are thus offered an illustration of Lincoln's rhetorical talents, engaging even the most humble men in familiar conversation, and diffusing any potential conflict with the subterfuge of self-deprecating humor and personal anecdotes. When Lincoln says that his last barber hung himself, we know we are in the presence of the Western tall-tale and the moment for serious discussion of racial injustice has passed. Two white soldiers interrupt this exchange to tell Lincoln that they heard him at Gettysburg. They then proceed to recite the famous Gettysburg Address, first one soldier and then the other taking up the recitation. As they are ordered back to their company, only one black soldier remains, and he finishes the speech as the soundtrack reverentially hushes and a respectful piano solo accompanies his recitation as he walks off. We are left with a Lincoln hagiographically half-lit from behind as the music and light both fade.

This first scene deftly captures the dual nature of the film's project, evoking on the one hand the iconic and national Lincoln, the man whose speeches are memorized by soldiers and generations of schoolchildren, and on the other hand, the human and personal Lincoln, who takes the time to have personal conversations with Union soldiers in a military camp, even allowing disgruntled black soldiers to vent their grievances to him without resentment. This is the sovereign who mixes with the populace, lowering himself to the level of the humblest infantryman while retaining the dignity of the head of state as he sits on a crate in the midst of barrels and ammunition. The next two scenes continue in the vein of showing Lincoln at his most humble and domestic: one where he tells his wife Molly about a dream and another where he takes his little son Tad to bed by lying down on the floor beside him first. The film's desire to show a Lincoln at his most intimate and accessible is apparent, and the touching scene of Lincoln on the floor could not make this clearer or more visually literal. A devoted husband and father, Lincoln seems saintly from the start. The first overt sign of trouble is when the eldest son Robert returns and is rudely dismissed by Lincoln who is deep in conversation about the war. In fact, the next hour and a half of the film is devoted mainly to statecraft, Lincoln's conversations with his Secretary of State William Seward, his contentious cabinet, and his political allies and rivals, as he maneuvers the Thirteenth Amendment into a debate and a ratifying vote. Just as Lincoln dismisses Robert from his office, so the film places the domestic on a back burner while the political theater of the Senate and its behind the scenes workings are displayed.

Lincoln: *The Pathos*

However, the last third of the film builds to a dramatic climax as a series of increasingly emotional moments are initiated with an explosion of the conflict with Robert that has been brewing since he arrived. Taking Robert to a military hospital but unable to persuade him to step inside, Lincoln plays father to the young men missing legs and arms while his own son waits outside and finally follows a mysterious leaky wheelbarrow to the hospital's dumping ground for amputated arms and legs. Shaken and weeping, clearly ashamed of his own fear of injury, Robert confronts Lincoln with his determination to enlist. Here the film's emotional meter jumps to a new level as Lincoln slaps Robert then tries to embrace him and is violently shaken off.

The ideological stakes of this scene are higher than they might initially seem since Lincoln is more than just any father worried about the safety of his child. He is a man who has sent hundreds of thousands of sons to their deaths on the battlefields of the Civil War, and his refusal to sacrifice his own son can be read as a grave failure of moral courage and as an unfair attempt at personal exemption from the cruel lottery of war. I believe that this too is offered by the film as one of the reasons why Lincoln must be redeemed. And indeed, the film begins the redemption immediately, if we understand it in terms of the melodramatic logic of suffering. Though Lincoln attempts to prohibit Robert from enlisting, Robert refuses both his authority and his affection in one brutal rejection, leaving Lincoln standing alone, head bowed down.

The emotional punishment, we could almost say crucifixion, of Lincoln continues in the next scene, when he and Molly argue. Molly reproaches Lincoln for Robert's enlistment (which we know he tried to prevent) and accuses him of having wanted to put her in a madhouse because she was heartbroken over the death of their other son Willie. The film shows him stoically enduring Molly's accusations, and gives him the last word in the argument. With Molly kneeling histrionically before him, Lincoln explains with extraordinary calmness and self-insight that he "couldn't tolerate you grieving so for Willie because I couldn't permit it in myself," and that he had to stifle and hide his grief for Willie in order to carry on with his duties as president.

With this revelation, critical for a melodramatic reading of Lincoln as silent sufferer, he describes wanting to crawl into the coffin with Willie, and still feeling that same intensity of grief every day. He concludes by telling Molly that she alone can "lighten the burden." With the trope of grief as a heavy burden, the film tacitly introduces an image of Lincoln as Christ carrying his cross, an image that links the melodramatic focus on suffering with a Civil Religion reading of Lincoln as national martyr. In addition to his grief for Willie, Lincoln must cope with Molly's emotional self-indulgence, Robert's resentment, and the lack of support and understanding of his plans by his own cabinet. In short, the film depicts Lincoln as both solitary and afflicted, a classic example of the virtuous victim of melodrama. In keeping with the myth of Lincoln as the Great Heart, the toll of the war is depicted as weighing on him as much as the grief for his own son. Thus the film shows him awake at 3 in the morning, anxiously signing pardons in his secretaries' bedroom, wishing to spare at least some lives among deserters sentenced to hang.

The two most emotionally climactic scenes of the film are the passing of the Thirteenth Amendment and the assassination, and both are conventionally melodramatic but in directly opposed ways. In keeping with the temporal logic of melodrama, as described by Linda Williams, the first moment can be read as a just-in-time rescue, a standard feature of the melodramatic plot, while the second is the too-late melodramatic death. Both scenes are linked, however, by their depiction of characters weeping and their invitation to the film audience to weep as well. The first is the dramatic vote count in the Senate that culminates in the ratification of the Thirteenth Amendment. As the final count is tallied, the film cuts the speaker off in mid-sentence and instead shows Lincoln with little Tad in his office as he begins to hear the bells ringing in the town. Lincoln looks otherworldly as light from the window bathes him in a saintly glow. The film then cuts to the senate floor, where people are jubilantly throwing papers, laughing and crying at once, in a carnivalesque scene of celebration. There is a close-up of Mrs. Keckley, Mrs. Lincoln's dress maker and confidante, weeping and smiling as she looks upwards in silent thanks. Then we see a crowd outside the White House, waving American flags and throwing hats into the air as they cheer and shout.

This scene, which continues for several minutes, functions as a prototypically melodramatic moment, where the plot stops so that characters and viewers can be moved to tears together: here to tears of joy or national pride. The important thing is that viewers and characters are emotionally in tune during this scene and one of the driving objectives

of melodrama – to dissolve the boundaries between characters and between viewers and to allude to a moral occult – has been achieved. The
moral occult evoked by the scene is the unfolding of the national narrative of democracy and equality, as one of the most cherished myths of
American Civil Religion. The passing of the Thirteenth Amendment is
charged with mighty national portent, as it represents a step towards the
realization of the ideals of the Declaration of Independence. Here we
see the collapse of the melodramatic narrative into the Civil Religion
one. In the melodramatic frame, we have the temporality of "in the nick
of time." With just two votes to spare, the two-thirds majority vote has
been achieved, the slave population has been rescued, and the characters
and viewers exult. In the Civil Religion framework, we have what appears as the successful workings of the state, an affirmation of the ideals
of the Declaration of Independence and a correctly executed modifica-
tion of the Constitution: in short, a successful state ritual and an affirmation of the virtue of the collectivity.

The other major melodramatic moment is Lincoln's assassination.
However, before that scene, sandwiched between the ratification of the
Amendment on 31 January and the fateful departure to the theater on 14
April, there are two more low-key but important scenes in which the
film grows heavier both with emotion and ideological import: Lincoln's
meeting with the delegation from the Confederate States, and his visit to
a battlefield. In the first scene, he asks the South to surrender and scolds
the delegates for having "not kept faith" with the "democratic process,"
explicitly conflating religious and political rhetoric. When the delegates
reply by accusing him of having kept the Union intact not with ballots
but with bullets, arguing that "your Union, Sir, is bonded with cannon-
fire and death," Lincoln makes a speech very reminiscent of the Gettysburg Address. As the film pans in for a close-up, a lone oboe in the
background scores the scene and cues the audience to know that what
Lincoln is saying is Important and True. And what he articulates at this
moment is the essence of the moral occult aspect of Civil Religion. He
says that "we have shown the world" – and one can note how making
visible, legible, and producing recognition, the core drives of melodrama, are central to this speech – that there is a "great invisible
strength in a people's union." He continues, "we have shown that a
people can endure awful sacrifice and yet cohere," invoking the central
tenets of Civil Religion and nationalist ideology in general, which is that
sacrifice and national coherence are linked. The "yet" seems to imply an
opposition, but, as the Gettysburg Address expressed, and many social
theorists have argued, national or group coherence in fact *depends* on

sacrificial violence.[9] Thus, turning the reproach of the Southern delegation about the hundreds of thousands who have died during his administration into a Gettysburg moment, Lincoln uses precisely those deaths
as proof and moral guarantors of the legitimacy of the cause they died
for. The words that allude to the occult or religious dimension of the
national project are the "great invisible strength." The existence of invisible but powerful forces guiding events and giving sense and meaning
to them – in a secular but somehow spiritual way – is precisely the core
of the melodramatic mode as much as the Civil Religion one, and the
locus of their overlapping objectives.

Lincoln's visit to a battlefield after a battle brings us full circle to the
beginning of the film, as it were, except it is not the same battle, and
now we witness, with Lincoln, the results. The scene is gray, somber,
dark, still, and Lincoln rides through it grimly. We see the Union and
Confederate dead lying together, indiscriminately, piled on top of each
other, surrounded by smoke and rubbish and destruction. It is a hellish
landscape once more, only this time instead of the roar of battle, we
have a piano solo, scored by John Williams, titled, curiously "Remembering Willie," alluding to the Lincolns' dead son. The title of the piece
suggests that Lincoln's grief for his own dead son merges here with his
feelings for the dead sons of the nation in a classical melodramatic move
of breaking down barriers through pathos. As the audience already
knows that Lincoln carries the cross of grief for Willy, this scene suggests that Lincoln's cross actually is freighted with grief for all the other
sons that have died in the war. Not surprisingly, in the next scene, as
Lincoln talks with Grant he looks so exhausted and shaken by what he
has just witnessed on the battlefield that Grant tells him that he looks
"ten years older." The screenplay confirms that this is true and that
make-up artists had been asked to make it clear: "He has grown older,
the skin around his eyes is cobwebbed with fine creases, and his hair's
thinner, softer, suffused with grey" (http://www.imsdb.com/scripts/-
Lincoln.html). Here we have again the logic of melodrama, where the
virtuous victim's virtue is made manifest by making his suffering visible
and recognizable.

If the ratification of the Thirteenth Amendment follows the melodramatic logic of the just-in-time rescue, then the assassination is
framed in terms of a temporality of the too-late. Hence the night of the
assassination is preceded by a sunny carriage ride, where the Lincolns
make plans for travel in the future and Lincoln tells Molly reassuringly,

---

[9] Most notably, Girard, Burkert, and Marvin and Ingle.

"we must try to be happier." The film draws on the audience's sense of historical irony since we know that the Lincolns will not travel anywhere, and that they will not be happier, because it is "too late": the assassination will happen that very night. The aesthetic choices informing the representation of this event are also cued for maximum emotional impact. In principle, the assassination of Lincoln can make for a colorful narrative, with the handsome actor John Wilkes Booth sneaking up on Lincoln from behind at the Ford Theater while the Lincolns watch a comedy, then getting tangled in the red, white and blue banners as he leaps on stage to cry "Sic temper tyrranis" and "I have done it, the South is avenged." Spielberg's film sidesteps all these historical details and goes for pure emotion instead. What it shows is little Tad breathlessly watching a play in another theater and then his reaction to the news that his father has been shot. Like the ratification scene, this moment is also clearly meant to make the viewer weep as the camera closes in on the child screaming again and again in anguish at the loss of the beloved parent. The screen is dark except for Tad's anguished face, an image of pathos. The film then cuts from Tad's shrieks to Mary's face also distorted with weeping, then to one of the many men weeping around his bed during the almost comically heavy-handed deathbed scene where Lincoln lies in the middle, bathed in light. At this point Spielberg abandons realism altogether and presents Lincoln superimposed on a flame like a god or a saint. In dying, the virtuous victim of the melodramatic plot merges with the national martyr and we begin to hear his voice and recognize (or some will) the Second Inaugural Address.

Lincoln: *The Ending*

In ending with this particular speech, the film not only bookends its narrative with Lincoln's two most famous speeches, the only two speeches inscribed on the Lincoln Memorial, but he ends with the speech where Lincoln approaches most closely the tone and rhetoric of a preacher. This makes a certain narrative sense, since the speech is placed after his death, as if he's crossed over to another register, where the political and the religious co-mingle, which is indeed the peculiarity of that Inaugural Address. This is Lincoln's most religious speech, and the film picks it up towards the end, leading up to the most famous last lines, where the first words that we hear clearly are: "fervently do we pray, that this mighty scourge of war may speedily pass away." Not only does it explicitly mention praying, but with the word "scourge" it evokes a medieval instrument of religious self-punishment. In stark counter-distinction to the oft-quoted words that will follow, urging charity for all, here Lincoln imagines divine judgment upon the South and possibly America as whole, with the notion of "every drop of blood drawn with the lash . . . paid by another drawn with the sword." This is the logic of the Old Testament, with its moral equation of an eye for an eye, and this is the God of the Puritans, whose will directly guides the unfolding of history in the United States. If the anecdote about Lincoln attributing the Civil War to Stowe is apocryphal, here we see Lincoln unmistakably shifting responsibility for it onto God himself.

More importantly, however, by invoking this kind of theological understanding of American history, Lincoln is also reminding his audience of the Puritan's notion of a covenant. An angry god is one who loves the people he is chastising and cares about the bond they have with him. By implication, then, the chastised people can really believe themselves a single people, bound by divine covenant to each other as much as to this personal and engaged, if momentarily displeased and vengeful, God. In this very specifically American way, Lincoln offers a definition of Union that is explicitly theological and hearkens back to the religious and cultural origins of the United States. It also indirectly sets the stage for a more charitable attitude towards the South on the part of the Republican North, by implying that the South is already being punished by God. Moreover, as Lincoln's remarks must be understood to mean that the North has been punished as well, since it too has lost hundreds of thousands of men, the implication is that it too was somehow guilty. If both sides have been punished by God, there is no need for human retribution, which allows Lincoln to end his sermon on a note of healing, charity and care for the widow and orphan, and calling for a "just and lasting peace among ourselves and with all nations."

The general rhetorical impact of this speech is to lend Lincoln an aura of great moral and religious authority. The words "pray," "God, "Lord," and a quotation from the Bible, "the judgments of the Lord are true and righteous altogether," stand out for the film viewer, leaving him with the impression that Lincoln is like a prophet. Visually, the scene is staged like a famous photograph of the inauguration, where Lincoln is barely visible in a sea of faces. As a result, his voice seems to emanate from the people itself, or from some invisible source, like a voice of God, as film voice-off narration is sometimes called. I have argued that Civil Religion offers melodrama a powerful partner because both paradigms operate on the assumption that a moral occult exists and can make sense of the world. Both discourses offer the hope of redeeming suffering and death by bestowing an invisible meaningfulness on what otherwise seems as a tragic waste of life. In the case of Civil Religion, or even just simple patriotism, the moral occult that is invoked is that of the nation itself. According to this logic, it is the nation and its continuity in time and its meaningfulness that redeems the lives that are sacrificed in its name. It is no accident therefore that the last word of this speech, and the last word of the film, is "nations." With all the earmarks of a religious sermon, what Lincoln is ultimately urging devotion to is not God, Old Testament or New, but the nation and system of nations that has replaced religion as the main way of organizing human collective life.

With this final image of Lincoln addressing the crowd like a preacher, invoking an angry and righteous god, the film reveals something else about one of the many roles of cinema in American culture. I would argue that by mixing an emotional experience with a historical and ideologically freighted narrative, film can serve as a kind of ritual or liturgy in the national civil religion in which emotions of patriotism, belonging, pride, and connection to a social reality called the nation are rekindled and reaffirmed. It is undeniable that film combines many traditional elements of ritual – collective participation, heightened emotion, music, and the use of collective symbols, tropes, myths and references – to tell a story about the history and values of the collectivity. It is also clear from these remarks why melodrama would be particularly useful to mediatized ritual: by synchronizing moods and emotions through music as well as narrative and focusing attention on a serious (earnest) dramatic story, melodrama can heighten the intensity of "emotional energy" created by the film ritual (Collins 49). Thus, for better or for worse, *Lincoln*, with its melodramatic construction and attention to Lincoln's charismatic state performances, can be understood as a ritual of collective revitalization, drawing on both melodrama and civil religion to create a potent exercise in national mythopoesis.

References

Anderson, Benedict. *Imagined Communities.* London: Verso, 1982.

Bellah, Robert. "Civil Religion in America." *Daedalus: Journal of the American Academy of Arts and Sciences* 96 (1967): 1-21.

———. "Durkheim and Ritual." *The Robert Bellah Reader.* Eds. Robert N. Bellah and Steven M. Tipton. Durham: Duke University Press, 2006: 150-180.

Billig, Michael. *Banal Nationalism.* London: Sage, 1995.

Brooks, Peter. *The Melodramatic Imagination: Balzac, Henry James, Melodrama, and the Mode of Excess.* New York: Columbia University Press, 1985.

Burkert, Walter. *Homo Necans: The Anthropology of Ancient Greek Sacrificial Ritual and Myth.* Trans. Peter Bing. Berkeley: University of California Press, 1983.

Collins, Randall. *Interaction Ritual Chains.* Princeton and Oxford: Princeton University Press, 2002.

Cristi, Marcela. *From Civil to Political Religion: The Intersection of Culture, Religion, and Politics.* Ontario: Wilfrid Laurier University Press, 2001.

Durkheim, Emile. *The Elementary Forms of the Religious Life.* Trans. Joseph Ward Swain. New York: The Free Press, 1915, 1965.

Elsaesser, Thomas. "Tales of Sound and Fury: Observations on the Family Melodrama." *Monogram* 4 (1972): 2-15.

Fleming, Mike. "Mike Fleming's Q&A with Steven Spielberg." http://www.deadline.com/2012/12/steven-spielberg-lincoln-making-of-interview-exclusive (accessed on 15 March 2014)

Gentile, Emilio. *Politics as Religion.* Trans. George Staunton. Princeton: Princeton University Press, 2001.

Girard, René. *Violence and the Sacred.* Trans. Patrick Gregory. Baltimore: Johns Hopkins University Press, 1977, 1972.

Goodwin, Doris Kearns. *Team of Rivals: The Political Genius of Abraham Lincoln.* New York: Simon and Schuster, 2005.

Grimstead, David. *Melodrama Unveiled: American Theater and Culture, 1800-1850.* Berkeley: University of California Press, 1976.

Haberski, Raymond, Jr. *God and War: American Civil Religion Since 1945.* New Brunswick: Rutgers University Press, 2012.

Kushner, Tony. *Lincoln.* Film Shooting Script. http://www.imsdb.com/scripts/Lincoln.html (accessed on 29 July 2013).

Marvin, Carolyn and David W. Ingle. *Blood Sacrifice and the Nation: Totem Rituals and the American Flag.* Cambridge: Cambridge University Press, 1999.

Pahl, Jon. *The Empire of Sacrifice: The Religious Origins of American Violence.* New York: New York University Press, 2010.

Roshwald, Aviel. *The Endurance of Nationalism.* Cambridge and New York: Cambridge University Press, 2006.

Soltysik, Agnieszka M. "Melodrama and the American Combat Film." *Passionate Politics: The Cultural Work of American Melodrama from the Early Republic to the Present.* Eds. Ralph Poole and Ilka Saal. Newcastle: Cambridge Scholars, 2008.

Tompkins, Jane. *Sensational Designs: The Cultural Work of American Fiction, 1790-1860.* New York: Oxford University Press, 1985.

Vollaro, Daniel. "Lincoln, Stowe and the 'Little Woman/Great War' Story." *Journal of the Abraham Lincoln Association,* Vol. 30, No. 1, 2009: 18-34.

Weinstein, Cindy. "Introduction." *The Cambridge Companion to Harriet Beecher Stowe.* Ed. Cindy Weinstein. New York: Cambridge University Press, 2004.

Williams, Linda. *Playing the Race Card: Melodramas of Black and White from Uncle Tom's Cabin to O. J. Simpson.* Princeton: Princeton University Press, 2001.

Notes on Contributors

NANCY ARMSTRONG is Gilbert, Louis, and Edward Lehrman Professor of English at Duke University. Her books include *Desire and Domestic Fiction: A Political History of the Novel* (Oxford University Press, 1987), *The Imaginary Puritan: Literature, Intellectual Labor, and the Origins of Personal Life* (University of California Press, 1992; co-authored with Leonard Tennenhouse), *Fiction in the Age of Photography: The Legacy of British Realism* (Harvard University Press, 1999), and *How Novels Think: The Limits of Individualism, 1719-1900* (Columbia University Press, 2005). She edits the journal *Novel: A Forum on Fiction* (Columbia University Press, 2005).

SARAH CHEVALIER is Senior Teaching and Research Associate at the English Department of the University of Zurich. Her research interests are the social and regional varieties of English, onomastics, bi- and multilingualism, language attitudes and language acquisition. She is the author of a monograph which explores the formation, use and social meanings of personal names, *Ava to Zac: A Sociolinguistic Study of Given Names and Nicknames in Australia* (Francke, 2006). Her most recent publications are concerned with the role of social context in the acquisition of three languages by very young children, "Active Trilingualism in Early Childhood: The Motivating Role of Caregivers in Interaction" (*International Journal of Multilingualism*, 2012) and "Caregiver Responses to the Language Mixing of a Young Trilingual" (*Multilingua*, 2013).

JONATHAN CULPEPER is Professor of English Language and Linguistics at Lancaster University, UK. His research spans pragmatics, stylistics and the history of English. His recent major publications include *Impoliteness: Using Language to Cause Offence* (Cambridge University Press, 2011) and *Pragmatics and the English Language* (Palgrave, 2014; co-authored with Michael Haugh). He is co-editor-in-chief of the *Journal of Pragmatics*.

FRANCESCA DE LUCIA is currently teaching American literature at Zhejiang Normal University in Jinhua, China. She holds a *licence ès lettres* from the University of Geneva and a Diploma in American Studies from Smith College. She obtained a PhD from the University of Oxford, where the title of her thesis was "Italian American Cultural Fictions: From Diaspora to Globalization." She has published articles on different aspects of ethnicity in American literature.

REGULA KOENIG has an MA in English from the University of Bern. She was employed as a researcher in the Swiss National Science Foundation project "Life (beyond) writing: Illness narratives" (University of Basel) from 2009 to 2013 and worked with the reflective writing corpus. She has presented her work at numerous conferences and has published together with Franziska Gygax, Miriam A. Locher and Victoria Tischler.

ERZSI KUKORELLY is *chargée d'enseignement* in the English department of the University of Geneva, where she teaches eighteenth-century literature and cultural studies. She obtained a doctorate from that institution in 2008, which discussed issues of reading, authorship and authority in Samuel Richardson's *Pamela in Her Exalted Condition,* the sequel to *Pamela, or Virtue Rewarded.* She has published essays and book chapters on eighteenth-century literature and gender studies.

ANDREAS LANGLOTZ is Senior Lecturer in English Linguistics at the University of Lausanne and *Privatdozent* in English and General Linguistics at the University of Basel. His research interests include cognitive and socio-cognitive linguistics (with a special focus on figurativity and linguistic creativity), interpersonal pragmatics (theorising and analysing the situated construction of relational meaning), conflict talk, verbal humour, language and emotion (with an emphasis on emotional display in relational work), and phraseology. He is the author of the monograph *Idiomatic Creativity: A Cognitive-Linguistic Model of Idiom-Representation and Idiom-Variation in English* (John Benjamins, 2006) and works as Review Editor for the *Yearbook of Phraseology* (De Gruyter).

MIRIAM A. LOCHER is Professor of the Linguistics of English at the University of Basel, Switzerland. She worked on linguistic politeness and the exercise of power in oral communication (*Power and Politeness in Action,* Mouton, 2004) and advice-giving in an American Internet advice column (*Advice Online*, Benjamins, 2006). She edited a collection of papers on impoliteness (*Impoliteness in Language*, Mouton, 2008, with D. Bousfield), on *Standards and Norms of the English Language* (Mouton, 2008, with J. Strässler), on computer-mediated communication and politeness (*Journal of Politeness Research*) and edited the handbook of *Interpersonal Pragmatics* (Mouton, 2010, with S. Graham). She is currently working on illness narratives in a joint project with the medical humanities of the University of Basel, on linguistic identity construction in Facebook with B. Bolander, and on the connection between emotional display and relational work with Andreas Langlotz.

SANGAM MACDUFF is an Assistant in Modern British Literature at the University of Geneva. He read English at Trinity Hall, Cambridge University, before completing his Masters in English Literature and Creative Writing at the University of Edinburgh. He also holds a Post Graduate Certificate in Education from the Institute of Education, University of London. He has published several short stories in literary anthologies, including *V: New International Writing* from Edinburgh (Edinburgh University Press, 2007). He recently contributed to the James Joyce Broadsheet (October 2013) and wrote a chapter for *Joyce in the World of Publishing* (W. Brockman and T. Mecsnóber, eds, Rodopi, 2014). He is currently writing his doctoral thesis on James Joyce's Epiphanies.

LEYLA MARTI is currently an associate professor in the Department of Foreign Language Education at Boğaziçi University, Istanbul, Turkey. Her main research interests include cross-cultural communication, speech acts, politeness and indirectness. She has published in the *Journal of Pragmatics* on indirectness and politeness and co-authored an article on impoliteness in *Intercultural Pragmatics*.

DANIEL MCCANN is a Leverhulme Early Career Fellow in English Literature at the University of Oxford, and a Non-Stipendary Junior Research Fellow at St Anne's College, Oxford. He completed his doctorate at Queen's University Belfast. He has published on the interaction between medieval religion and medicine, the connection between heaven and health, and is currently preparing a monograph on medieval ideas of therapeutic reading and affective response. His other research looks at the importance of language in texts such as the *Cloud of Unknow-*

ing, and explores the importance of purgation in medieval religious writings.

MEILIAN MEI is associate professor of College of Foreign Languages at Zhejiang University of Technology, China. Her research spans pragmatics, stylistics and second language acquisition. Her recent major publications include *A Pragmatic Study of Fictional Communication* (Zhejiang University Press, 2008) and *A Study of English Signs with No and Only* (Journal of Xi'an International Studies University, 2013).

MINNA NEVALA is Senior Lecturer of English Linguistics at the University of Helsinki, Finland. Her research interests include historical sociolinguistics and pragmatics, especially, person reference and address. Currently she is involved in two research projects, *Dynamics of Change in Language Practices and Social Meaning* (1700-1900) and *Language of Evaluation: Constructing the Social Margins in England, 1650-1900* (both University of Helsinki). She is the author of *Address in Early English Correspondence: Its Forms and Socio-Pragmatic Functions* (Société Néophilologique de Helsinki, 2004), and one of the compilers of the *Corpora of Early English Correspondence* (CEEC-400).

PATRICIA RONAN is lecturer and *Privat-Docent* at the Department of English at the University of Lausanne, Switzerland. Her main research interests are the languages of Britain and Ireland, their variation and their historical development, as well as the linguistic and cultural results of contacts between the different population groups in these areas. She has recently published a monograph entitled *Make Peace and Take Victory: Support Verb Constructions in Old English in Comparison with Old Irish* (John Benjamins Publishing Company, 2012)and edited a volume on linguistic contact in Ireland, *Ireland and its Contacts/L'Irlande et ses contacts* (Centre de linguistique et des sciences du langage, 2013).

GILA A. SCHAUER is Professor of English and Applied Linguistics at the University of Erfurt, Germany. She received her PhD from the University of Nottingham. Her main research interests are interlanguage pragmatics, intercultural communication, cross-cultural pragmatics and impoliteness research. She is the author of *Interlanguage Pragmatic Devel-*

opment: The Study Abroad Context (formerly Continuum, now Bloomsbury, 2009), as well as of several articles and book chapters.

AGNIESZKA SOLTYSIK MONNET is Professor of American Literature at the University of Lausanne. She has published a monograph, *The Politics and Poetics of the American Gothic* (Ashgate, 2010), and several edited volumes, including *Writing American Women* (Gunter Narr, 2009, with Thomas Austenfeld) and *The Gothic in Contemporary Literature and Popular Culture* (Routledge, 2012, with Justin Edwards). Her publications include articles on American popular culture, war literature and melodrama. She is currently working on a research project focusing on the re-enchantment of war and militarism in American culture in the post-World War II era.

ENIT KARAFILI STEINER was educated at the University of Zurich and University of California, Los Angeles. Her monograph *Jane Austen's Civilized Women: Morality, Gender and the Civilizing Process* was published by Pickering and Chatto in 2012. She is also editor of Frances Brooke's *The History of Lady Julia Mandeville* (Pickering and Chatto, 2013) and of a collection of essays, *Called to Civil Existence: Dialogues on Mary Wollstonecraft's A Vindication of the Rights of Woman* (Rodopi Press, 2014). Her fields of interest include the novel and its relationship with the philosophical thought of the Enlightenment, Romanticism, women's writing of the18th and 19th centuries, theory of criticism. She is working on a project that examines the extent to which cosmopolitan thought is part of utopian imagination.

STEPHANIE TRIGG, a Fellow of the Australian Academy of Humanities, is Professor of Literature at the University of Melbourne and one of the Chief Investigators of the Australian Research Council Centre of Excellence for the History of Emotions. She is editor of *Wynnere and Wastoure* (Oxford University Press, 1990) and author of *Congenial Souls: Reading Chaucer from Medieval to Postmodern* (University of Minnesota Press, 2002) and *Shame and Honor: A Vulgar History of the Order of the Garter* (University of Pennsylvania Press, 2002). She is currently working on the expression of emotion on the face in literary texts from Chaucer through to the present.

Index of Names